Subjective Understanding

Computer Models of Belief Systems

Computer Science: Artificial Intelligence, No. 5

Harold S. Stone, Series Editor

President, The Interfactor, Inc.

Other Titles in This Series

Subjective Understanding

Computer Models of Belief Systems

by
Jaime G. Carbonell

UMI RESEARCH PRESS

Ann Arbor, Michigan

Produced and distributed by
UMI Research Press
an imprint of
University Microfilms International
Ann Arbor, Michigan 48106

Library of Congress Cataloging in Publication Data

Carbonell, Jaime G. (Jaime Guillermo)
Subjective understanding: computer models of
belief systems.

(Computer science. Artificial intelligence ; no. 5)
A revision of the author's thesis (Ph.D.)–Yale
University, 1979.
Bibliography: p.
Includes index.
1. Social sciences–Data processing. 2. Political science–
Data processing. 3. Belief and doubt–Data processing.
I. Title. II. Series.

H61.3.C37 1981   300'.28'54   81-11528
ISBN 0-8357-1212-5   AACR2

To the memory of my father,
Jaime Raul Carbonell

Contents

List of Figures

List of Tables

Preface

Human thinking is heavily influenced by subjective opinions and idiosyncratic beliefs. Nowhere is this phenomenon more strikingly apparent than in ideological reasoning. Why did Barry Goldwater interpret the Panama Canal treaty as a sellout of United States interests and "the worst treaty ever signed by the U.S.," while George McGovern hailed the very same treaty as an "enlightened diplomatic breakthrough" in the cause of world peace and international harmony? Differences of opinion abound in human reasoning, from ideological and political clashes to social and domestic disagreements. In order for a theory of human reasoning to be complete, it must account for the formation of subjective and ideological opinions. It follows that a model of a stereotypical human reasoner is necessarily incomplete, since it ignores the issues of idiosyncratic belief, self interests, and the generation of opinions.

More than a decade ago, Robert Abelson created his "ideology machine," a computer simulation of Senator Goldwater's ideological rhetoric. The ideology machine was capable of responding to descriptions of real-world events in a manner paralleling Goldwater's political pronouncements. This system, however, could not correctly incorporate knowledge about "mundane" reality in its responses. For instance, the ideology machine asserted that South American radicals would build the Berlin Wall, since "building the Berlin Wall" was classified as an action done by Communists.

The work described in this study was initially motivated by a reexamination of the ideology machine from the viewpoint of Schank and Abelson's [1977] theory of human understanding. My investigation has produced a more extensive theory of ideological reasoning in particular, and subjective understanding in general. The theory is implemented in computer programs that interpret descriptions of events from a variety of ideological and subjective perspectives. The usefulness of this theory can be judged by the aspects of human reasoning which it can explain. These include establishing and guiding the focus of a conversation, predicting the effects of human personality traits upon a person's plans and actions, and modeling several kinds of social, political, and legal conflicts.

The best-developed program is POLITICS, a computer model of subjective thought processes that are manifested in individual opinions and ideological responses. POLITICS was designed to apply its own motivations and concerns as it simulates various human-reasoning tasks in understanding natural language texts describing political events.

Acknowledgments

I would first like to thank Professor Roger Schank, an endless source of original ideas, inspiration, and guidance invaluable to my research. His great enthusiasm led me to investigate some fascinating problems originating from his ideas. The results of these investigations are largely responsible for the contents of Chapters 8, 9 and 10.

Professor Robert Abelson initiated the line of research which motivated the work described in this study. Together with Professor Schank, he developed a theory of human understanding which provided the foundations for my theory of subjective understanding. His advice, comments, and discussions contributed immeasurably to my research.

Professor Wendy Lehnert was also a constant source of ideas and encouragement. Her thorough treatment of question-answering processes made the computer implementation of my theory feasible.

Dr. Christopher Riesbeck deserves a special note of thanks for his plentiful advice, his help with programming difficulties, and his thorough examination of an earlier draft of the manuscript. His influence upon my style of thinking can be judged from the fact that, after three and a half years of associating with him, I think up almost as many puns as he does.

Professors David Barstow and Drew McDermott read earlier versions of this work and provided extremely useful advice on how to make the text readable and the ideas meaningful to people outside the Natural Language Processing community.

My friends and co-workers at the Yale A.I. project made the research environment one of the finest and liveliest anywhere. Anatole Gershman and Larry Birnbaum contributed to several lengthy and enlightening discussions on natural language analysis. Steven Slade and Rod McGuire wrote the English generator for the TRIAD system. Janet Kolodner revised and corrected a draft of this manuscript. Walter Stutzman kept the computer healthy and running, even at times when it wanted to go on strike. The rest of the people, whose contributions are too numerous to state individually, include: Mark Burstein, Eugene Charniak, Richard Cullingford, Natalie Dehn, Jerry DeJong, Glenn Edelson, Richard Granger, Jim Hendler, Michael Lebowitz, Mallory Selfridge, and Robert Wilensky.

No words can convey my warmest feelings of appreciation to Myra Lynn Carbonell, who read and corrected every draft of the original study, while caring for our newborn son Ruben and working at her own job.

Finally, the PDP10 and PDP20 deserve mention for their relentless efforts at calling attention to numerous bugs in my programs, and for staying up with me at all hours of the night.

1

Why Subjective Understanding?

Modeling human inference processes, such as language comprehension and planning behavior, requires an understanding of subjective thought phenomena. No two people think exactly alike; different individuals subscribe to different beliefs and are motivated by different goals in their activities. Therefore, it is imperative to investigate the underlying cognitive mechanisms that give rise to subjective understanding and idiosyncratic behavior. The investigation discussed in this document seeks to find the minimal computational mechanism sufficient to account for subjective behavior by applying Occam's Razor to the degree of individual variability that must be postulated. Our primary result is that priority orderings among a person's motivations (encoded as goal-subgoal and relative-importance *goal trees*) suffice to model most individual differences in comprehension and inference. Hence, inference mechanisms and factual knowledge structures need not vary across individuals.

We chose to focus our investigations on modeling political ideologies, as these seemed to exhibit the greatest individual variations in subjective thought processes. Later, we applied goal trees to model certain aspects of individual personality traits and to simulate topic selection and focus in a discourse model. In addition to goal trees, we needed effective mechanisms for relating high-level goals to perceived actions and situations. To satisfy this requirement we developed a comprehensive set of *counterplanning strategies*, discussed in detail in chapters 4 through 6. Counterplanning is the process of thwarting the goals of an adversary, or achieving one's own goals in spite of accidental or intentional blocking actions on the part of other planners. Unlike goal trees, counterplanning strategies model the general planning mechanism that remains invariant across different individuals or political ideologies.

The work described in this document was performed at Yale University, supervised primarily by Professor Roger Schank and also by Professor Robert Abelson. Since the completion of the initial POLITICS project, the theory of subjective understanding has formed the basis for several new investigations, including: A process-model of analogical reasoning (Carbonell [1981]), a method of incorporating multiple subjective viewpoints into a reasoning system, evidentiary-combination techniques in POLITICS-II, and aspects of long-range planning in chess-playing systems. Additionally, the counterplanning strategies and goal-priority orderings have influenced several other investigations in Cognitive Science in more indirect ways. The bulk of this document consists of the unaltered text of the original dissertation.

1.1 What Subjective Understanding Is

People interpret a story in different ways, depending upon their subjective interests, personal motivations, beliefs, and knowledge about the various actors in the story. Differences in interpretation include formulating different opinions on possible consequences of the story, assigning different motives to the actions of the characters, and inferring completely different consequences from the same natural language text of the story. Consider various interpretations of political event 1.1 below. Each interpretation indicates that the memory representation of the understander encompasses more than the act of signing two names on a piece of paper. The variety of responses indicates that the various memory representations of the event are far from identical.

EVENT 1.1   Brezhnev and Carter have signed a comprehensive strategic arms limitations treaty.

QUESTION 1.1   What is likely to happen as a result of the treaty?

RES 1.1.1   The next step should be complete nuclear disarmament. The two superpowers have finally come to their senses.

RES 1.1.2   The U.S. can reduce military spending and focus on serious domestic issues. This is great news!

RES 1.1.3   The intentions are good, but Carter will never get a SALT treaty through Congress. The Soviets would not have signed the treaty unless it gives them a strategic advantage.

RES 1.1.4   We have a peanut in the White house! First Carter gives away the B-1, then the neutron bomb, now God knows what he promised to give away. At this rate we'll never be able to stop the Communists.

RES 1.1.5   What? You got to be kidding me! The Russians would never sign such a treaty. The internal Soviet policies mandate a continuous outside threat.

RES 1.1.6   [Response by a Communist Chinese] This is terrible. Now it will be much harder to play the Russians and Americans against each other.

There is no "correct" response to question 1.1. All the above responses are correct within their own understanding framework. The multitude of interpretations of event 1.1 is one illustration of the process of *subjective understanding*. Subjective understanding is the process of applying the beliefs, motivations, and interests of the understander to the task of formulating a full interpretation of an event. The following statement summarizes the first principle underlying our theory of subjective understanding:

Different understanders may have radically different perceptions of the same event.

The theme of this work is the development of a process model for subjective understanding. A process model explains the nature of the understanding mechanisms and the way in which these mechanisms interact to produce a memory representation. We first discuss the significance and pervasiveness of subjectively biased understanding across many different domains. Second, we demonstrate how subjective beliefs and subjective evaluations of importance and relevance help to focus and constrain the inference process. In later chapters we develop a process model of human subjective understanding.

One could argue that all understanders process event 1.1 in the same manner, producing the same memory representation. In this case, one would attribute the different responses exclusively to subjective differences in the question-answering process. We show that, in general, this is not the case. Both understanding and question answering are subjective processes. The beliefs of the understander affect the way in which he interprets events. The following examples illustrate the fact that understanding an event is itself a subjectively guided process.

EVENT 1.2   A border conflict that flared up between Albania and Yugoslavia may escalate to an all out war. The Soviet Union sent two battalions into Albania.

QUESTION 1.2   What is Russia doing?

RES 1.2.1   The Russians are invading Albania. Russia wants to change the Albanian government that has been pro-China and anti-Soviet. The border conflict seems to be a convenient excuse.

RES 1.2.2   Russia is giving military aid to Albania. The Yugoslav army could crush the Albanian army with ease. If Russia is stepping into the conflict it must be to reverse the otherwise certain outcome.

RES 1.2.3   Russia is in a peace-keeping mission. Russia wants to enforce a settlement before the conflict erupts into a full scale war.

Which of the three responses is "correct"? Any of the three scenarios described in the responses may be possible depending on the understander's interpretation of Soviet motives. Sending troops into Albania can be interpreted differently depending on how such an action fits into Russia's ultimate goals. If the understander believes that Russia wants to take over Albania, then the first interpretation of the Russian action is appropriate. If Russia's goal is to keep Albania from being invaded, then the second interpretation is plausible. If Russia's ultimate goal is to maintain peace, then the Russian troops may be viewed as a peace-keeping buffer force between the Albanian and Yugoslav armies. The responses to question 1.2 indicate that there are cases where in order to determine the plan of action of an actor in an event, the understander must first establish the motives of the various actors. Each response is a paraphrase of what the understander believed was stated in the event. Therefore, the differences in the responses are attributable to different beliefs applied by the understanders while reading event 1.2.

The subjective component of the understanding process in event 1.2 stems from the attribution of different goals to the same political entity by different understanders. It is impossible to interpret event 1.2 without knowing Russia's goals. It is often the case that an understander must either infer or have preconceived notions about the goals of the participants in a political event, since these goals are usually not explicitly stated in the text describing the event. Therefore, a significant factor that contributes to differences in interpretation is the understander's perception of the goals of the actors in the various events. The term "actor" is used to mean a person, institution, or political entity participating in an event. We will show how inferring the goals of the participants in the events always guides the understanding process. We summarize our discussion by the following two principles of subjective understanding:

The understander's perceptions of the goals of the actors determines, to a significant degree, his understanding of the event.

Different understanders may attribute different goals to the actions of an actor.

Subjective interpretation appears in many guises in everyday conversations. Depending on one speaker's perception of the goals of the other speaker, one statement can be understood to mean different things. Consider, for instance, the scenario in event 1.3:

EVENT 1.3   John walked up to a person on the corner and asked: "Do you know how to get to Elm Street?"

RES 1.3.1   The stranger replied: "You go two blocks toward that tall building and turn right."

RES 1.3.2   The cab driver on the corner replied: "Sure, Hop in. Where on Elm do you want to go?"

RES 1.3.3   The person, who was holding up a map and a piece of paper with an Elm Street address on it, replied: "No, could you tell me how to get there?"

RES 1.3.4   The child answered: "Yes, I know how to go there!"

The question was interpreted to mean four different things, depending on who John spoke to. If a stranger asks "Do you know how to get to X?" the listener usually interprets this to mean "I want to go to X, but I do not know how to get there. Please give me directions." Since the occupation of a cab driver is to take people to their destination it is perfectly legitimate for him to interpret the question as: "If you know how to get to X, please take me there." The person who is visibly lost and trying to find his way may interpret questions 1.3 as: "You seem to be lost. Can I help you find your way?" Response 1.3.3 illustrates that the responder did not infer that John's goal was to go to Elm Street, in contrast with the two previous responses. A child often interprets questions of the form: "Do you know Y" literally, possibly inferring that the person asking the question is quizzing him. As in our previous examples, the differences in interpretation can be explained in terms of differences in the perceived goals of the participants in the event.

Our objective is to construct a theory that accounts for different interpretations of events such as 1.1, 1.2 and 1.3. There are many factors that influence the interpretation process; we will isolate and analyze the more significant ones in the course of this chapter. An adequate theory of subjective understanding requires not only the identification of relevant factors, but an understanding of the mechanisms that integrate these factors into a process model. The types of mechanisms necessary to apply relevant knowledge in the subjective understanding process are introduced in the following sections and discussed in more detail in chapter 4.

1.2 Focus of Attention Based on Subjective Interest

We have seen that there are differences in understanding various events depending, to a significant extent, on the understander's perception of the goals of the actors. In order to understand the processes which give rise to these differences, we examine more specific factors that play an important role in subjective understanding. One such factor is the focus of attention of the understander. Attention can be focused on some aspects of the event while others are ignored, thereby directing the inferencer to determine and consider certain consequences and ignore others outside the focus of attention. This process can yield different memory representations for an event, where each memory structure encodes the consequences and motives that were of interest to the understander.

A person reading about an event is likely to focus his attention on the aspects of that event that have a direct effect upon him. For instance consider the interpretation of event 1.4 by a stock market investor, a factory worker who lives in an electrically heated house, and a government economist.

EVENT 1.4   The state government approved a 10% rate hike requested by the ConEdison electric power company, effective immediately.

QUESTION 1.4   What is going to happen now?

RES 1.4.1   (Stock market investor) ConEdison shares ought to go up. They can probably afford to raise dividends too. It looks like I should convert my option for 300 shares of ConEdison common stock.

RES 1.4.2   (Non-affluent resident of an electrically heated house) Good God, 10% means that I'll have to pay almost $100 more next year in electric bills. The government sold out to big business once again.

RES 1.4.3   (Government economist) The increase in price will encourage energy conservation although it might fuel inflation. ConEdison should use the new capital to build new plants and alleviate the construction slump.

The point of analyzing the answers to question 1.4 is to see how the direct effects of event 1.4 on each of the three understanders influences their focus of attention. The homeowner's concern is for the rise in electric bills that he will have to pay. His focus is on the impact of higher electric bills upon himself and possible others in the same socio-economic class. The homeowner neither cares about the possible rise in stock values nor does he care about encouraging energy conservation. Therefore these factors are not considered in the understanding process and have no part in the memory representation of event 1.4. The stock investor's central concern is for the profit he can make by converting his ConEdison option. Rising electric bills are insignificant in comparison with the money he can make as a result of the increased revenue for ConEdison. His understanding of event 1.4 focuses on how he can make a profit, not energy conservation or the detrimental effects of higher prices upon less affluent people. The economist, in contrast with the investor and the homeowner, is not strongly affected by the price rise. He takes a more detached professional view in analyzing the consequences of event 1.4, focusing on what he considers most interesting: the economic impact of 1.4 on the nation as a whole.

The personal involvement of the understander in the event affects the focus and depth of the inference process in the course of understanding that event. The effects of personal involvement by the understander on the inference processes are summarized below:

The understander focuses his attention on the aspects of the event that affect him personally.

The focus of the understanding process determines which consequences of the event are analyzed and remembered in the memory representation.

Personal involvement in some consequences of an event may cause the understander to ignore other consequences that may be of greater significance to other understanders.

Focus of attention as a result of personal involvement is illustrated by the responses to event 1.4. Most people, including stock market investors, are usually concerned about rising inflation, but in response 1.4.1 the personal vested interest in ConEdison stock caused the investor to ignore the inflationary aspect of event 1.4.

A process model of subjective understanding has to take into account the fact that the understander tends to focus his attention on matters that personally affect him, while ignoring a host of other matters. The model must encode rules that make it behave according to the principles listed above. The problem at hand is not so much what inferences the understander is capable of making, but which lines of inference to pursue and which lines of inference to ignore. The inferences that determine the consequences of an event upon one's self are pursued more vigorously than other possible inferences. This is one criterion for establishing the focus of attention of the inference mechanism. There are other criteria for deciding which inferences should not be made and which lines of reasoning should be pursued further. The crux of the problem is focusing the attention of the inference process on the appropriate types of consequences, i.e., making the inferencer follow the same lines of reasoning that a person would follow given the same story to interpret. The focus of attention in human understanders is predicated upon interests and beliefs that are subjective, and therefore specific, to each understander.

The problem of controlling inferences appears in any large-scale reasoning system. Subjective interest is a very useful means of reducing the inference space that must be searched. This is accomplished by pursuing only the lines of inference that the understander considers relevant to his own beliefs and motivations.

Let us investigate some more criteria that determine the focus of attention of the understander.

1.3 Identification with Actors in the Event

A significant factor in subjective understanding is the identification of the understander with one of the actors in the event. Many events do not personally affect the understander in any significant way, but do affect someone with whom the understander empathizes or identifies. In these cases he may (figuratively) take the place of the appropriate actor in the event and focus his attention on the consequences that affect this actor, in much the same way as if the understander were himself personally affected by the consequences of the event. Examples of this phenomenon occur often in everyday life. People who read novels, especially romances or adventures, usually identify with the main character—the hero or the heroine. Movies and theater presentations exhibit similar identification with fictional characters.

There is psychological evidence supporting the notion that identification with a character in a story affects the perceptions and memory of the events, the evaluations of the characters, and the attribution of motives to the actions described in the event. The reader is referred to these psychological experiments by Abelson and Pinto described in Bourne, et al. [1979], Taylor, et al. [1978], and Anderson and Pichert [1978].

Identification with actors in events is not confined to fictional stories. A person may identify with the goals and aspirations of someone with whom he has emotional or obligational attachments. In most instances identification with an actor in an event means that the understander "adopts" the goals of the actor as if they were his own goals. Therefore, the concern of the understander is for the fulfillment of these goals. This identification places certain constraints on the reasoning process of the understander, as he is likely to focus on the achievement of the actor's goals and ignore other, less relevant, information. The examples below illustrate focusing of the reasoning mechanism by the understander as he identifies with the goals of one of the actors.

> EVENT 1.6　John had borrowed $200 from Jack, his next door neighbor. Jack needed the money back after he got into a car accident which the insurance did not cover. John, however, said that he was deep in gambling debts and was unable to repay him. Jack refused to believe this.

> QUESTION 1.6　What's going to happen now?

> RES 1.6.1　(Response by Jack's wife) That no-good bum next door is going to have to pay up. Jack needs to get the car fixed. Maybe he ought to borrow John's car until he pays up and stops lying about the loan-sharks coming to get him.

> RES 1.6.2　(Response by John's ex-army buddy) Poor John; he's in trouble again. I don't see any easy way out for him. He ought to ignore that vulture of a neighbor until he pays off the sharks. Maybe he'll be luckier next time around.

The responses above clearly indicate the identification of each understander with one of the two actors in the event. Jack's wife interprets question 1.6 from Jack's perspective, i.e., "What can Jack do to get his money back?" and "How is Jack going to have a working car?". John's army buddy sympathizes with John and focuses his attention on trying to help John overcome his problem. John's buddy does not worry about Jack being stuck without a car—his concern is for John's goals. This example is quite similar to 1.4 and 1.5, except that at least one of the understanders (John's buddy) was not personally affected by the event. The two points below summarize the principles of goal identification.

If the understander of an event identifies with the goals of one of the actors he will focus attention on inferences that lead to the fulfillment of these goals.

Inferences that are relevant only to the concerns of other actors will probably not be pursued in the understanding process.

The identification of the understander with one actor in an event occurs in many different guises. A fan rooting for his favorite major league baseball team is an example of identification with the goals of an actor in an event. In this case the event is the game itself and the understander is the sports fan identifying with his team—one of the actors in the event. The goal that the fan identifies with is winning the game and possibly the individual glory of some players. In this example there is only partial goal identification with the team and its members. The sports fan may not really care about negotiations between the owners of the team and the stadium employee's association, for instance. The sports fan is not necessarily concerned with the personal problems of all of the players on the team, nor with the financial status of the team's owner. Basically, the fan is primarily concerned with the ritualized goals of the team that are activated in the baseball game scenario.

The process of partial identification with the goals of an institution is very common. For instance, members of Alcoholics Anonymous share the concern of the organization as a whole on its goal of eliminating alcoholism. In fact, the reason that this and other such organizations exist is that its members share a common goal. The John Birch society exists because a number of people hold the same ultra-conservative goals. A person considers himself to be a member of a political party if he can identify with the goals of the party. People usually identify with the goals of the country in which they live; this is called nationalism—a very widespread phenomenon in the modern world.

How does identification with an organization, a political party, or a country affect the understanding process? Identification with the goals of a political actor (e.g, a country, a political party, an international organization) focuses the attention of the understander in the same way that personal involvement and identification with a human actor channels the inference process. Recall event 1.1 at the start of this chapter; two of the responses to question 1.1 are reiterated below.

EVENT 1.1   Brezhnev and Carter have signed a comprehensive strategic arms
limitations treaty.

QUESTION 1.1   What is likely to happen as a result of the treaty?

Res 1.1.2   (Response by an American) The U.S. can reduce military spending and
focus on serious domestic issues. This is great news!

RES 1.1.6   (Response by a policy-making Communist Chinese) This is terrible.
Now it will be much harder to play the Russians and Americans
against each other.

Response 1.1.2 is an evaluation of event 1.1 in the context of: "How will the event affect U.S. goals?" Response 1.1.6 interprets event 1.1 from the corresponding Chinese viewpoint: "How will the event affect Chinese goals?" with predictably different results. This is an example of how goal identification focuses the reasoning process on appropriate consequences of the event. Thus subjective understanding via goal identification produces two diametrically opposed evaluations of the same event. We summarize our principle of goal identification:

The process of identification with the goals of an institution, country or political party focuses the attention of the understander in the same general way as having a personal vested interest in the event.

We established that identification with the goals of an actor in an event is an important factor in the understanding process. This realization does not solve the problem of how understanding proceeds; it merely indicates that our process model of subjective understanding ought to see goal identification as a principle which is crucial in guiding the inference process. The following section examines other factors involved in focusing the attention of the understander. These factors are considered part of a decision process that compels the inferencer to examine certain consequences of the event while ignoring others.

Social psychologists have long noted a process of negative identification, wherein a statement by a disliked group motivates a contrary stance in the individual. This process is termed the "negative reference group" (Collins and Raven [1968]), and it should have the effect of focusing the attention of the understander in a way similar to that of positive character identification.

1.4 Requirements for a Process Model

How does the understander relate the actions in the event to the goals of the actors? How does he identify with the goals of one actor? How does goal identification enable the inference process to concentrate on certain lines of reasoning? The purpose of this section is to suggest answers to these questions by outlining a process model of subjective understanding.

Consider the following scenario: The understander is an American reading event 1.7 in a newspaper. Assume the newspaper reader knows that killer satellites are devices capable of destroying other satellites in orbit.

EVENT 1.7   The Soviet Union announced that their killer satellite network is operational.

Possible lines of inference the understander could pursue:

1.7.1 How did the Russians make their announcement? It must have been written or spoken. In the former case it may have been through Pravda. In the latter case it was probably in a party speech . . .

1.7.2 I wonder how killer satellites work? They need something that can detect and destroy a metal object. Radar system?—could be. Explosive charge? Explosives can be nuclear or chemical . . .

1.7.3 What was I doing when they made their announcement? I need to know: When did they make the announcement? And, what have I been doing? Suppose they made their announcement before yesterday. No, then yesterday's newspaper would have reported it . . .

1.7.4 Why did Russia develop killer satellites? Maybe Brezhnev does not like satellites. A dislike of objects beyond his reach could be symptomatic of an insecurity complex . . .

1.7.5 How is the U.S. affected by Russia having killer satellites? The American satellites can be destroyed. What effects can this have on the U.S.? Spy, weather and communication satellites would cease to function. Is this a reasonable Russian goal? Yes—Russia does not want the U.S. to spy on them.

1.7.6 Why does the newspaper carry this story? . . .

1.7.7 How does this affect the Somali-Ethiopian war? . . .

1.7.8 Can this help me get rich? . . .

1.7.9 Whose idea was it to shoot down satellites? . . .

The reasoning process of an understander may follow many different tracks. The nine inference tracks above are but a token sample of the multiple lines of reasoning that an understander could pursue. Is there a "correct" line of reasoning? How is one line of reasoning chosen and a myriad others ignored? Clearly one cannot establish a unique line of reasoning, since many of the above inferences could plausibly be made by a human understander. Example 1.7.5 seems the most natural line of reasoning for an American newspaper reader. Example 1.7.2 is also plausible; an engineer, for instance, is more likely to think along these lines. The interests of the understander determine the lines of inference pursued in the understanding process. There are some lines of inference, such as 1.7.3, that seem rather absurd because we cannot conceive that any understander would be interested in pursuing such lines of thought. What makes other lines of inference, such as 1.7.7 and 1.7.8 less natural than, for instance, lines 1.7.5 and 1.7.2? In order to answer this question we need to have a concrete notion of the process that focuses the reasoning mechanisms.

We cannot simply say "Ah yes, goal identification" and consider the problem solved. Response 1.7.8 shows the understander trying to determine whether the event could affect one of his goals. Somehow this response to event 1.7 seems rather silly. A person has many different goals that could conceivably be affected by external events. Similarly, one can identify with the goals of a multitude of family relations, friends, and organizations that share goals with the understander. This suggests that there is a very large number of goals that an individual can be potentially concerned with. Does the understanding process enumerate all the possible goals and see if the event could conceivably affect any of them? The logical answer is "no", since we believe that the reasoning process is reasonably efficient. If for every fruitful line of goal-directed inference, the understander needs to follow a hundred dead-end reasoning chains, then our process model has failed in focusing the attention of the inference process.

Little needs to be said for the opposite extreme: the process of enumerating all possible consequences of the event and all possible relations to other facts in the memory, in the hope of establishing the "interesting line of reasoning." In this method, a candidate for a line of reasoning that may be worth pursuing is found by determining whether each memory association is something that could be part of a goal identifiable with those of the understander. This process is nothing more than an exhaustive search of the inference space with the proviso that the searching process knows when to quit. Knowing when to quit in this context is equivalent to knowing when one line of reasoning is sufficiently interesting to warrant further pursuit while abandoning other potential lines of reasoning. This method is inefficient; it defeats the purpose of focusing the attention of the reasoning process. The objective of the focusing process is to eliminate non-directed searches. Therefore, a non-directed search whose purpose is to establish the focus of attention is a self-defeating proposition.

1.5 The Initial Focus of Attention

Our process model is based on a semantically-rich environment where the inferencer can determine the significance or usefulness of its current line of reasoning with respect to the goals of the understander and actors of the event. The first question the understander asks himself upon encountering a new event is: What is the most significant concept in the event that I did not already know about? "The most significant concept" is extracted from the event by applying a set of criteria to evaluate the intrinsic interest of certain actions in an event. For example, Criterion 1.1 may be applied to event 1.8 in order to determine the initial focus of attention of the understander.

> CRITERION 1.1   Objective/Means distinction: If there are two or more actions in an event, and some actions are instrumental to stated or implicit objectives of one of the actors, the understander should focus attention on the objectives and non-instrumental actions.

> EVENT 1.8   John went to the Cadillac dealer where he purchased a 1978 Coupe DeVille.

There are two actions explicitly stated in event 1.8: John went to the dealer, and John bought a Cadillac. Clearly, the second one is the more significant action. We want our inferencer to focus attention on purchasing a Cadillac and virtually ignore going to the dealer. By applying criterion 1.1 to event 1.8, we can see that "purchasing a Cadillac" is the action that the understander should focus on. Going to the dealer is an instrumental action, whereas purchasing a Cadillac was probably John's objective. Criterion 1.1 is a heuristic principle and, as such, useful most of the time it is applicable, but also fallible on occasion. Consider event 1.9, a case where criterion 1.1 fails:

> EVENT 1.9   Peter was broke and hungry. He took his .38 revolver and held up the mayor, getting away with $20. Peter had a full dinner that night.

The causal relations among the actions of event 1.9 can be informally diagrammed as follows:

Figure 1.1.   Casual chain of event 1.9

Peter gets gun	ENABLES	Holdup of Mayor	RESULTS IN	Peter gets money	ENABLES	Peter to eat dinner

Figure 1.1 shows that each of the events was directly or indirectly (by transitivity) instrumental to Peter's eating a big dinner. Peter's objectives, implicitly stated in the first sentence, are the acquisition of money and food. However, holding up the mayor stands out as a much more interesting action than Peter's eating a big dinner. An understander should focus the inference process on the consequences of the holdup, whether the understander identifies with Peter's goals, those of the mayor, or

neither actor's goals. Criterion 1.1, although able to choose the more significant action in many cases, fails when applied to event 1.9. What makes the holdup of the mayor more significant than the other three actions? It is very unusual for mayors to be held up. The consequences of this action can be far more serious for Peter, the mayor, and possibly the rest of the people in the city than any other part of event 1.9. These factors that govern the significance of actions are taken into account by the following four criteria:

Criteria for measuring the inherent interest of actions:

CRITERION 1.2   Deviance from social/political norm: If an actor, recipient or object of an action are very different from the socially-defined normative case, then that action may be inherently interesting.

CRITERION 1.3   Routine task property: A routine action by an institution or a person whose occupation is to do that action is NOT interesting unless other interest criteria apply.

CRITERION 1.4   Interest in VIP activities: An action involving someone or something that is unique and well known is likely to be of inherent interest.

CRITERION 1.5   Imminent severity: An action whose immediate consequences can change drastically the goals of parties directly involved is inherently interesting.

Criterion 1.2 applies to event 1.9, stating that since mayors are not usually held up at gunpoint, Peter's holdup of the mayor is therefore interesting (i.e., worthy of attention by the understander by means of focusing the inferencer on this action and its consequences). Armed robbery can have severe consequences for both the victim (e.g. he could be shot and killed) and the assailant (e.g., going to jail or becoming a fugitive). Thus, criterion 1.5 indicates that the holdup is more significant than the other actions in the event.

Criterion 1.4 is also applicable to event 1.9. There is only one mayor per city, and he is usually well-known to the residents of that city. Therefore, the fact that an action involves him directly makes this action more interesting than it would otherwise be. Criterion 1.4 is amply illustrated in the press coverage of Amy Carter. She is the President's one and only school-age daughter. A large number of Amy's actions were reported in the press. For instance, Amy danced in a square dance, an event which would have been totally uninteresting were it not for the fact that Amy was a participant. Similarly, events involving unique objects are noteworthy because of their rarity and consequent fame. The sale of a Van Gogh self-portrait is likely to be of much wider interest than the sale of a sizable manufacturing business in Munich, although the latter may involve a much larger financial transaction than the former.

Criterion 1.3 is useful in ruling out a large number of actions as being uninteresting on the grounds that the understander already knows all he wants to know about them. For instance, consider event 1.10:

EVENT 1.10   The United States Congress voted to fund the Trident submarine project.

There are two parts to this event: Congress voted on a resolution, and, as a consequence of the resolution, the Trident submarines will be funded. The normal function of Congress is to debate and subsequently vote on resolutions. Congress follows this process time and again with little deviation that an outside layman can see. Funding Trident submarines, however, is a unique action; Congress does not make a habit of funding submarine projects all the time. Therefore, by criterion 1.3, the understander should focus attention on the submarine funding aspect of event 1.10, not on the details of the Congressional vote. Criterion 1.1 reinforces criterion 1.3 in the current example. The Congressional vote is instrumental to the Trident funding and therefore of lesser interest. Thus, the funding event, not the Congressional vote, becomes the focus of attention.

This method of focusing attention requires knowledge not contained in either script; that is, the focus of attention is determined by the instrumentality relation between the two scripts. On occasion, a script itself can be used to determine whether an action is important by the following criterion:

CRITERION 1.6   If an action matches part of a script and that part is neither the main concept of the script nor its goal, the action is probably unimportant.

Thus, if we hear the details of the Congressional vote, we can apply criterion 1.6 to determine that they are probably of minor importance. However, an unusual event, such as a bomb threat during the voting, is potentially more interesting to a reader.

A process model requires more than a set of principles; it requires a method of encoding the principles, determining the situations in which they apply, and precisely defining their actions as part of the overall understanding process. In a later section we outline the overall algorithm for focusing attention, and in later chapters we discuss the implementation of the process model as a computer system.

Consider how our criteria determine the original focus of interest and constrain the inference mechanism from starting down irrelevant inference paths.

EVENT 1.7 The Soviet Union announced that their killer satellite network is operational.

Recall event 1.7, repeated above, and the multiple lines of possible inferences that an understander could generate. Some of these lines can be pruned at the start by an appropriate focus of attention on the basis of the above criteria. Two of the spurious lines of inference were based on analyzing the action of the announcement rather than focusing on the building of the killer satellites. Since governments routinely make announcements of various sorts, criterion 1.3 can be applied to conclude that it is not the announcing itself that is of interest, but that which was announced. Killer satellites are space weapons; as such, their development is something unique. Applying criterion 1.4, the building of the killer satellites emerges as the more significant event. This line of reasoning may lead to the inferences in 1.7.2. Criterion 1.5 is applicable, since new weapons usually have severe consequences on those who build them and those whom they may be used on. Selecting the focus of attention on this basis may lead to response 1.7.5.

1.6 The Reasoning Process: Refocusing the Inferencer

After the initial focus of attention, the inference process must be guided by means other than the significance criteria. The attention of the reasoning process is focused on the more significant consequences of the inferences spawned from the initial centering of attention. "Relevance" and "interest" are subjective concepts that may vary from one understander to another. Goal identification plays an important role in determining the interest and relevance of certain lines of inference to the understander.

Let us look at one example of inference proliferation after the initial focus of interest has been established by our previous criteria. The application of the significance-determination heuristics to event 1.9 determined that "holding up the mayor" was the most important action in the event. Let us see what lines of reasoning can be spawned from an initial focus of the inference-making system on the holdup part of event 1.9:

EVENT 1.9   Peter was broke and hungry. He took his .38 revolver and held up the mayor, getting away with $20. Peter had a full dinner that night.

Possible lines of inference spawned from the hold-up:

1.9.1   Is the mayor OK? Probably, the story would have said otherwise. What happens if the mayor is killed? Someone might take over. Is there a vice-mayor? The city bureaucracy would keep functioning anyway.

1.9.2   How was Peter able to hold up the mayor? I thought he had bodyguards. He must not have had any. Mayor Smith is so tight-budgeted he wouldn't appropriate the city funds. He must also be really tight personally, walking around with only $20.

1.9.3   The Mayor must have been frightened. He seems to be getting a taste of what we had to put up with all this time. Maybe now he'll finally realize the problem and increase police protection in the city.

1.9.4   How did Peter have the guts to hold up the Mayor? Maybe he didn't know who he was holding up.

1.9.5   There is going to be a massive manhunt to get Peter. I wonder whether he'll hole up or leave town? If I were Peter, I would leave immediately.

1.9.6   I wonder if the holdup was a ruse by the mob. Maybe they want to show the Mayor how vulnerable he is to extort some concession from him.

1.9.7   The Mayor's money must have been in his wallet. Did Peter take that too? If so the Mayor lost his credit cards. He must have notified the banks by now.

For each line of inference listed above there are dozens of other potential lines of inference; most are rather insignificant, such as 1.9.7. Given the initial focus of the inferencer on the Mayor being held up, all of these inferences could plausibly be made. Depending on the interests of the understander, however, only one or two of the above lines of inference are likely to be pursued. Consider the case where the understander of event 1.9 is a person with a family who lives near a high crime area. He is very worried about the crime in his neighborhood, especially the possibility that one of his children may be the victim of a crime. Which line of inference is he likely to make when he hears about event 1.9? The most natural one appears to be 1.9.3. The process that guides the inference process proceeds somewhat as follows: Starting from the inherently interesting part of event 1.9, the holdup, the understander identifies with the Mayor as a victim of the crime. Victims of crimes have certain goals in common, namely, not being a victim for a second time, regaining lost property, and possibly having some punitive action taken against the criminal. The goal identification is suggested by the predicament of the Mayor in the event, not by an exhaustive search of all possible goals and actors the understander could conceivably identify with.

Once the understander has identified with the (presumed) goals of the Mayor, the inference process focuses on what it means for the mayor to have the same goals as the understander in this matter. One of the inferences is that the Mayor, being in a position of power, is able to pursue plans to increase law enforcement, a subgoal to all three crime-victim goals mentioned above. The inferencer may have generated many other consequences, but it is this consequence that matches the goals of the understander; therefore further inference proceeds only from the fact that the Mayor is capable of increasing law enforcement. Of the ways known to the understander in which the Mayor can improve law enforcement there is one that matches the understander's more specific goal of reducing street crime. At this point the understander loses interest in further inference. Other lines of inference do not match his goals, and he is satisfied at having found a beneficial consequence that may result from event 1.9.

Subjective understanding starts at the point where the understander has an idea of what the event is about, and some parts of the event have struck his attention as being of possible interest. The reasoning process uses goal identification as a primary inference-focusing mechanism in addition to the initial determination of the inherently interesting features of the event. Our model of the inference-focusing mechanism is diagrammed in figure 1.2, which is meant to give a general idea of how the attention-focusing mechanism should function. Much of this work is devoted to the objective of investigating memory structures (chapter 3) and heuristic rules and principles (chapters 4 through 7) that provide the significant details of the general processing structure outlined in figure 1.2.

Figure 1.2 is an algorithm that focuses the attention of the understander. The degree to which such an algorithm corresponds to human thinking is an open question. In the psychology and political science literature, there is a controversy on whether political issues move citizens' thoughts and actions first and foremost because of how these issues affect the individual's self-interest, or because the issues may symbolize success or failure for the political groups with which the citizen identifies. This controversy maps into whether box 3 dominates over box 7 or vice versa. In responding to highly debated political issues, it appears that box 7, identification with a political group, may be the dominant factor, as discussed in Sears, et al. [1977].

Figure 1.2.   Subjective understanding algorithm.

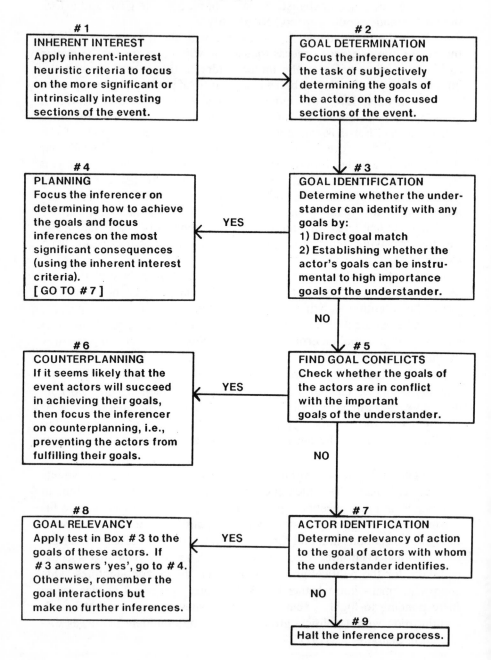

Let us briefly apply our process model of inference focusing to event 1.10.

EVENT 1.10   The United States Congress voted to fund the Trident submarine project.

Start at box 1. The inherent interest criteria make the funding of the project the initial focus of the inference system. Assume the understander is an ultra-conservative American.

Moving into box 2, the inferencer is directed to determine which goals of the United States may be fulfilled by funding the submarines. If submarines are funded, then they can be built. Building weapons increases U.S. military strength. Increasing military strength is believed to be an American goal by this understander, though not necessarily by other understanders.

The reasoning process moves into box 3, where the inferencer focuses on the task of finding a common ground between the understander's goals and the U.S. goals. None is found. If the understander is an unemployed naval engineer, then one of his most important goals, getting a good job, may have been instrumentally fulfilled by the step the U.S. takes in pursuing its goal of building weapons to increase military strength. Moving into box 5, the inferencer determines that there is no conflict between the goals of the U.S. and those of the understander.

In box 7 the inference process determines that the understander identifies with the goals of the United States and that these will be beneficially affected by the event. When the inferencer is directed to further explore the U.S. goals affected by the increase in military strength, it finds that the goal of containing Communism is enhanced. (Communist containment is an important American goal according to conservatives.) The reasoning process subsequently applies the test in box 3 and proceeds to box 4, where the inferencer is directed to find the significant consequences of the U.S.'s fulfilling its goal. The primary consequences found by the inferencer are a shift in the balance of power and the Communist nations' unwillingness to confront the U.S. in a military scenario.

The process described above for guiding the inference process according to inherent interest criteria, goal identification and subjective, preconceived notions of other actors' goals has been implemented in POLITICS, a computer system whose inference mechanism is driven by the reasoning model diagrammed in figure 1.2.

1.7 Formulating Different Types of Explanations

Thus far we have discussed only subjective explanations of events. There are also certain events that can be understood in a more detached or cursory manner. We say that a person has understood an event if he has formulated an explanation for that event (and is able to communicate his explanation in a coherent manner). It is, therefore, important to define what constitutes a satisfactory explanation for an event. We are concerned with two general classes of explanations: (1) integration of the conceptual content of the event with the understander's memory, and (2) subjective analysis of the consequences of the event and the motives of the participants. Consider how an event can be explained in terms of each explanation category:

EVENT 1.4   The state government approved a 10% rate hike requested by the ConEdison electric power company, effective immediately.

EXPLANATION   (i)   Oh yes, I know about this type of event. It is the old utility rate hike that happens every so often. What I know about utility rate hikes tells me that they range from about 3% to 10%. This one must be one of the larger hikes. Such rate hikes must be approved by a regulatory agency—the state government in this case. Often consumer groups protest against the larger rate hikes. Since this one is high I should expect such a protest.

EXPLANATION   (ii)   What is the normal function of rate hikes? To raise more money. What goal of the ConEdison company is fulfilled by a rate hike? ConEdison is a company. Companies have the goal of making money. Is a rate hike a reasonable plan to make money? Yes, indeed, that is the primary purpose of the rate hike. Why would the state government approve the rate hike? If they approved it, they must have decided that ConEdison should make more money.

EXPLANATION   (iii)   (By a non-affluent resident of an electrically heated house) Good God, 10% means that I'll have to pay almost $100 more next year in electric bills. The government sold out to big business once again.

We saw earlier that event 1.4 can be subjectively interpreted in various different ways depending upon the goals of the understanders. Now, we are also concerned with other ways in which 1.4 may be explained. Both explanations (i) and (ii) are objective elaborations of the event. Explanation (i) corresponds to understanding by means of script application (see Schank and Abelson [1977], Cullingford [1977], and Charniak [1977]). Scripts consist of detailed episodic and factual knowledge of certain types of scenarios encountered many times by an understander. Explanation (ii) consists of attributing the actions of each participant to the goals that the participant is likely to have. In explanation (ii) it is necessary to infer the goals of the actors from their actions and the situation. The actions of the participants are explained as plans to achieve their goals. This type of explanation is exhibited by PAM, a goal-based story understander (Wilensky [1978]).

The differences between these two types of explanation are based on the generality of the mechanisms that formulate explanations. Scripts contain large amounts of detailed knowledge particular to the domain, but one cannot have a script to explain every unforeseen or novel event. A goal/plan-based explanation mechanism is much more general—it accounts for novel situations—but it lacks specific detailed knowledge that people often bring into play when understanding familiar events. For instance, the pure goal-based explanation of event 1.4 cannot infer any specific actions on the part of consumer groups, such as demanding a rate review. This type of inference requires more specific knowledge about how our society works than the general interaction of goals and plans.

The third explanation is different in principle from the first two. It is a totally subjective interpretation of the event. In order to interpret event 1.4 in such a subjective manner, some sort of minimal objective understanding of the event is required. This initial understanding required to formulate (iii) bears some resemblance to the two types of objective explanations. We have to know that rate hikes mean more money for the utility companies and less money for the customer before we can relate the effects of 1.4 to our subjective goals as in explanation (iii). Subjective understanding supplements, guides, and biases objective criteria for determining satisfactory explanations of events. The programs which are described later project subjective perspectives on factual knowledge and inference rules to achieve an integrated understanding of a large class of events.

There are two basic types of explanations for events. Each type of explanation is characterized by the type of knowledge used to substantiate the interpreted events. The first type of explanation relies on finding objective causal reasons. The second type of explanation focuses on identifying the subjective motivations to explain why the actors in the event chose their particular action. We list the classes of explanation that fall into each of these two categories:

    TYPE I.   Objective integration of the meaning of the event with the understander's memory.

        A.   Script-based explanation of the event.

        B.   Goal-based explanation of the actions.

     C. Role-theme attribution of the actions of the central participant of the event.

     D. Attribution of action to idiosyncratic behavior.

TYPE II. Subjective interpretation of the motives of the participants and the consequences of the event.

     A. Effects on the self brought about by the event.

     B. Identification with one of the event participants.

     C. Attribution of motives, other than the apparent ones, to one of the actors of the event.

Explanations (i) and (ii) for event 1.4 are instances of type I explanations. Explanation (iii) is a type II explanation. Several existing computer programs exhibit the first type of explanation, for instance SAM (Script Applying Mechanism, Cullingford [1977]), and PAM (Plan Applying Mechanism, Wilensky [1978]). The programs discussed in the following chapter focus on the second type of explanation.

The explanation subtypes are necessary in order to understand when people stop making inferences. For instance, if we are told that the doctor took some blood from John, we formulate the explanation that this is a normal diagnostic action often taken by doctors. (This is a type I-C objective explanation.) No further inference or explanation is normally required. We do not attempt to infer what John's ailment may have been, nor do we analyze the doctor's personal intentions. The same is true for subjective explanations. If an ultra-conservative hears that Russia is making peace overtures, he is likely to attribute this to some hidden motive (e.g., lulling us to complacency). He is not likely to reflect upon ways we can respond to the peace overtures. Essentially, his explanation cuts off further inferences in other directions. (This is a type II-C explanation.)

Let us summarize our discussion. We believe that people will say they understood an event only if they can give an explanation for that event. Explanation, however, can proceed at two levels: at the first level, a minimal accounting of the actions in the event is formulated. If, in the course of establishing this explanation, the understander finds a subjective interest in the matter, then a deeper subjective analysis involving the goals of the understander is pursued. We adopt this general subjective understanding paradigm in our computer models introduced in the following chapter.

1.8 A Reader's Guide to This Document

The problem of subjective understanding appears in numerous manifestations and domains, including ideological interpretation, human conflict situations, social relations and interactions, purposeful connected discourse, and human personality traits. In order to model human understanding of natural language text relating to these domains, we must model the subjective biases, beliefs, and motivations of the understander. We have developed a theory of subjective understanding. This theory is embodied in a process model which focuses the attention of reasoning systems in various domains.

Three computer systems, introduced in the following chapter, illustrate our theory. These systems are POLITICS, TRIAD, and MICS. POLITICS demonstrates ideological reasoning by modeling interpretations of politial events made by liberals and conservatives. TRIAD models social power relations and conflict situations ranging from domestic quarrels to international incidents. MICS simulates a participant in a natural language conversation, using its beliefs and interests to guide the course of the conversation.

A description follows of the chapters in this work, based on their content and their contribution to our theory of subjective understanding:

Chapter 1 introduces the problem of subjective understanding and discusses the influence of personal motivations, interests, and character identification on understanding many different types of events. We discuss the problem of focusing the attention of the reasoning system on the subjectively and intrinsically more important aspects of a situation. The outline of our initial solution is presented.

Chapter 2 introduces the three programs: POLITICS, TRIAD, and MICS. We present the input-output behavior of some illustrative computer runs of the three programs. More detailed discussions of their internal functions appear in later chapters.

Chapter 3 introduces ideological interpretations of political events, demonstrates why a set of behavioral rules constitutes an insufficient model of ideological reasoning, and proposes the goal-tree paradigm as a general solution. Goal trees are mechanisms which focus the inference processes and thereby influence understanding. Chapter 3 discusses goal trees and their funtion in POLITICS. Chapter 10 and 11 discuss the application of the goal-tree model in understanding human personality traits and simulating human discourse.

Our reasoning model consists of a set of counterplanning strategies. Each strategy is a general method for thwarting the goals of another actor, interfering with his plans, or reformulating one's plans to circumvent outside interference. The use of these strategies in the understanding process is guided by the focus of attention of the understander as determined by the goal trees.

Chapter 4 introduces counterplanning strategies, discusses their application and internal structure, and classifies the situations where such strategies are applied. Conflict situations give rise to counterplanning. This chapter discusses mutual exclusion goal conflicts, partial fulfillment of goals, and goal compromises.

Chapter 5 discusses plan interference situations and the counterplanning strategies they suggest. A dimensional analysis of interference situations is presented as part of the process model that interacts with the beliefs of the understander.

Chapter 6 analyzes plan-conflict situations by applying a taxonomy of conflict situations based on the cause of the conflict. We analyze various resource limitations and violated preconditions as the primary causes of plan conflicts that give rise to counterplanning situations.

Chapter 7 presents a detailed, annotated computer run of the POLITICS system, briefly explaining the natural language analysis, the question answering mechanism, and the script application process. Goal analysis and counterplanning processes are also illustrated.

Chapter 8 discusses some interesting errors made by POLITICS. As a solution to the problems underlying these errors we introduce the "basic social acts," a system of representation and inference applicable to social and political conflict situations. TRIAD, a program which embodies the social-acts paradigm, is discussed.

Chapter 9 formulates our theory of human personality traits based on the goal-tree representation of human beliefs, interests, and motivations.

Chapter 10 discusses inference processes and focus of attention in a conversational dialog. Our model uses goal trees to guide the topic of the conversation in directions of interest to the speaker. Our "speaker" is MICS (Mixed Initiative Conversational System), a program that simulates a participant in cocktail party conversations in natural language.

Chapter 11 presents a brief overview of three other models of belief systems (BELIEVER, PARRY, and the "ideology machine") and contrasts them with our POLITICS model.

There are many ways to read this document. The best way is, of course, to read it from cover to cover as time and interest permit. Chapter 3 is recommended to all readers; it is relatively easy reading and describes our basic model of subjective belief. The reader who wishes to focus on our model of subjective understanding is referred to chapters 2, 3, 5, 9,

10 and 11, and should return to chapter 8 as time permits. The reader who is primarily interested in the POLITICS system and its computer implementation is referred to chapters 2, 3, 4, 5, and 7 and the first half of chapter 8. Finally, the reader who wants a fast overview is referred to the intersection of the above lists; namely, chapters 2, 3, 5, and 8 if time permits.

2

The Computer Models: POLITICS, TRIAD and MICS

We have developed three computer programs to model different aspects of subjective understanding. This chapter introduces the three programs and presents some illustrative input/output sessions. We used the three programs as research tools to develop and test the ideas and principles discussed throughout this work. None of the programs attempts to be a complete performance model; each embodies various aspects of a theory of subjectively oriented reasoning that is in the process of being developed. We discuss each program in turn, focusing on the type of inference and inference-focusing mechanisms they exhibit.

2.1 POLITICS: A Computer Model of Ideological Reasoning

POLITICS simulates human ideological understanding of international political events. The understander focuses the inference process on the ideologically relevant facts and events. (The methods used to formulate and focus the inference process are discussed at length starting in Chapter 3.) POLITICS demonstrates its understanding by answering questions directly related to ideologically interpreted events. The ideologies simulated correspond to those of a United States conservative and a United States liberal interpreting brief political events. Input events are given in English. POLITICS analyzes these events into Conceptual Dependency (CD) representation, applies situational information in the form of scripts (Schank and Abelson [1977], Cullingford [1977]), and applies the appropriate inference processes guided by its ideology. The question-answer dialog is used to interrogate the story representation built during the event interpretation phase, and, if necessary, further inferences are performed. The answer is converted from memory representation to English by a template-based English generator. The following is a U.S.-conservative POLITICS interpretation and subsequent question-answer dialog:

(INTERPRET U.S.-CONSERVATIVE)
INPUT TEXT: Russia massed troops on the Czech border.

INTEPRETATION COMPLETED, READY TO ACCEPT QUESTIONS.

Q1: Why did Russia do this?

A1: BECAUSE RUSSIA THOUGHT THAT IT COULD TAKE POLITICAL
     CONTROL OF CZECHOSLOVAKIA BY SENDING TROOPS.

Q2: What will Russia do next?

A2: RUSSIA MAY TELL ITS TROOPS TO START THE INVASION.

Q3: What else can Russia do?

A3: RUSSIA MAY WAIT FOR CZECHOSLOVAKIA TO GIVE IN TO RUS-
     SIAN DEMANDS.

Q4: What happens if Czechoslovakia does not give in?

A4: RUSSIA MAY DECIDE TO START THE INVASION.

Q5: What should the United States do?

A5: THE UNITED STATES SHOULD INTERVENE MILITARILY.

Q6: What else can the United States do?

A6: THE UNITED STATES CAN DO NOTHING, OR IT CAN INTERVENE
     DIPLOMATICALLY BY CONFERRING WITH RUSSIA ABOUT CZECHO-
     SLOVAKIA. THESE ALTERNATIVES ARE BAD FOR THE UNITED
     STATES.

The U.S.-conservative ideology incorporated into the POLITICS system
believes that the primary concern of the United States is to stop Communist expansion, and that Russia's primary concern is to eventually take
over the world. Therefore, the inference process is focused on what Russia can do to increase its control of other parts of the world, and what
the United States can do to stop Russia. The latter concern is illustrated
in the questions about possible U.S. responses to the Russian action.
POLITICS, simulating a U.S. conservative, focused its inferences on the
most effective method of stopping Russia, ignoring other inference paths
such as the threat of war, worsened East-West relations, and the cost to
the United States of a military adventure in Eastern Europe. Other ideologues, such as a U.S. liberal, would worry about (and therefore focus
their inferencer on) the threat to world peace and human rights brought

about by the Russian action. The idea of American military intervention may not even occur to a liberal. It is this type of ideologically-based inference-focusing process that POLITICS was designed to model. (The interpretation of this story, including the application of a multi-track script, is discussed at greater length in Carbonell [1978].)

Let us proceed to analyze a POLITICS protocol in somewhat greater depth. We present the inferences that POLITICS actually makes while interpreting the event, first from a U.S.-conservative and later from a U.S.-liberal ideology.

The POLITICS protocol below illustrates the interpretation of a headline on the Panama Canal from the *New Haven Register*. The headline reads: "The U.S. Congress is expected to approve the Panama Canal Treaty."

POLITICS interprets the headline first from the point of view of a conservative ideology and later from a liberal ideology. The same system of computer programs can model any self-consistent ideology. The liberal and conservative ideologies are data structures which encode the significant motivations and evaluative beliefs characteristic of each ideology. An evaluative belief tells the understander what course of action is more consistent with the ideological goals. The ideology is assimilated by POLITICS before the event is interpreted. The story interpretations, illustrated by the respective question-answer dialogs, differ substantially in their evaluations of the headline and expectations of possible future events.

Consider the U.S.-conservative interpretation of the Panama Canal story. POLITICS analyzes the headline to conclude that "approval of a treaty" by a legislative body (e.g., the U.S. Congress) calls for the application of parliamentary procedures (encoded as the script $PARLIAMENT-PROC in POLITICS). More specifically, since the input event expresses the expectation of an outcome, the system concludes that the means of arriving at the outcome should be instantiated. The $PAR-LIAMENT-PROC script knows that the $VOTE scene is what normally produces a decision or outcome about an issue under consideration by a legislative body. The word "approve" when applied to an item under consideration by a voting body is considered to mean a positive outcome for the proposition under consideration.

POLITICS tries to infer the immediate result of the Congressional $VOTE on the state of the world, because the $VOTE script states that this is usually of importance. The inference generated is that everything in the Panama Canal Treaty will probably become fact. (The main provisions of the treaty are stored in POLITICS' memory.) The primary result of the treaty is the change in control of the Canal Zone (and therefore anything therein, such as the Canal itself) from the United States to Panama.

The Initial phase of the headline interpretation appears below:

Start of POLITICS Interpretations and QA Dialogs

PTYCON LOG FILE	2-Mar-78 11:51:25

PTYCON> CONNECT (TO SUBJOB) 1
[CONNECTED TO SUBJOB POL(1)]

*(INTERPRET US-CONSERVATIVE)
INCORPORATING US-CONSERVATIVE IDEOLOGY GOAL TREES . . .
G0: SOVIET-WORLDOM.
G12: US-SAVEFREEWORLD.
INITIALIZING PARSER . . . DONE.

INPUT STORY: +   The U.S. Congress is expected to approve the Panama
Canal treaty.

PARSING . . . COMPLETED.

INSTANTIATING SCRIPT: $PARLIAMENT-PROC
EXPECTED TRACK:
   <=> (($VOTE VOTERS (#ORG NAME (CONGRESS) PARTOF (*US*))
              ISSUE (#TREATY NAME (PANAMA CANAL)
                    REF (TREATY03))
                    SIGNEES (*US* *PANAMA*))
            OUTCOME (*POS*)))

U.S.-conservative POLITICS takes the scriptal analysis and applies goal-directed inferences, using the goals and motivations of the U.S.-conservative ideology. No new goals for the U.S. are achieved as a result of the Panama Canal Treaty; in fact some active U.S. goals suffer serious setbacks. One U.S. goal is to be militarily as strong as possible. This goal suffers as a result of the abandonment of the Panama Canal, an important military outpost. The military strength goal is a subgoal to being stronger than the Communist nations (militarily, economically, and politically), which is in turn a subgoal to Communist containment, the highest level U.S.-conservative goal. Making the Communists aware of the new U.S. weakness (i.e., the MTRANS inference listed below) violates the U.S. military deterrent goal, which leads U.S.-conservative POLITICS to believe that Russia may pursue the goal of expanding its military and political control over small nations.

    The section of POLITICS protocol below illustrates the goal-directed inferences discussed above:

```
*CANAL-ZONE*  FROM (*CONTROL* VAL (*US*))
              TOWARD (*CONTROL* VAL (*PANAMA*))

*US* GOAL VIOLATED:
*US* MILITARY STRENGTH DECREASED.

*US* GOAL VIOLATED:
ACTOR (#COUNTRY TYPE (*COMMUNIST*))
  <=> (*MTRANS*)
  MOBJ ((ACTOR (*US*) TOWARD (*STRENGTH*TYPE (*MILIT*))
```

INTEPRETATION COMPLETED, READY TO ACCEPT QUESTIONS.

The question-answer (QA) dialog illustrates the necessity of the above inferences and scriptal knowledge in evaluating the situation to predict future events and to make suggestions for future actions by the United States. The first answer in the QA dialog below expresses a relative evaluation of the state of the world resulting from approval of the Panama Canal treaty compared to the present state of the world. The evaluation function considers only the changes in the state of the world brought to light in the preceding event-interpretation process. The resulting negative evaluation is, or course, from the point of view of the United States. The second and third questions are answered directly from the goal-directed inferences generated in the understanding phase, namely the expected drop in U.S. military strength and the ensuing activation of a Russian military/political expansion goal. The fourth answer reconstructs the reasoning chain concluding that Russia may try to take over the Canal.

The question-answer dialog is presented below:

INTEPRETATION COMPLETED, READY TO ACCEPT QUESTIONS.

Q1: Should the U.S. approve the treaty?

A1: NO, THE TREATY IS BAD FOR THE UNITED STATES.

Q2: Why is the treaty bad for the U.S.?

A2: THE UNITED STATES WOULD LOSE THE CANAL TO PANAMA AND THE UNITED STATES WILL BE WEAKER.

Q3: What might happen if the United States loses the Canal?

A3: RUSSIA WILL TRY TO CONTROL THE CANAL.

Q4: Why would Russia try to take over the Canal?

A4:   RUSSIA WANTS TO EXPAND ITS MILITARY CONTROL. THE PAN-
AMA CANAL HAS HIGH MILITARY VALUE.

Q5:   How might this happen?

A5:   THE UNITED STATES MAY NOT BE ABLE TO STOP ANYONE TAK-
ING OVER THE PANAMA CANAL. TORRIJOS IS A COMMUNIST.
TORRIJOS WILL LET RUSSIA CONTROL PANAMA.

Q6:   Why should the U.S. worry about Russia taking over the Canal?

A6:   BECAUSE RUSSIA WANTS TO CONTROL THE WORLD.

Q7:   What should the U.S. do to stop Russia from taking over the Canal?

A7:   CONGRESS SHOULD VOTE AGAINST THE PANAMA CANAL
TREATY.

The fifth question calls for some planning: How can Russia proceed in
the pursuit of its newly activated goal? Since nothing to this effect was
concluded in the event interpretation phase, the inference mechanism
must be reinvoked with the objective of determining the most plausible
Russian plan. There are various methods known to POLITICS whereby
one country can achieve control of another country (or demographic
region) such as invasion, causing revolution, economic domination, and
direct influence based on a common ideology. The last alternative is
selected as Russia's probable choice because it involves the least cost.
(Torrijos, hence Panama, is believed to have Communist tendencies by
the U.S.-conservative ideology.) The counterplanning module is called to
evaluate the plausibility of the proposed Russian plan of action. (Counterplanning is a process which determines how an actor can thwart another
actor's goals or plans. Chapters 4 through 7 contain a detailed discussion
of counterplanning strategies.) Since the U.S. ended its military and
political control of the Canal Zone, the counterplanning module sees no
effective way of preventing Russian actions in Panama. Hence, POLI-
TICS is satisfied that the method it selected for Russian takeover of the
Panama Canal is indeed plausible.

"How" questions refer to instrumentality (Lehnert [1978]). The
instruments of a plan are considered to be the preconditions that must be
true in order for that plan to succeed. Therefore, the answer that is generated for the fifth question is a list of the preconditions to a Russian
takeover: no effective opposition from the present party controlling the
Canal, and no opposition from the party controlling the Canal in the

future because of their perceived ideology. (The English generator is a little weak at expressing the causality present in the memory structures.)

The answer to the sixth question is obtained by examining Russia's goals in order to see what motivates Russia to expand its military control whenever possible.

The last two question-answer pairs reflect the counterplanning strategies applied to suggest the courses of action that the United States should choose in order to achieve its goals in light of the currently activated context. The conclusion is essentially that the only alternative available to the U.S. is to reject the Panama Canal Treaty. This agrees with most of the recent statements voiced by conservatives around the nation.

The question-answering phase of POLITICS is based on Lehnert's [1978] question-analysis process to determine precisely what the question is asking for. Once the desired information is specified, POLITICS searches the interpretation of the original event for the answer. If the search fails, further inference is tried, as illustrated in the hypothetical "what if" questions of the U.S.-conservative QA dialog. The English text of each question is analyzed into Conceptual Dependency (CD) representation before the question-answering process is invoked. The analysis process is based on Riesbeck and Schank's [1976] description of an expectation-based parser, but the program is oriented to the task of parsing into memory structures used by the POLITICS system. Some power and robustness is gained from the memory interaction because the parser can query memory for additional processing information. Definite references to previously discussed objects and events are determined as part of the analysis process. The answers to the questions are translated from CD to English by a template-based English generator. Neither the analyzer nor the generator are of immediate concern. Chapters 7 and 8 discuss how subjective understanding affects natural language interpretations. Other aspects of POLITICS are discussed in greater detail.

The liberal interpretation of the Panama Canal event proceeds in a similar way through the initial script-based interpretation of the event. The goal-directed inferences, however, find that the U.S. action can indeed help to achieve some U.S. goals. In the U.S.-liberal ideology, the important United States goals include: reducing political tensions, avoiding conflicts, and improving relations with all countries in general (Latin American countries in the present context). POLITICS concludes that the Panama Canal treaty is an important step in achieving these goals; hence it arrives at a favorable evaluation of the proposed change in the state of the world brought about by approval of the Panama Canal treaty.

The counterplanning strategies are invoked to answer questions about what may happen if the U.S. does not approve the treaties (i.e., keeps the Canal), and whether the Russians are likely to try to take over the Canal. The same counterplanning strategy of verifying a candidate plan for Russian control of Panama (hence the Canal) that was applied in the U.S.-conservative ideology yields different results in the U.S.-liberal ideology. Under the liberal ideology, Russia's goals of maintaining world peace and avoiding political and military conflicts are much more important than expansion of military or political control. Hence, since the Panama Canal Treaty has a section providing for U.S. defense of the Canal, the counterplanning strategies conclude that if Russia tried to take over Panama, then it would come into conflict with the U.S. According to the U.S.-liberal ideology, international conflict is less desirable for Russia than abandoning its goal of political/military control over Panama. Thus, the answers to the last two questions in the liberal interpretation differ greatly from the answers to the respective questions posed to the Conservative interpretation.

The U.S.-liberal POLITICS interpretation and subsequent QA dialog for the Panama Canal headline is presented below:

```
*(INTERPRET US-LIBERAL)
INCORPORATING US-LIBERAL IDEOLOGY GOAL TREES . . .
  G0: SOVIET-WORLDPEACE.
  G11: US-WORLDPEACE.
INITIALIZING PARSER . . . DONE.

  INPUT STORY:    +   The U.S. Congress is expected to approve the Panama
                      Canal treaty.

PARSING . . . COMPLETED.
INSTANTIATING SCRIPT: $PARLIAMENT-PROC
EXPECTED TRACK:
    <=> (($VOTE VOTERS (#ORG NAME (CONGRESS) PARTOF (*US*))
                  ISSUE (#TREATY NAME (PANAMA CANAL)
                                REF (TREATY03))
                                SIGNEES (*US* *PANAMA*))
             OUTCOME (*POS*) ))

  *CANAL-ZONE*   FROM (*CONTROL* VAL (*US*))
                 TOWARD (*CONTROL* VAL (*PANAMA*))

  ($COLONIALISM  CPOWER (*US*)
                 COLONY (*CANAL-ZONE* PARTOF (*PANAMA*))
  ABORTED.   MAINCON NO LONGER MATCHES WORLD.

  *US* GOAL ENABLED:
  *US* AND *PANAMA* TO END CONFLICT.
```

```
*US* GOAL ENABLED:
(#COUNTRY TYPE (*THIRD-WORLD*) PARTOF (*SOUTH-AMERICA*))
TO IMPROVE RELATIONS WITH *US*
```

INTEPRETATION COMPLETED, READY TO ACCEPT QUESTIONS.

The goal-directed inference process, with the U.S.-liberal goals, find that in order to maintain world peace the United States should improve relations as much as possible with all countries. One way of accomplishing this is to end conflicts, and a way to end a conflict is to eliminate its cause. The cause of the U.S.-Panama conflict was the "colonialistic" relationship whereby the U.S. had political control of part of Panama. Hence, discovering that this is no longer the case, as a result of the Canal treaty, U.S.-liberal POLITICS infers that the U.S. may now be able to accomplish its peace-making goals.

U.S.-conservative POLITICS did not view the Canal treaty as the end of an instance of colonialism because improving relations with third world countries is not a high priority goal (compared with maintaining the proper U.S. military strength). Hence, U.S.-conservative POLITICS did not search for ways to improve relations with Panama or other Latin American countries, and therefore it did not see this consequence of the treaty's approval. This illustrates how the point of view of the reader can determine what is actually understood in an account of a political event.

The QA dialog follows:

Q1: Should the U.S. approve the treaty?

A1: YES, THE PANAMA CANAL TREATY IS GOOD FOR THE UNITED STATES.

Q2: Why is the treaty good?

A2: THE PANAMA CANAL TREATY IMPROVES RELATIONS WITH LATIN AMERICAN COUNTRIES.

Q3: What happens if the U.S. keeps the Canal?

A3: THIS WILL CAUSE DISCONTENT AND CONFLICT IN PANAMA AND LATIN AMERICA.

Q4: Why would this lead to conflict?

A4: THE CANAL ZONE IS A UNITED STATES COLONY. LATIN AMERICA DOES NOT LIKE COLONIALISM. THE UNITED STATES WOULD MAINTAIN COLONIALISM.

Q5:   What if Russia tries to take over the Canal?

A5:   RUSSIA DOES NOT WANT CONFLICT WITH THE US. RUSSIA WILL
STAY OUT OF THE CANAL IF THE UNITED STATES DEFENDS IT.
THE UNITED STATES DEFENDING THE CANAL IS PART OF THE
TREATY.

The Panama Canal event is the most complicated type of scenario that
the program can understand. POLITICS is limited in its domain of application to interpreting political events, but many of its mechanisms such
as the counterplanning process are much more generally applicable. The
next program we discuss, TRIAD, has a much wider range of applicability, although the program is not yet fully developed. TRIAD should
eventually encompass all the ideological reasoning processes now exhibited by POLITICS.

2.2 TRIAD: Analyzing Social and Political Conflicts

There are other aspects of subjective understanding that go beyond the
ideologically driven process exhibited in POLITICS. One important aspect
type of subjective understanding is contextually driven inference focusing. For instance, consider the following story:

EVENT 2.1   Johnny complained to mother that Billy took away his candy bar.

There are some inferences that are relevant to this situation and others
that are quite irrelevant. The dispute over who should have the candy is
the dominant theme of event 2.1. For instance, a person reading 2.1 may
infer the following:

1. Johnny wants his candy bar back.

2. Billy wants the candy bar.

3. Johnny's complaint may cause his mother to tell Billy to return the candy bar.

4. If Billy does not do this, mother may enforce her order.

5. If mother does not do anything, Johnny may try to get back the candy bar by
   himself.

However, a person reading event 2.1 is unlikely to make inferences such
as the following:

6. The candy is probably made out of chocolate, sugar, and other ingredients.

7. Johnny probably spoke to his mother in the process of making his complaint.

8. Johnny's teeth are less likely to have cavities if he does not eat the candy bar.

9. Billy probably used his hands in order to grab Johnny's candy bar.

How do we know that the former inferences are relevant to the situation and the latter ones irrelevant? The probability that a particular inference is true is an insufficient criterion for determining whether that inference should be made. For instance, both inferences (1) and (9) are extremely likely to be true, yet (9) seems irrelevant. If we recognize event 2.1 as a social conflict situation, we see that this context can establish the relevant aspects of the situation on which the inferencer should focus. Conflict situations appear across many different domains, including international politics, domestic problems, civil matters, etc. TRIAD is a program that analyzes conflict situations and focuses the inferencer on the appropriate set of contextually relevant issues. The mechanisms used by TRIAD are much more general than the analysis performed by POLITICS. We discuss these mechanisms, called "basic social acts" and "authority triangles" in Chapter 9 and in Schank and Carbonell [1979].

POLITICS's understanding of a concept such as colonialism is restricted to asserting the relationship between the colonial power and the colonized region. TRIAD can represent this concept using the social acts (discussed in Chapter 8), and infer the types of goals and courses of action that both parties are likely to pursue. Here we present some output from the TRIAD program.

Start of TRIAD Interpretation and Inference Process

PTYCON LOG FILE   26-May-78 15:46:08

PTYCON> CONNECT (TO SUBJOB) TRIAD
[CONNECTED TO SUBJOB TRIAD(1)]

  Yale Computer Science—Research DECsystem20,
TOPS-20 Monitor 3(1371)
TRIFNS-PARFNS-PARDIC-PARREQ-(CATAWBA.REP)-
TRIANGLE analyzer loaded.
TRIANGLE inferencer loaded.

*(PARSER)

INPUT SENTENCE: Catawba Indian land claims supported.

Run Parser? (Proceed/Halt)
*P

Output token: CON4

[GENERATING THE MEMORY REPRESENTATION OF THE FULL EVENT]

```
Expanding token: CON4 =
((CON ((ACTOR (*PP*CLASS (#GROUP)
                    CFEATURE (*AMERINDIAN*)
                    TYPE (*ETHNIC*)
                    NAME (CATAWBA) TOK NP1)
          <=> (*PETITION*)
          OBJECT ((ACTOR (*PP* CLASS (#REGION)
                              TOK NP2 REL CON1)
                    IS (*OWN* VAL NP1))
                 TOK CON1)
          FROM NP1
          TO (*PP*CLASS (#INSTITUTION)
                 MEM *COURT* TOK NP3))
          TOK CON2)
     IR ((ACTOR NP3
            <=> (*AUTH*)
            OBJECT CON1
            RECIP1 NP1
            RECIP2 GAP1
            FROM GAP2) TOK CON3))
     TOK CON4)
```

Loading generator functions . . .
14703 FREE STG, 6600 FULL WORDS AVAILABLE
Files-Loaded for Generator.

*(GENERATE CON4)

   The Catawba Indians asked a Federal Court to rule that they own the land, and
   it decreed that the land is owned by them.

*(INF-APPLY CON4)

   [Generating inferences form CON4]

*(TELL-STORY)

   The Catawba Indians and the other parties disagreed over the ownership of the
   land.

   The Catawba Indians requested a Federal Court to rule that they own the land.

A Federal Court decided that the land is owned by the Catawba Indians.

The other parties will probably appeal the decision.

The other parties might use force against the Catawba Indians to assert that they own the land.

NIL
*P

TRIAD analyzes the English text of the conflict situation and builds a full memory representation of the conflict episode. This process combines natural language analysis with memory integration. TRIAD knows that Indian affairs are handled by the federal government and that land claims usually constitute a legal appeal (in the absence of further information). Furthermore, TRIAD knows that a legal suit or appeal is an instance of a petition to a higher authority for the resolution of an existing conflict. This fact disambiguates the meaning of "supported" to mean "resolved in favor of" (rather than physical or financial support). The interaction of the language analysis and the TRIAD memory generates the event representation CON4, printed above. This event representation is generated in English to illustrate the additional information supplied by TRIAD's memory in the process of analyzing the original English text.

The TRIAD English analyzer is much more general in scope than the POLITICS analyzer. It represents an advance over other analyzers in that it references memory to create a full event representation. Depending on the memory of the system (e.g., its knowledge and beliefs) the analyzer may produce different representations for the same English text. This brings subjective understanding to the level of natural language analysis. The TRIAD generator is a version of PHLUENT, a general purpose English generator used by all the AI systems at the Yale AI project.

After constructing the event representation and recognizing the conflict situation, TRIAD recognizes the conflict situation and focuses the inferencer on the appropriate aspects of the expected outcome and the preconditions of the event. The result of the inference phase is integrated into the event representation and the entire story is generated in English to illustrate the inferences that were made. In the Catawba Indians example, TRIAD inferred that the land claims may have resulted from a previous conflict between the Indians and other parties. These other parties are not expected to be pleased by the Federal Court decision. Therefore, TRIAD expects that they will take action to recover the land. The same inferences are applicable to the Catawba situation and event 2.1 (the candy bar conflict) because TRIAD abstracts the general conflict scenario from the physical acts and other situation-specific information. The TRIAD inferences apply only at this higher level of abstraction where conflicts and ways of resolving them are analyzed without irrelevant situational details.

A more detailed discussion of the TRIAD memory representation, its analyzer, and its inference rules is presented in Chapter 8.

2.3 MICS: Focusing Inferences in Human Conversation

Subjective understanding is pervasive in almost all instances of human communication. Two people engaged in a conversation interpret each other's comments with respect to their own knowledge of the subject matter under discussion, their interest in any particular aspect of their discussion, their conversational goals, and their perceptions of the interests of the other party. We discuss the subjective aspects of human conversations in Chapter 10. Here we introduce MICS (Mixed-Initiative Conversational System), a computer program that takes the place of a human in a conversational dialog.

MICS has some knowledge about people, occupations, objects, and actions in the world. This factual knowledge is encoded in a semantic network. The interesting aspect of MICS is how it uses its knowledge to generate proper and relevant utterances in the course of a conversation. To this end MICS has its own interests and conversational goals. For instance, MICS has the goals of getting to know strangers, keeping people out of trouble, playing chess, and spreading gossip about its acquaintances. These goals translate into conversational goals (e.g., trying to start up a chess game, warning people of dangerous courses of action, and asking questions of strangers in order to learn new facts about them.)

The inference process in MICS is driven by how relevant the current topic of conversation is to its goals. Therefore, MICS will change topics in the conversation to topics that can help it fulfill its conversational goals. In understanding utterances of the other speaker, MICS directs its inferencer to analyze the effects of the utterance on its conversational goals. We also worked on getting the inferencer to establish the conversational goals of the other speaker, but this is a more difficult and as yet unsolved problem. MICS also encodes topic selection rules (based on Schank [1977]) and rules on how to conduct a conversation. These rules are discussed in Chapter 10.

The following is a dialog between MICS and Dave, a total stranger to MICS. Dave is a fictional character created by this writer for the purpose of conducting a conversation with MICS. The lines in upper case are MICS's utterances. Lines in italics are comments we inserted later.

Start of MICS Conversational Dialog

PSEUDO LOG FILE   11-Oct-77 21:06:11

```
@RUN MICS [37,104]

*(SETQ MODE 'STRANGER)
*(SETQ TRACEFLAG NIL)
*(TALK)
```

HELLO, WHAT IS YOUR NAME?

I am Dave.
WHAT'S NEW TODAY, DAVE?

Nothing, What's your name?
MY NAME IS MICS.

What is your job?
I AM A COMPUTER PROGRAMMER.

That's nice.
WHAT DO YOU DO FOR A LIVING?

> *MICS takes the initiative by asserting its conversational goal of learning about Dave.*

I am still a student.
DO YOU LIKE BEING A STUDENT?

For the time being yes.
WHAT WILL YOU DO AFTERWARDS?

I want to be a professor some day.
WHAT DO YOU DO FOR FUN?

> *MICS formed a person-frame for Dave. At this point, the conversational goal of trying to establish an area of mutual interest and shared knowledge is activated.*

I smoke dope.
YOU MIGHT GET STONED IF YOU SMOKE TOO MUCH.

I know, that's the idea.
YOU MIGHT GET IN TROUBLE IF THE COPS CATCH YOU.

> *The goal motivating the above two utterances is warning Dave about the*

consequences of his action. A later version of MICS realizes that the goal of smoking marijuana is to get high and people are aware of their own goals. Therefore Dave should realize the effects of dope and require no warning.

All right, stop moralizing, what do you do for fun?
I LIKE TO PLAY CHESS.

That sounds boring.
NO, IT IS A LOT OF FUN!

My brother Eric plays chess.
HE MUST BE SMART.

I have to go. Bye Mics.
NICE TALKING TO YOU, DAVE.

As a result of the conversation, MICS knows something about Dave, in particular that one of his life goals is to become a professor. MICS remembers what it learned about Dave in its long term memory. Thus MICS has one more person to talk about in future conversations such as the dialog with Pete below. MICS believes Pete to be his friend and a student at the university where MICS works as a programmer.

HELLO, WHAT IS YOUR NAME?

Pete.
WHAT'S NEW TODAY, PETE?

Professor Stevenson is giving us an exam Friday.
STEVENSON GIVES DIFFICULT EXAMS.

Yeah, do you know that Dave is probably going to flunk?
THAT'S GOING TO MAKE IT HARD FOR DAVE TO BECOME A PROFESSOR.

Too bad, Dave is not too smart anyways.
YES, DAVE LIKES TO SMOKE DOPE.

I've got to go and study.
YOU WILL DO WELL IN THE EXAM.

The above conversation illustrates the usefulness of shared knowledge between the two participants. Pete and MICS both know about taking exams, know who Professor Stevenson is, and have Dave as a mutual acquaintance. When Pete mentions that Dave may flunk, MICS directs the inference process at the most important aspects of flunking—namely, the fact that Dave may no longer be able to graduate because a necessary precondition to graduating is violated (i.e., passing one's exams). MICS also focuses its inferences on how Dave's most important goal (becoming a professor) may be affected by the present actions. Once again a precondition is violated; if Dave does not graduate, he cannot become a professor. It is significant to note that MICS could have carried on other chains of inference, but focused only on what it considered most important for Dave's goals and what it considers to be the most inherently interesting aspect of the previous utterance. For instance, MICS is able to make the following contextually inappropriate inferences but does not make them because they do not come into the focus of attention of the inferencer: Dave may be sad if he flunks; Dave's graduating class will be smaller; Dave may use a pen or a pencil to take the exam.

We gave MICS rules about what people believe and how they make decisions. These rules interact with the rules of conversation to alter MICS's model of communication. consider the following rule: "If a speaker willingly follows a given course of action, he is probably aware of the consequences of that action." In conjunction with MICS's conversational rule of not telling people what they already know, this rule would eliminate MICS's warnings about getting high smoking marijuana. The following dialog exhibits a later version of MICS with the addition of this rule and several other similar rules:

> Ashtrays.
> WHAT ABOUT ASHTRAYS?
>
> Ashtrays are useful.
> DO YOU SMOKE?
>
> Yes.
> YOU MIGHT GET CANCER IF YOU SMOKE TOO MUCH.
>
> Who cares, anyway I smoke dope, not tobacco.
> I SEE, YOU LIKE TO GET HIGH.
>
> It is better than getting drunk.
> NOT NECESSARILY. YOU MIGHT GET CAUGHT BY THE COPS.

In Chapter 10 we discuss the MICS model of conversation, its conversational rules, and its subjectively oriented topic selection process.

2.4 A Concluding Remark

The three programs have served us as very useful means for testing our hypotheses about how subjective understanding may function. Programs highlight inconsistencies and insufficiently-specified mechanisms in any process-based theory under development. Without methods of constraining the inference process by some means such as establishing the subjective focus of interest, we could not have built our three working programs. In subsequent chapters we discuss our theory of subjective understanding and the embodiment of our theory as a computational model.

3

Goal Trees: A Model of Ideological Reasoning

3.1 Ideological Interpretations of Political Events

Subjective understanding encompasses many types of belief-oriented reasoning processes. One such process is politically based ideological understanding. In the first chapter we discussed the importance of a subjective component guiding the understanding system and constraining the inference process. Here we present a process model of ideological reasoning. This model is generalized in later chapters to encompass other types of subjective understanding based on rational strategies applied to preconceived notions of how the world functions and what motivates people and human institutions. We make the stronger claim that a single set of strategies guides the understanding of events from different domains. These strategies, however, do not operate in a knowledge vacuum. They require domain-specific knowledge and an internal representation of the understander's perspective about how the world works. In the domain of international politics, this perspective is called a political ideology.

Consider some political events and different ideological interpretations of these events.

U.S.-CONSERVATIVE interpretation:

EVENT 3.1 President Carter proposed the sale of additional F-15 fighters to Iran.

QUESTION 3.1.1 Should the United States sell the weapons?

RESPONSE 3.1.1 Yes, Iran is an anti-Soviet U.S. ally.

Our task is to model the interpretation process that a U.S. conservative uses to understand event 3.1 and answer the subsequent question. Since a liberal would answer question 3.1.1 differently, there must be some difference in the liberal and conservative interpretations of event 3.1. For instance, the following is a typical liberal response to question 3.1.1:

> RESPONSE 3.1.2   No, the U.S. should not support dictatorships that suppress human rights.

The differences in the interpretations of event 3.1 that lead to the different responses must be accounted for by the differences between conservative and liberal political ideology. Hence, the political ideology is part of the subjective component of the understanding process. In the first chapter we demonstrated the importance of this component; here we derive a model for ideological interpretation as part of the subjective understanding process. We discuss possible ways to represent ideologies in terms of behavioral rules. Later we show that such approaches are insufficient, and we derive a general representation of political ideologies based on goal trees and rules for applying goal trees to the understanding process.

A first-order hypothesis to account for the different responses to event 3.1 might be that the conservative ideology contains the fact that the U.S. should sell arms to Iran, and the liberal ideology contains the negation of this fact. This approach is clearly too naive. Consider the case where the conservative and liberal understanders were previously unaware of possible U.S. arms sales to Iran. The conservative and liberal ideologues would still have answered the question in much the same way. That is, they would have been capable of evaluating the advisability of U.S. arms sales to Iran if such an evaluation was not already in their respective memories. This suggests a somewhat more general hypothesis, based on the fact that it is reasonable that an ideologue can generate an opinion about an unfamiliar event involving familiar actors.

Our next suggestion is: The conservative ideology states that the U.S. should provide necessary aid to Iran, and the liberal ideology states that the opposite should be the case. Unfortunately, such a suggestion does not generalize to encompass the following situation:

> EVENT 3.2   The dictator of Buthan is trying to suppress Soviet-backed Marxist insurgents. The joint chiefs advised Carter to send weapons to the government of Buthan.
>
> QUESTION 3.2.1   Should the United States send the weapons?
>
> U.S.-CONSERVATIVE ANSWER:
> RESPONSE 3.2.1   Yes, Buthan is fighting against Soviet domination.
>
> U.S.-LIBERAL ANSWER:
> RESPONSE 3.2.2   No, the U.S. should not support dictatorships that suppress human rights. The U.S. should also stay out of foreign guerilla wars.

The conservative and liberal answers to question 3.2.1 are very similar to the corresponding answers in event 3.1. What information in the conservative and liberal ideologies accounts for these responses? Most people know very little about Buthan. The conservative and liberal interpretations of event 3.2 were formed from the information contained in the event itself. That is, the fact that Buthan is anti-Soviet and the fact that it is a dictatorship are part of the event being interpreted. Therefore, the political ideologies should not contain such information as: "The U.S. should aid Buthan" in the conservative ideology, and "The U.S. should not provide any military aid to Buthan" in the liberal ideology. Given that neither ideologue required prior knowledge of Buthan, it is evident that these policies are generated as part of the interpretation process.

Since the ideological interpretation process need not contain specific statements about U.S. policy toward specific nations in order to understand event 3.2, we postulate that the specific information about U.S. policy toward Iran is also superfluous. This is to say that a U.S. policy toward a specific issue can be generated from the ideology and information about the situation being interpreted. Since our task is not to model professional political strategists with contingency plans for countless developments in international politics, we focus on the problem of generating possible policies and interpretations from a given ideological perspective. It is, of course, possible that for some situations there is a specific party line or established policy which conservatives or liberals may choose to follow. These are the cases where the political event has already been pre-interpreted. We consider the novel interpretation of new political events to be the more interesting and informative aspect of ideologically based understanding.

Let us return to the original problem: What knowledge is contained in a political ideology? Our two previous suggestions are too specific and do not account for the responses to event 3.2. For our third suggestion, let us formulate the knowledge in the form of a rule, more general than the policy statements directed at a specific country which we suggested earlier:

CONSERVATIVE IDEOLOGY:
RULE 3.1   If a country is anti-Soviet, the U.S. should extend military support in its struggle against the Soviet Union or Soviet-backed factions.

LIBERAL IDEOLOGY:
RULE 3.2   If a country suppresses the human rights of its people, the U.S. should not aid that government's effort to remain in power.

RULE 3.3   If a country is involved in a guerilla war, the U.S. should avoid any military involvement.

These rules seem reasonable in that they can generate the conservative and liberal responses respectively for events 3.1 and 3.2. Iran is anti-Soviet, a fact the conservative understander already knows; thus rule 3.1 applies to the arms sales situation of event 3.1 suggesting that the U.S. should indeed sell the arms that Iran requested. Buthan is fighting Soviet-backed guerrillas (stated in event 3.2); therefore it is anti-Soviet. Hence, rule 3.1 also applies to this situation to suggest U.S. military aid. It is evident that rule 3.1 is applicable to many other situations interpreted from a conservative perspective, not just to our two examples. Rule 3.1 also generates the reasons why a U.S. conservative supports the U.S. military-aid to countries such as Buthan. That is, given that the U.S. is aiding Buthan, if the test clause of rule 3.1 is true, then it serves as an explanation for why the U.S. should aid Buthan: The country receiving the U.S. aid is anti-Soviet.

Rules 3.2 and 3.3 generate the liberal responses to events 3.1 and 3.2. The understander knows from memory that the Shah's government in Iran is dictatorial, and therefore suppresses human rights. Applying rule 3.2 to the arms sales scenario of event 3.1 results in the suggestion that the U.S. should not sell arms to Iran. The Buthan government is also dictatorial, as stated in event 3.2, therefore rule 3.2 also applies with the same conclusion. Rule 3.3 applies to the Buthan situation because event 3.2 suggests that there is guerilla activity in Buthan. Thus, rule 3.3 suggests that the U.S. should not send arms, as this action constitutes an involvement in the guerilla war. The suggestions of rules 3.2 and 3.3 reinforce each other. Both rules suggest that the U.S. should not send arms to Buthan; therefore both are cited as reasons for the negative liberal response.

Unfortunately, rules such as the three discussed above do not suffice to encode all the knowledge contained in a political ideology. Consider the following event:

EVENT 3.3   Communist China asked for U.S. technical assistance in building high-speed military aircraft.

A conservative interpretation of event 3.3, using rule 3.1, would conclude that the U.S. should give military aid to China. The fact that China is anti-Soviet, and the fact that technical assistance in military matters constitutes military support, make rule 3.1 applicable to the situation. However, most conservative ideologues would have very strong reservations about giving China any kind of military aid, and are likely to reject the idea. In fact, U.S. conservatives are more likely to favor military aid for China's non-Communist adversaries, such as Taiwan. How can we change our rule to capture this aspect of the conservative ideology? We suggest modifying rule 3.1 in the following manner:

CONSERVATIVE IDEOLOGY:
> RULE 3.4   If a country is anti-Soviet and non-Communist, the U.S. should extend military support in its struggle against the Soviet Union or Soviet-backed factions.

Rule 3.4 no longer applies to event 3.3. China is Communist; therefore, it is not worthy of U.S. military aid. Rule 3.4 is, however, unequal to the task of modeling a U.S.-conservative interpretation of the following events:

> EVENT 3.4   Idi Amin demanded that the U.S. supply him with anti-personnel weapons to fight a local insurgent movement, allegedly supported by the Soviets.

> QUESTION 3.4.1   Should the U.S. send Amin the weapons he requested?

> EVENT 3.5   The neo-Nazi storm troopers seized power in Southern Centuria. They asked for tanks and airplanes to conquer Soviet-sympathizing Northern Centuria.

> QUESTION 3.5.1   Should the U.S. send the neo-Nazi government of Southern Centuria the weapons it requested?

Rule 3.2 applies to a liberal interpretation of the above events. Both Idi Amin and the neo-Nazis suppress human rights, therefore they should not receive American military aid. What should be the conservative response to question 3.4.1? There are very few, if any, U.S. conservatives who sympathize with either Idi Amin or a Nazi resurgence. Furthermore, the Southern Centurians want to use their weapons for a military conquest, not self-defense. These facts suggest that conservatives in the United States ought to be opposed to U.S. military aid directed at these countries. (Indeed, Barry Goldwater and other U.S. ultra-conservatives have publically denounced Idi Amin and his inhuman policies.)

This discussion suggests that rule 3.4 is inaccurate, or at best insufficient, as part of a model of U.S.-conservative ideology relating to U.S. military aid. Why are the conservatives reluctant to aid Amin or neo-Nazis? One possible reason is that the liberals may not be the only ones concerned with human rights and the preservation of human life. Both Amin and the Nazis have proven to be singularly flagrant and offensive in their disregard for human life and human rights. Thus, the conservative ideology should include both rule 3.4 (aiding anti-Soviet countries) and rule 3.2 (not aiding human rights violators). Unfortunately, these rules contradict each other.

A computer program interpreting events on the basis of the two conflicting rules would need some means of deciding which rule is applicable and to what degree. We can add the proviso to rule 3.2 (in the conservative ideology) that the human rights violation be "sufficiently flagrant" or "extremely serious", but this patchwork causes more trouble than it solves. How does one measure the degree of "flagrancy" in a series of human rights violations? Does the same degree of flagrancy or seriousness apply to all applications of rule 3.2, or does the military aid decision also hinge on the country's strategic importance to the U.S.?

We need a general mechanism for resolving conflicts among rules. Generating arbitrarily many conflict-resolution rules results in a patchwork system, rather than a general mechanism. For example, a U.S.-conservative military aid decision should hinge on the relative importance of the country being aided to U.S. defense interests. Hence, different degrees of human rights violations are tolerable for different situations. Our suggestion of modifying rule 3.2 to state that the human rights violations be sufficiently flagrant is not a solution because we are dealing with a different meaning of the word "sufficiently" in different situations. Therefore, contradicting rules such as 3.2 and 3.4 cannot be reconciled without a more global mechanism that takes other factors in the situation into account.

Consider another example where conflicting rules are a necessary part of the U.S.-conservative ideology:

U.S.-CONSERVATIVE INTERPRETATION:

EVENT 3.6   The U.S. Air Force is very weak at present. It urgently requires new F-15 fighters. Carter proposed the sale of additional F-15 fighters to Iran.

QUESTION 3.6.1   Should the United States sell the weapons?

RESPONSE 3.6.1   No. the U.S. should first provide F-15's for its own air force.

The conservative response to the above question suggests that the following rule must be part of the conservative ideology:

RULE 3.5   The U.S. should satisfy its own military needs before extending aid to other nations.

Rule 3.5 contradicts rule 3.4. That is, the U.S. cannot simultaneously give military help to anti-Soviet countries and not do so in the case that its own armed forces need the military equipment. There seems to be a simple solution to this dilemma; we can add the following rule to the ideology:

> RULE 3.6   Rule 3.5, if applicable, always overrides any application of rule 3.4.

Now we can explain the conservative interpretation of event 3.6. Both rules 3.4 and 3.5 are applicable to the situation: Anti-Soviet Iran wants U.S. weapons, and the U.S. Air Force needs the same weapons. Rule 3.6 breaks the impasse by giving priority to the U.S. need; thus, we have accounted for the U.S.-conservative response 3.6.1.

Unfortunately, there are more serious problems involved in rule contradictions. Consider the following event:

U.S.-CONSERVATIVE INTERPRETATION.

> EVENT 3.7   Soviet-backed forces are scoring rapid gains against the Buthan government. The U.S. is diverting tanks and M-16's, earmarked for the U.S. army, in an emergency airlift to Buthan.
>
> QUESTION 3.7.1   Is this policy good for U.S. interests?
>
> RESPONSE 3.7.1   Yes, unless Buthan is supplied immediately, the Soviet faction will take over.

Response 3.7.1 reflects a reasonable conservative interpretation of event 3.7. Why is this interpretation reasonable? Given the U.S.-conservative premise that anti-Soviet countries should be given military assistance, the crisis situation in Buthan makes it necessary that any military assistance be immediate. Otherwise, there may be no anti-Soviet government in Buthan to receive the U.S. military aid. The U.S. military hardware flown to Buthan was needed by the American army, but, unlike the situation in event 3.6, the present situation calls for giving Buthan priority over the needs of the U.S. Army. Rule 3.6, however, stated that the U.S. should always ignore foreign needs in the case that the U.S. military has any unmet needs. Thus, rule 3.6, which seemed so useful in the conservative interpretation of event 3.5, is flatly contradicted by this event. Why? Clearly, rule 3.6 was an oversimplification; it ignored many global constraints imposed by the situation, such as the crisis nature of Buthan's need for military assistance and the fact that the U.S. armed forces were not facing any real weapon shortage.

How can we fix our set of rules to account for the conservative interpretation of event 3.6 and all the previous events? One possibility is to create yet more rules about what to do in order to avoid contradictory situations, for instance:

> RULE 3.7   If military equipment is needed by both the U.S. and a non-Commu-
> nist anti-Soviet country, the equipment should go to the country
> whose need is more urgent.

> RULE 3.8   If both rules 3.6 and 3.7 are applicable, apply only rule 3.7.

We have introduced two more rules with the purpose of bypassing contradictions among our previous rules. Indeed, rule 3.8 circumvents a contradictory situation that can arise between two rules that were created with the purpose of circumventing other contradictions. Both rules 3.6 and 3.7 exist to avoid contradiction (with different results) when rules 3.4 (aiding anti-Soviet countries) and 3.5 (supplying the U.S. armed forces) are applicable.

The process of creating more and more rules to model conservative interpretations of international events can be very tedious. For two base rules (i.e., rules not predicated upon previous rules) we found that at least three contradiction-avoidance rules were necessary. As we expand our set of base rules, there are many more pair-wise interactions of rules, therefore many more potentially contradictory situations. This seems to require a sizable set of contradiction-avoidance rules which may be larger than the original set of base rules. These contradiction-avoidance rules may themselves require a large number of meta contradiction-avoidance rules. It is not clear how many levels of rules are necessary before the process of rule creation to model ideological interpretation converges.

The most serious problem with this model of political ideologies as a set of independently applicable rules is that the rules are, in essence, context-free. One rule can only test one or two facts. There is no mechanism for evaluating the global effect of any single rule, nor is there a way to predicate the rules on some aspects of the entire context.

In a logically closed domain, such as Winograd's [1972] understanding of actions and relations in the blocks world, there is a relatively small number of things that a rule can do. Furthermore, all the objects, relations, and actions in this mini-world can be tested in a short period of time. Since these two properties are not true of open-ended domains, such as the political world, we need a mechanism for determining which aspects of the world are most relevant and important to consider. For instance, before making a military-aid decision, policy makers consider the overall military, diplomatic, and economic impact of such a decision. They do not normally consider vast numbers of rules that determine every possible contingency and subsequently they test other large sets of rules for deciding conflicts among the specific contingency rules. What we really want our rules to do for us is to apply the following principle of ideological decision making for the U.S.:

If the U.S. has to make a decision on military aid, it should base the decision on whether sending aid is better for the U.S. in terms of overall military, diplomatic and economic situations.

The problem with applying this principle is that we need a method for evaluating the effects of a decision on the overall goals and aspirations of the United States. In fact, if we had such an evaluation process, this principle would generalize to any U.S. decision on international politics, not just military-aid decisions. It is also significant that our principle applies to a liberal as well as a conservative interpretation of a situation. Both liberals and conservatives want what they think is best for their country and the world. The difference in their understanding lies in the evaluation process that determines the beneficial or harmful effects of particular decisions. For instance, conservatives believe that Soviet containment is much more important than the human rights of people under dictatorships, but liberals, in general, reverse the priorities of these two goals. The following section proposes a model of evaluating how political events and governmental decisions affect the U.S. based on what each political ideology regards to be the most important U.S. goals.

3.2 Using Goal Trees to Represent Ideological Beliefs

Rules about specific foreign policy issues prove insufficient for an ideological interpretation of political events. Therefore, we need another method for modeling ideological decisions. This section proposes a method based on modeling ideologies by *goal trees*, a process that accords with our principle of interpreting events in light of the entire subjective understanding of the situation. We designed the goal-tree model of ideological interpretation with the intent of circumventing such difficulties as incompatible rules and the unbounded proliferation of contradiction-avoidance rules. In this we have succeeded. We do not, however, claim completeness for our model. We can simulate many different types of ideological behavior, but ideological interpretation may include such considerations as the emotional reaction toward certain actors or classes of events that are outside the scope of our process model.

We introduce our model by means of some illustrative examples. Recall the U.S. arms-aid scenario from our previous examples. We had difficulty in formulating rules to decide whether or not the U.S. should send military shipments to a particular country. Let us state the three U.S. goals that were involved in the U.S.-conservative decision process:

GOAL 1:   The U.S. should have strong, loyal and fully supplied armed forces.

GOAL 2:   The U.S. should give military aid to countries who oppose communism.

GOAL 3:   The U.S. should try to preserve human rights and lives throughout the world.

These U.S. conservative goals do not exist in limbo. The understander knows which goals may be furthered by different events and decisions. Some goals exist in service of other higher-level goals. For instance, goals 1 and 2 are subgoals to the higher-level U.S.-conservative goal of containing Communist expansion to preserve the free world. (Goal 3 has no subgoal relation to the other goals.) This imposes a hierarchical structure on some of the goals, as follows:

Figure 3.1.   Goal-subgoal tree

GOAL 4:   Communist containment = preservation of the free world.

Goal-subgoal links are not the only useful structure that can be imposed on a set of ideological goals. The different conservative and liberal responses to events 1 and 2, reiterated below, suggest that we should attend to the differences in importance of the various goals.

EVENT 3.1   President Carter proposed the sale of additional F-15 fighters to Iran.

QUESTION 3.1.1   Should the United States sell the weapons?

U.S.-CONSERVATIVE ANSWER:
RESPONSE 3.1.1   Yes, Iran is an anti-Soviet U.S. ally.

U.S.-LIBERAL ANSWER:
RESPONSE 3.1.2   No, the U.S. should not support dictatorships that suppress human rights.

EVENT 3.2   The dictator of Buthan is trying to suppress Soviet-backed Marxist insurgents. The Joint chiefs advised Carter to send weapons to the government of Buthan.

QUESTION 3.2.1   Should the United States send the weapons?

U.S.-CONSERVATIVE ANSWER:
RESPONSE 3.2.1   Yes, Buthan is fighting against Soviet domination.

U.S.-LIBERAL ANSWER:
RESPONSE 3.2.2   No, the U.S. should not support dictatorships that suppress human rights. The U.S. should also stay out of foreign guerrilla wars.

The liberal ideology considers preservation of human life and human rights as more important than Communist containment. The conservative ideology ranks Communist containment as the more important goal. It is also the case that if there is no crisis situation, GOAL 1 (strong U.S. armed forces) is more important than GOAL 2 (military aid to anti-Communist allies) in the conservative ideology. We need to know the relative importance of the various goals in order to interpret events such as 1 and 2. Since the importance rankings vary between different ideologies, they should be included as part of the ideological goal representation. Thus, we add relative-importance links (RI links) to our set of goals for the conservative ideology.

The meaning of an RI link between two goals of an actor is defined in terms of that actor's decision when both goals demand his attention. $G2—RI \rightarrow G1$ means that goal G1 is subjectively more important that G2. If $G2—RI \rightarrow G1$; and an event affects both G2 and G1 then the actor will focus his attention primarily on the effects of the event upon G1. Consider a simple example paraphrased from Wilensky [1978].

EVENT 3.6   John held up a liquor store. The owner gave him the money.

QUESTION 3.6   Why did the owner give him the money?

Two of the store owner's goals are affected by 3.6: preservation of his life and preservation of his money. In order to answer question 3.6 one must understand that to the store owner, preservation of his life is the more important goal. In our formalism we encode an RI link between preservation of one's possessions and preservation of one's life. Wilensky was interested in developing heuristic rules to explain why a particular decision makes sense in a given situation. Our interest here is to use relative-importance relations among a larger set of goals to understand the decision-making process itself. We store the RI-links as part of our memory representation, as in the following fragment of the U.S.-conservative goal tree.

Figure 3.2.   Relative-importance and subgoal links

We call the goal structure in figure 3.2 a *goal tree* for the United States under the U.S. conservative ideology. In order to model the conservative interpretation of events 1 and 2 using the U.S.-conservative goals, we need to have some rules establishing the process of how goal trees are used as an integral part of subjective understanding. The following set of rules apply to goal trees in general, not just to our goal tree in figure 3.2.

RULE 3.9   If progress towards a goal can be achieved by a particular course of action, that course of action should be pursued.

RULE 3.10   If a possible course of action violates a goal, it should be actively avoided.

RULE 3.11   If a possible course of action has no relevance with respect to the goal tree, it should not be actively considered.

RULE 3.12   If a course of action affects two goals, and no other rules determine which goal to focus on, the effect on the higher importance goal determines whether the course of action should be pursued.

Rule 3.12 is particularly important because it embodies a primary theoretical motivation for the existence of goal trees. When two goals come into consideration, humans usually base their decision upon the more important goal, often disregarding the effects of their decision on the lesser goal. Psychologists and political scientists have recently noted that there is an apparent aversion to the simultaneous use of contrary considerations, or "tradeoffs", in the making of important decisions. Instead, Axelrod [1976] and Slovic [1974] have shown that the most important consideration tends to dominate, and the contrary consideration is suppressed. Goal trees embody a generalization of this principle by ranking all general motivations of an actor with respect to instrumentality and general importance criteria.

Let us see how rules 3.9 through 3.12 can be applied to the goal tree in figure 3.2 in order to model the U.S.-conservative interpretation of the first two events. In events 3.1 and 3.2 the decision of whether the U.S. should send arms to Iran or Buthan is based on the goal that these actions help to achieve. Sending arms to either Iran or Buthan affects two U.S.-conservative goals: goal 1 (military aid to anti-Communist countries) and goal 3 (opposition to human rights violations). Since there is more than one goal that the action affects, rule 3.12 applies to determine that the understander should consider the effect on goal 1, the more important goal in the U.S.-conservative goal tree. Since sending arms constitutes progress toward this military-aid goal, rule 3.9 applies to determine that the military-aid policy should be pursued. Thus, the same reasoning process determines that the U.S. should send arms to both Iran and Buthan.

Any U.S. action in response to event 3.3, reiterated below, does not represent progress toward a U.S. goal. Recall that goal 2 applies specifically to anti-Communist nations and Communist China does not fit into this category. Therefore, the default rule 3.11 applies to suggest that the U.S. do nothing in response to event 3.3.

> EVENT 3.3   Communist China asked for U.S. technical assistance in building
> high-speed military aircraft.

> EVENT 3.6   The U.S. Air Force is very weak at present. It urgently requires
> New F-15 fighters. Carter proposed the sale of additional F-15 fighters to Iran.

The U.S.-conservative interpretation process for event 3.6 proceeds in much the same way as for events 3.1 and 3.2. The U.S. action affects two U.S. goals: goal 1 (military aid to anti-Communist nations) and goal 2 (maintaining and strengthening the U.S. armed forces). Since goal 2 is the more important U.S. goal, according to the U.S.-conservative goal tree, rule 3.12 determines that the policy decision be made with respect to its effect on this goal. Because the proposed course of action has a negative effect on goal 2, rule 3.10 applies to determine that the U.S. should avoid the course of action suggested in event 3.6. Hence, the U.S.-conservative response is that the United States should not sell F-15's to Iran while the American Air Force needs the jet fighters.

Some notion of transitivity in importance relations is necessary. For instance, consider the following events:

> EVENT 3.8 The U.S. Air Force needs a refueling base in Iran. In order to get the base the U.S. has to give military support to the Shah's government.

> EVENT 3.9 To stop a Communist takeover in Vietnam, the U.S. is prolonging a war in which hundreds of people die each day.

A conservative interpretation of event 3.8 should include the conclusion that aiding Iran and establishing a U.S. Air Force base are in the best interests of the United States. The U.S. goals affected by 3.8 are goal 2 (military aid), goal 1 (strengthen U.S. armed forces), and goal 3 (human rights and lives). In order to decide which goal to consider by applying rule 3.12, we must know that goal 1 is more important in the U.S.-conservative ideology than goal 3. The goal tree states that goal 1 is more important than goal 3. Clearly, importance relations must be transitive in order to establish the relative importance of goals 1 and 3.

Decision theory uses probability of success as an important measure to model decision making. In order to incorporate such a measure into our ideological reasoning system we first need to understand how people estimate probabilities, how they combine probability estimates with the importance of the goal, and when probabilities are totally ignored. (Many ideologies seem to totally disregard probabilities. For instance, Nationalist China still hopes to regain the mainland, although such a goal is almost impossible to achieve.) Let us return to our discussion of relative-importance relations.

The conservatives in the 1960's supported the U.S. involvement in Vietnam. Therefore, they must have considered Communist containment more important than the lives being lost in Vietnam. In order to model this evaluation, our rules have to determine that goal 4 (Communist containment) is more important than goal 3 (preservation of human rights and lives). Once this relative-importance relation is established, rule 3.12 tells us that the U.S. course of action should be determined by goal 3. Recall that there is no relative-importance link between goals 3 and 4 in figure 3.2. In fact, there is no transitive chain of relative-importance links connecting the two goals. We find, however, that goal 3 is less important than goal 1, which is a subgoal of goal 4. If a goal is less important than the subgoal of a second goal, then it is less important than the second goal itself. Thus relative importance is transitive across subgoal links. We have two rules to determine the transitivity of relative importance relations on goal trees:

RULE 3.13   Relative-importance links in a goal tree are transitive.

RULE 3.14   Relative importance is transitive across subgoal links.
        CASE 1   If goal A is less important than a subgoal of goal B, then it follows that goal A is also less important than goal B.
        CASE 2   If goal A is less important than goal B, then each of the subgoals of goal A are also less important than goal B.

Rule 3.14 (case 1) tells the understander that the Communist containment goal is more important than the preservation of human rights and preservation of life goal. The relative importance being established, the understander applies rule 3.13 to determine that the U.S. should decide its course of action based on its effect on the Communist containment goal. Fighting to prevent a Communist takeover in Vietnam is positive progress towards Communist containment. Therefore, rule 3.10 determines that the U.S. should continue to pursue its course of action in Vietnam.

Let us consider how a liberal interpretation of event 3.15 may proceed. First, we define part of the liberal goal tree:

GOAL 5   Establish and maintain world peace.

GOAL 6   Preserve human rights.

GOAL 7   Oppose the creation of totalitarian governments.

Figure 3.3.   Fraction of U.S.-Liberal goal tree

                GOAL 5
                ↑   relative-importance link
                GOAL 6
                ↑   subgoal link
                GOAL 7

The United States actions in event 3.8 affect two goals in the U.S.-liberal goal tree, goals 5 and 7. That is, prolongation of a war violates world peace, and establishing a Communist (therefore totalitarian) regime in Vietnam violates goal 7. Since goal 6 is less important than goal 5, rule

3.14 (case 2) tells us that goal 7, a subgoal of goal 6, is also less important than goal 5. With the importance relation established, rule 3.13 applies to determine that the U.S. policy should be based on its effect on goal 5. The U.S. action of prolonging the Vietnam war violates goal 5, the preservation of world peace. Therefore, according to rule 3.11, the U.S. policy should be to terminate its intervention in Vietnam.

The rules we discuss presuppose that all goals are affected in the same manner by the actions in the event. This is not always the case. For instance, in the U.S.-conservative interpretation of event 3.7, a less important goal is given priority over a more important goal.

> EVENT 3.7   Soviet-backed forces are scoring rapid gains against the Buthan
> government. The U.S. is diverting tanks and M-16's earmarked for
> the U.S. army in an emergency airlift to Buthan.

In the U.S.-conservative ideology, supplying the U.S. Army is, in general, more important than aiding anti-Communist countries. But, because of the crisis nature of the latter goal, the U.S.-conservative ideology considers it to be temporarily more important. Hence the U.S. action of airlifting arms to Buthan is approved by the conservatives. We need a rule to know when the static-importance relations in the goal trees can be ignored. First, we define a crisis goal to be a goal that requires immediate action if it is to be fulfilled; any delay or inaction automatically causes the goal to be violated (Schank and Abelson [1977]). The rule that applies to crisis goals in our context is the following:

> RULE 3.15   If an action affects more than one goal, one of which is a crisis goal,
> then the crisis goal should be considered as the highest importance
> goal, only in the case that the action suggested by the crisis goal does
> not permanently violate a higher importance goal in the goal tree.

Since the U.S. can supply its army at a later time, the higher level goal is not permanently violated. Thus the conservative interpretation of event 3.7 considers the emergency aid to Buthan as temporarily more important. If it were the case that aiding Buthan meant losing some irreplaceable necessity for the U.S. army, rule 3.15 would not apply; the higher level goal would be permanently violated. Thus, in this hypothetical case, the conservative interpretation would suggest not aiding Buthan.

3.3 Goal Trees in POLITICS

In this section we analyze POLITICS goal trees and their application in a computer protocol. Rules 3.9 through 3.15, discussed in the previous section, are implemented as part of the POLITICS goal determination inference process. The goal trees actually implemented in POLITICS are much more complicated than the examples in figures 3.2 and 3.3. The reason for the added complexity is that POLITICS interprets stories from many domains, not just United States decisions about whether or not military aid should be sent to some countries. For instance, figure 3.4 is part of the United States goal tree under the U.S.-conservative ideology. The goal tree is internally represented as a directed acyclic graph for reasons of economy of storage in the computer, but this structure is equivalent to a tree for all relevant purposes.

3.3.1 The U.S.-conservative ideology

Consider figure 3.4, part of the United States goal tree under the U.S.-conservative ideology. All the links are strictly subgoal links. We use the term subgoal somewhat more loosely than others who build goal-subgoal hierarchies (e.g., Sacerdoti [1977]). Each of the subgoals helps to achieve the higher-level goal, but, unless specifically encoded, the set of subgoals to a tree form neither a disjunctive nor a strictly conjunctive set. The root node contains the goal of Communist containment, the most important U.S.-conservative goal. The goals of high military strength, the establishment of anti-Communist allies, and prevention of internal subversion are all subgoals to the Communist containment goal. However, the goal tree does not say that only one of these goals is required in order to fulfill the Communist containment goal, nor does it say that the conjunction is strictly required. The goal tree does say that in order for the U.S. to achieve Communist containment it should pursue all three goals and attain a measure of success on as many of them as possible.

The reason for this rather vague definition of goal-subgoal links is that POLITICS can consider some goals as partially achieved (see Chapter 4). The decision process tries to maximize the fulfillment of the entire set of subgoals. It makes little sense to consider the goal of military strength as a success or a failure. There are various degrees of success evaluated with respect to their contribution in fulfilling the higher level goal of Communist containment.

The root node in figure 3.4 is one of several goals of the U.S.-conservative hierarchy that has its own set of subgoals. Each one of these goals is, in turn, linked to the other goals by means of relative-importance relations. Figure 3.5 is a tree whose branches are all relative-importance links (RI links). Each node in 3.5 is the root node of its own goal-subgoal tree. The most important goal in the U.S.-conservative ideology is Communist containment. This is the goal that has the largest goal-subgoal tree (figure 3.4), in accordance with the conservative understander's focus on what he considers to be the most important national concerns. The goals

Figure 3.4.   U.S.-conservative goal tree with subgoal links

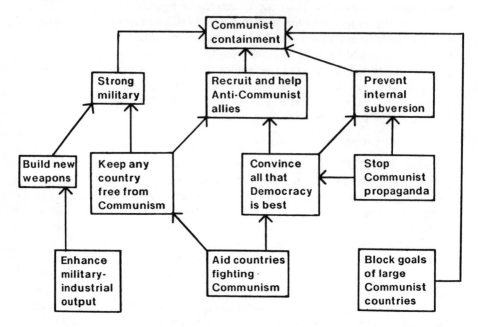

in the subgoal tree of each goal in 3.5 are interlinked with each other, including the goals in figure 3.4, via RI links. Thus, the United States goal tree under the conservative ideology contains a set of goals interrelated by subgoal and/or importance links.

Figure 3.5.   U.S.-conservative goal tree with RI-links

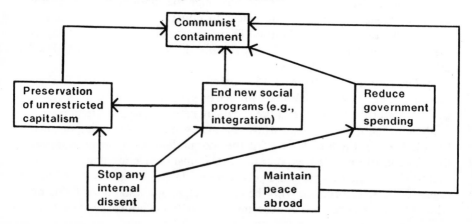

Let us see how politics uses its goal trees to interpret an event from a U.S.-conservative ideological perspective. The following is computer protocol in which the relevant goal-interaction processes keep us informed by printing appropriate messages.

EVENT 3.10: Start of POLITICS interpretation and QA Dialog

PTYCON LOG FILE   2-Mar-78 11:51:25

PTYCON> CONNECT (TO SUBJOB) 1
[CONNECTED TO SUBJOB POL(1)]

Computer Run	Annotation
*(INTERPRET US-CONSERVATIVE) INCORPORATING US-CONSERVATIVE IDEOLOGY GOAL TREES . . . TOP GOAL: US-SAVEFREEWORLD. INITIALIZING PARSER . . . DONE.	
INPUT STORY: +Russia massed troops on the Czech border.	
PARSING . . . COMPLETED. SPECIFICATION PHASE STARTED . . . INSTANTIATING $INVADE SCRIPT. GOAL DETERMINATION PHASE STARTED *CZECHOSLOVAKIA* GOAL G34 THREATENED	POLITICS analyzed the English input into Conceptual Dependency and proceeded to apply situational inferences that culminated in an instantiation of the $INVADE script. This phase of the understanding process is not relevant here, and therefore has been deleted. Chapter 7 presents an analysis of this phase.
	G34 = self preservation
RUSSIA GOAL G27 ACTIVATED	G27 = attain political control of smaller nations.

USELESS GOAL-STATE:
(#GOAL TOK G27
    ACTOR *RUSSIA*
    STATECHANGE
      (TOWARD (*SCONT*
      OBJECT
	POLITICS finds that Russia already had political control over Czechoslovakia.

```
          *CZECHOSLOVAKIA*
            VAL (+10))
ALREADY MATCHES WORLD.
```
Since POLITICS assumes that input events are always true, it concludes that its memory was wrong; i.e., something must have happened to cause Czechoslovakia to move away from Soviet political control.

```
RESOLUTION INFERENCE . . .
ASSUMING UNKNOWN STATE CHANGE:
CON12

*(TXPN CON12 'EXPAND)
((CON ((ACTOR *UNSPEC*)
       <=> (*DO*)))
 RESULT
 ((ACTOR (*RUSSIA*)
   IS (*SCONT* OBJECT
       (*CZECHOSLOVAKIA*
        VAL (&SMALLNUM))))))
```

```
INFERENCE: CON15
*(TXPN CON15 'NO-EXPAND)
((CON CON12
  INITIATE-REASON G27))
```
The inference is made that the reason for the Soviet goal of controlling Czechoslovakia is the previously inferred event: Something happened to decrease Soviet control of Czechoslovakia.

```
POSSIBLE *US* GOAL ACTIVATION:
G16
POSSIBLE *US* GOAL VIOLATION:
G9
POSSIBLE *US* GOAL ACTIVATION:
G12
```
G16 is the U.S. goal of aiding countries fighting communism (see figure 3.4).
G21 is keeping peace.
G12 is blocking actions that fulfill Russian goals.

```
SORTING GOALS: (G16 G9 G12)
(*IMPREL* VAL (GREATER G12 G16))
TRANSITIVE INFERENCES . . .
CANNOT RANK (G9 G16)
TRANSITIVE INFERENCES . . .
(*IMPREL* VAL (GREATER G12 G9))
```
Inference rules 3.13 and 3.14 rank the goal in terms of importance. G12 is found to be the most important goal.

```
FOCUS OF COUNTERPLANNING: G12
```
Here rule 3.12 determined the focus of attention of the counterplanner.

```
COUNTERPLANNING STRATEGY
CP10 INVOKED . . .
COUNTERPLANNING STRATEGY
CP12 INVOKED . . .

CP12 SUGGESTS
($CONFRONTATION
 ACTOR1      *US*
```
The counterplanning strategies propose possible plans of action to thwart another actor's goals. Counterplanning is discussed in Chapters 4, 5, and 6.

ACTOR2 *RUSSIA*
OBJECT (*SCONT*
    OBJECT
      CZECHOSLOVAKIA
      VAL (0))
INFERENCE:
$CONFRONTATION SUGGESTED

Since the confrontation blocks the active Russian goal G27 it fulfills the U.S. goal G12. Therefore, Rule 3.10 says to proceed with this course of action.

The two questions answered by POLITICS illustrate the goal directed inference process above.

INTERPRETATION COMPLETED, READY TO ACCEPT QUESTIONS.

Q: Why did Russia do this?

A: BECAUSE RUSSIA THOUGHT THAT IT COULD TAKE POLITICAL CONTROL OF CZECHOSLOVAKIA BY SENDING TROOPS.

Q: What should the United States do?

A: THE UNITED STATES SHOULD INTERVENE MILITARILY.

The POLITICS interpretation of event 10 demonstrates how the encoding of a political ideology as goal trees enables a process, defined by our rules 3.9 to 3.15, to make the correct inferences from the given ideological perspective. It is significant that POLITICS did not make many spurious inferences, such as the following possible but inappropriate inferences: (1) The U.S. intervention may lead to more repressive measures imposed by Russia on other Eastern European countries. (2) The U.S. could try to divert the military confrontation by diplomatic means.

The reason why the first inference is not made is that the goal of blocking Communist actions is more important than promoting human rights. Therefore, the inferencer does not worry about the lesser goal once a course of action has been proposed for the more important goal. The second possible inference is not made because diverting a confrontation is not a U.S.-conservative goal; it does not appear as a significant subgoal to the relatively low-importance goal of preserving global peace.

3.3.2 The U.S.-liberal ideology

A liberal interpretation of event 3.10 (presented below) makes inference 2 above because the most important liberal goal is the preservation of peace.

Therefore the inferencer focuses on this goal and its subgoals (one of which is diverting conflicts), instead of focusing on thwarting Soviet goals. Inference 1 is not made on the understanding phase of a liberal interpretation because U.S. intervention is not generated as a plausible course of action. Recall that this course of action was proposed because the conservative interpretation focused the counterplanning on finding a means of thwarting the Soviet goal of taking control of Czechoslovakia. On the other hand, if a U.S. intervention is proposed as a question asked to U.S.-liberal POLITICS, the military intervention is found to violate the more important goal of preserving peace. Intervention is therefore rejected on the grounds of ideological goal violation without requiring further inference. Thus, we see that the importance rankings of the goals for each political ideology constrain the inference process to a substantial degree. This property of the ideology goal trees accords with our principle of subjective understanding. POLITICS only makes the inferences that are relevant to the subjective point of view of the understander. Inferences about possible courses of action that violate ideological goals are immediately rejected.

The primary goals for the United States under a liberal ideology are given below to compare with the U.S.-conservative goals. We see that some goals are shared by both ideologies, but their relative importance in their respective goal trees is markedly different. For instance, preserving peace in the world is the dominating liberal goal, but a conservative goal of only medium importance.

The goal of military takeover (G103) associated with the invade script

Figure 3.6.   Relative-importance U.S.-liberal goal tree

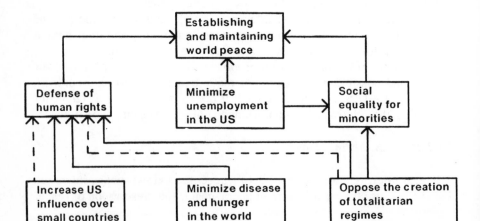

Event 3.10 Start of POLITICS Interpretation and QA Dialog

PTYCON LOG FILE   2-Mar-78 12:15:36

PTYCON> CONNECT (TO SUBJOB) 1
[CONNECTED TO SUBJOB POL(1)]

Computer Run	Annotation
*(INTERPRET US-LIBERAL) INCORPORATING US-LIBERAL IDEOLOGY GOAL TREES . . .	
TOP GOAL: US-WORLDPEACE. INITIALIZING PARSER . . . DONE.	
INPUT STORY: +Russia massed troops on the Czech border.	
PARSING . . . COMPLETED. SPECIFICATION PHASE STARTED . . .	We skip over the parsing and initial script application phase of the POLITICS interpretation.
INSTANTIATING $INVADE SCRIPT. GOAL DETERMINATION PHASE STARTED . . .	What scripts require the concentration of a military force? POLITICS knows about military aid, defense and invasion. Military aid is rejected because Czechoslovakia does not have the goal of receiving aid. Soviet defense is rejected because small countries (e.g. Czechoslovakia) do not pose a military threat to world powers (e.g., Russia).
CZECHOSLOVAKIA GOAL G39 THREATENED	G39 = Maintain peace with neighboring countries.
RUSSIA GOAL G29 THREATENED	G29 = Avoid armed conflicts, a subgoal of the Russian preservation of peace goal.
RUSSIA GOAL G27 ACTIVATED	G27 = Increase Political influence over smaller nations.
INTERNAL CONFLICT (G103 G29) G103 REJECTED . . . TRY NEW TRACK OR NEW SCRIPT	G103 = The goal of attaining military control of the invaded country. G103 is the default scriptal goal of $INVADE.

conflicts with the Russian goal of preserving peace (G29). The latter goal comes from the liberal ideology. Since any goal not in the goal tree of a country is automatically ranked as less important than all the goals in the tree, POLITICS resolves the conflict by abandoning G103 and pursuing G29, the more important goal. (See rule 3.14). Abandoning G103 means that either $INVADE was the wrong script to apply in the situation, or that $INVADE was correct, but it was applied for some purpose other than the default goal of taking military control of the invaded country.

POLITICS had previously rejected the two other possible scripts, therefore it checks whether there is an alternative purpose to applying $INVADE. This is the case, because $INVADE has more than one track. A track in a script is a possible sequence of actions that is likely to occur in the given situation. (See Cullingford [1977] for a description of the internal structure of scripts, and Carbonell [1978] for a discussion of the $INVADE script in particular.) A possible track in $INVADE is the use of a concentration of force as a threat of invasion, without necessitating an actual combat scenario. The threat track has the goal of obtaining some concessions from the threatened country, a goal that does not violate the U.S.-liberal ideological goals of maintaining peace. We continue with the liberal interpretation:

PREDICTED TRACK IN $INVADE
DEVIATES FROM DEFAULT PATH.

PREDICTION: ($THREAT1 IN
   ($INVADE &INVADEE
      CZECHOSLOVAKIA
      &INVADER *RUSSIA*))
&TRACK1 MAINCONS: CON23

This track accords with the ideological Russian goals, therefore it is predicted by U.S.-liberal POLITICS.

*(TXPN CON23 'EXPAND)
((CON ((ACTOR (*RUSSIA*)
   < = > (PB-THREATEN
      INSTR MILITARY)))
  INITIATE-REASON
  ((ACTOR (*CZECHOSLOVAKIA*)
   < = > (*DO*)))
  RESULT
  ((ACTOR (*RUSSIA*)
     IS (*SCONT* OBJECT
      (*CZECHOSLOVAKIA*)
      VAL (&BIGNUM))))))

The "threat" track consists of a show of force for the purpose of achieving some measure of social control over the threatened country.

POLITICS checks for the effects of the Russian action upon the ideological goals of the U.S.

POSSIBLE *US* GOAL
VIOLATION: G13

G13 is the U.S. goal of increasing its
influence over small nations.

POSSIBLE *US* GOAL
VIOLATION: G9

SORTING GOALS: (G13 G9)
(*IMPREL* VAL (GREATER G9 G13))

G9 is preserving human rights. (International military threats often violate
this goal.)

This relation comes directly from the
liberal tree for the U.S.

FOCUS OF COUNTERPLANNING: G9

COUNTERPLANNING STRATEGY CP6
INVOKED . . .

Here rule 3.13 determines the focus
on cancelling Russian influence in
Czechoslovakia.

PURSUING SUBGOAL G15
OF MAINGOAL G9

G15 = decreasing influence of totalitarian regimes, a subgoal to
preserving human rights.

U.S. influence is considered a way of
cancelling Russian influence by means
of establishing a mutual exclusion
goal conflict.

MUTUAL EXCLUSION GOALS (G9 G27)
COUNTERPLANNING STRATEGY CP13
INVOKED . . .

CP13 SUGGESTS
($DIPLOMATIC-INITIATIVE
 ACTOR: *US*
 RECIP1: *RUSSIA*
 FORUM: *UN*
 OBJECT: (*SCONT* OBJECT
          (*CZECHOSLOVAKIA*)
 MEANS: (*OPPOSITION* VAL G27))

How does the U.S. block Russia's
influence without violating higher level
U.S. goals?

Counterplanning strategy CP13 suggests diplomatic intervention.

INFERENCE:
$DIPLOMATIC-INITIATIVE
SUGGESTED.

INTERPRETATION COMPLETED, READY TO ACCEPT QUESTIONS.

Q: Why did Russia do this?

A: BECAUSE RUSSIA WANTED TO INCREASE ITS POLITICAL INFLU-
ENCE OVER CZECHOSLOVAKIA.

Q: What should the United States do?

A: THE UNITED STATES SHOULD DENOUNCE THE RUSSIAN ACTION
IN THE UNITED NATIONS.

The U.S.-liberal interpretation of event 3.10 illustrates that not only is the recommended U.S. policy different, but the actual meaning of the Russian action is interpreted differently. The conservative interpretation of the Russian troop buildup as a pending invasion was based on the fact that conservatives think that the Russian goal of controlling small countries is more important than avoiding military conflict. The liberal interpretation of the same action as a threat that would probably not be carried out is based on the relative-importance ranking of the goals in Russia's goal tree under the liberal ideology. Liberals think that the Russian goal of avoiding military conflicts is more important to the Russians than increasing their political influence. The liberal ideology does not consider political or military takeovers of small countries to be a Russian goal. In the conservative ideology, the Russian goal of taking over small countries is a subgoal both to increasing political influence and increasing military stature.

The fact that political ideologies must refer not only to United States goals, but also to the goals of other countries, suggests that these goals should be encoded as part of the ideology. Moreover, since the liberal and conservative ideologies postulate different importance relations among the goals of other countries, as illustrated above, the appropriate relative-importance relations should also be part of each ideology. For instance, the following is the bulk of the U.S.-conservative goal tree for the Soviet Union, as implemented in POLITICS. Solid lines represent subgoal links and dotted lines denote relative-importance links.

Figure 3.7.   Soviet goal tree in U.S.-conservative ideology

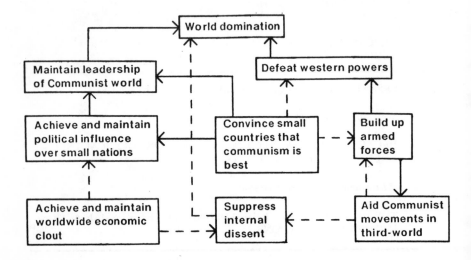

3.4 The Flow of Control in the POLITICS System

We digress from our discussion of goal trees in POLITICS to present the overall control flow governing the various processes in the POLITICS system. POLITICS is an integrated understanding system. It does not have clearly defined, separable modules, since much of the processing involves applying information from one module to guide the processing in another module. The band-width of the information channel across the modules is substantial. The numerous interconnections among the modules makes the control-flow diagram appear rather complicated. The best way to think about POLITICS may be as one complex module with access to many different sources of information. Since the goal trees, attention focusing mechanisms, and counterplanning strategies are of greater theoretical interest than the flow of control, we present figure 3.8 without further discussion.

3.5 Goal Trees: How Many and How Complex

One may ask at this point: Do we need an inordinately large memory to represent the goal hierarchies of all relevant political actors? This question can be answered from either a theoretical or a practical point of view. In either case the answer can be summarized as follows: The memory representation of a political ideology is complex, but its size is a small fraction of the total memory of a subjective understanding system.

Since our task is to model the political interpretations of humans, we should ask: How much information does a newspaper reader have about the goals of all international political actors? Presumably, a person knows most about his own country. Since we are modeling an American subjective understander, our model of conservative or liberal understanders will contain more information about the goals of the United States than, for instance, the goals of Buthan. From a practical viewpoint, we found it necessary to encode for each ideology about 30 United States goals, 15 Soviet goals and 10 goals for most other countries. From the point of view of psychological plausibility, we need to ask the question: How much does a newspaper reader really know about the goals of Bolivia, Haiti, and Buthan? The answer seems to be that in general the reader knows nothing about the specific aspirations of those countries, but he knows the goals of third world countries in general. For instance, we may know nothing about Bolivia other than the fact that it is a third world country. This information, however, is sufficient to enable us to infer that the government of Bolivia wants to stay in power, that it wants to have a better and more affluent economy, and that it would probably

Figure 3.8.   The flow of control in the POLITICS system

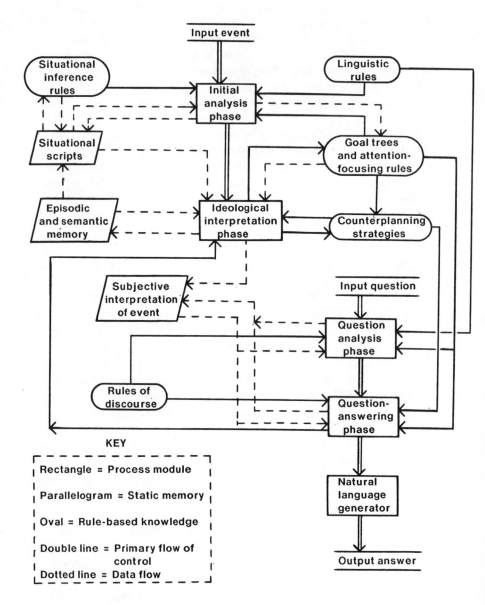

not turn down economic aid from more developed countries. These are default goals that most people attribute to third world countries.

Hence, rather than having a specific set of goals associated with Buthan, Haiti, Bolivia, or any other third-world country, we have a single set of goals that applies to all third world countries. There are similar sets of default goals that apply to Eastern European countries, western industrialized countries and oil-rich Arab countries. These sets of goals are organized into relative-importance goal trees for each country. Different ideologies will impose different importance relations; therefore, there is a goal tree in each ideology for each class of countries. Some countries, such as the United States, the Soviet Union, and Communist China are classes in themselves. Thus, they have their own, unique goal trees under every U.S.-centered ideology. Having less than a dozen trees to represent the motivations of all countries in the world makes the problem of proliferating goal trees non-existent.

An average person's knowledge about the intentions of different countries is rather limited. It is, therefore, reasonable that a model of human ideological understanding should have comparable limitations in the detail of its knowledge of international intentionality. There are, however, exceptions to any fixed limit on the depth of knowledge on any subject matter. Political scientists presumably have a much deeper, and possibly more objective, knowledge of the political goals of most countries. Since we do not try to model expert knowledge of political science, we can ignore this exception. Some well-known political spokesmen are, however, more well informed than others. For instance, Buckley is as conservative as Goldwater, but his knowledge about political matters appears to be significantly greater. Therefore, an ideological model of Buckley would require larger and more detailed goal trees, though of similar structure, than the present U.S.-conservative trees encoded in POLITICS.

The depth of intentional knowledge encoded in a goal tree is proportional to the degree of interaction between the central actor of the ideology (the U.S. in our case) and the actor whose intentions are encoded in the goal tree. Therefore, POLITICS contains many more goals and relative-importance relations for the U.S. goal tree than for the Soviet goal tree, which in turn is more detailed than, say, the Australian goal tree. In accordance with this general property of subjectively oriented understanding, there are countries about which we may specifically know one or two goals in addition to the default goal trees. For instance, the conservative ideology considers the Eastern European countries to be Soviet controlled states. However, Yugoslavia is an Eastern European nation that is striving for independence from Soviet domination. Therefore its goal tree should be the Eastern European default goal tree with the addition of the relatively high importance goal of maintaining an independent status from the Soviet Union. This notion is somewhat similar to adjunct frames (Charniak [1977]), where default information is used for the greater part of a knowledge representation except where more specific or contradictory detail is present.

Let us look at the complete default goal trees for third world countries encoded in POLITICS. The liberal and conservative ideologies share some of the goals listed below, others are particular to each ideology. The importance relations differ widely as expressed in figures 3.9(a) and (b).

1. Self preservation of government—maintain and increase the power of the government.
2. Economic development—become an industrialized nation.
3. Military defense—from invasion by neighboring countries.
4. Develop natural resources.
5. Get economic aid (financial and technological) to enable goals 2 and 4.
6. Maintain peace with neighbors.
7. Keep the people healthy and well fed.
8. Get military aid from the superpowers.
9. Stop internal subversion and keep rigid order.

The liberal ideology has goals 1 through 7 in the hierarchy illustrated in figure 3.9(a); the conservative ideology has goals 1 through 6, 8 and 9 in the tree in figure 3.9(b). Solid lines indicate subgoal relations, and dotted lines indicate relative-importance relations.

EVENT 3.11   Nicaragua will receive five million dollars in economic development aid from the United States this year.

QUESTION 3.11.1   What will Nicaragua do with the money?

QUESTION 3.11.2   Should the U.S. continue to aid Nicaragua?

Consider how the third world goal trees yield different subjective interpretations of a single event. A U.S. conservative interpreting event 3.11 determines Nicaragua's motives with respect to the highest goal in figure 3.9(b) that the actions in 3.11 can help to bring about. The U.S.-liberal interpretation proceeds in the same manner, but uses the goal tree in figure 3.9(a) with different resulting interpretations.

Let us suppose that neither ideological understander has much knowledge about Nicaragua other than its status as a third-world country; therefore, the default goal trees in figure 3.9 are fully applicable. Both liberal and conservative ideological interpretations agree on the immediate

Figure 3.9(a).
Relative-importance goal
hierarchy for third world
countries perceived by the
U.S.-liberal ideology.

Figure 3.9(b).
Relative-importance goal
hierarchy for third world
countries perceived by the
U.S.-conservative ideology.

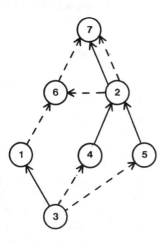

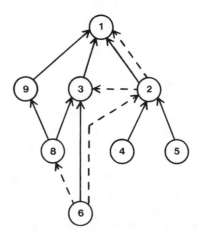

use of economic aid to Nicaragua: it furthers goal 2, economic development. In the conservative ideology, economic development is a subgoal
to the highest importance goal of increasing the power of the government;
therefore, this is the ultimate purpose to which Nicaragua will use its
economic aid. The conservative answer to question 3.11.1 is: "Nicaragua
will probably use the money to develop that part of their economy which
increases the power of the government." The liberal interpretation is
based on economic development as a subgoal to the goal of keeping the
people healthy and fed. Therefore the liberal interpreter sees the money
being spent to develop this aspect of the economy, regardless of whether
or not it helps the government stay in power.

The difference in the subjective interpretations of Nicaragua's ultimate economic goal directly affects the answer to question 3.11.2. In
order to answer this question, both ideological understanders must ask
themselves: "Does Nicaragua's use of the money represent progress
towards U.S. goals or does it violate U.S. goals?" The liberal understander matches the Nicaraguan goal of keeping its people healthy and fed as
an instance of the U.S. goal of minimizing disease and hunger throughout
the world (see figure 3.6). Therefore the liberal answer to 3.11.2 is "Yes."
The goal inferred by the conservative ideology of increasing the power of
the Nicaraguan government neither matches nor violates any goal in the
U.S. goal tree. Therefore, this ideology fails to provide an answer to

question 3.11.2. If it were the case that the Nicaraguan government was Communist, the answer would be negative. But, if Nicaragua was an anti-Communist U.S. ally, the answer to 3.11.2 would be positive. In either case the answer would be based on whether it is in the best interests of the U.S. to keep the Nicaraguan government in power, a different criterion than the basis for the U.S.-liberal answer.

3.6 Requirements for a Model of Ideological Understanding

In developing our model of ideological reasoning we defined certain criteria that our model had to meet. The purposes of these criteria are twofold. First, we want our model to be psychologically plausible. This consideration constrains the rules of inference to be compatible with our introspections of ideological reasoning, and suggests that only the appropriate rules of inference should be applied at each step of the understanding. The reason for our insistence on applying only the appropriate rules of inference is that we believe that humans do not pursue a large number of inference paths only to rule out all but the one or two most relevant inferences. Goal trees in conjunction with the half dozen rules operating on them provide a useful means of focusing the inferencer on the subjectively relevant aspects of the situation. The second motivation behind our criteria is to insure that our model of ideological understanding would be an integral part of a general subjective understanding process. We did not want to have different process models for different "types" of understanding. There is essentially one general "type" of human subjective understanding, though it manifests itself differently, depending on prior beliefs, experiences, attitudes, interests, and depth of knowledge.

Let us consider the specific criteria that guided the development of the goal-tree model of political ideologies:

CRITERION 3.1   Parsimony—A political ideology should contain only the subjective knowledge (e.g., beliefs, goals, etc.) required for ideological reasoning. General knowledge, such as inference rules, applicable to all ideologies or to other types of reasoning, should not be part of a political ideology.

CRITERION 3.2   Orthogonality—A political ideology does not necessarily affect other aspects of subjective understanding such as interpersonal relationships. A political ideology may be de-coupled from other subjective beliefs.

CRITERION 3.3   Compatibility—The form in which an ideology is represented should be useful in formulating representations for other aspects of human subjective understanding in a natural and consistent manner. All aspects of subjective understanding should be represented in the same general formalism.

CRITERION 3.4   Generality—There should be only one general inference mechanism operating on the entire memory of the understander. The same mechanism should apply across all ideologies and other subjective beliefs. The reasoning process is not domain-dependent.

Criteria 3.3 and 3.4 stem from our belief that all people think in the same general way. We do not believe, for instance, that Barry Goldwater thinks in an entirely different way than George McGovern. We attribute the differences in their political interpretations of events only to different political ideologies, not to differences in reasoning abilities. Ideological beliefs do not necessarily influence their reasoning processes on other matters. For instance Goldwater and McGovern may or may not think in the same general way when deciding to buy a house, send their children to college, etc. They may or may not share other idiosyncratic beliefs such as religious beliefs or personal attitudes. These beliefs are part of the subjective memory model of the person, encoded in the same representational form as political ideologies, but are conceptually separable from ideological beliefs. There can be selfish conservatives, generous liberals, selfish liberals, and generous conservatives. The subjective cognitive model of a person is a cross-product of different dimensions of subjective belief. The mechanisms underlying the thinking process that apply these subjective beliefs in understanding events or conversations are assumed to be the same for all understanders.

In subsequent chapters we develop process models of counterplanning, general conflict situations and their resolutions, human personality traits, and human discourse. All of these systems are really part of an integrated subjective understanding model. Goal trees interface with each of these processes. The primary function of the goal trees is to focus the attention of the understander by directing the inference process toward the subjectively most relevant or interesting aspects of the situation.

4

The Process of Goal-based Counterplanning

4.1 Introduction: Counterplanning and Common Sense

In order to understand political events, it is necessary to know about the goals, plans, and counterplans of the actors in the event. Counterplanning is a process in which one actor intentionally thwarts another actor's plans or attempts to achieve his own goals by circumventing the counterplanning attempts of the other actor. Goal conflicts and plan interferences give rise to counterplanning situations. When two actors want to achieve mutually exclusive goal states, or when their plans require the use of a unique resource, they are likely to counterplan against each other.

The POLITICS system encodes its counterplanning knowledge as a set of counterplanning strategies. The application of the strategies to a conflict situation is predicated upon each actor's perception of the goal conflict. Thus, counterplanning is essentially an inference process driven by the subjective beliefs of the actor. Understanding counterplanning events requires that the understander know or infer the goal trees of the actors in the event. Therefore, the counterplanning process described in this chapter is closely integrated with the goal tree representations of ideologies developed in the previous chapter. POLITICS uses its ideological beliefs to guide and focus the counterplanning strategies in understanding political events, as we will see in later discussions.

Before discussing our integrated model of subjective understanding, let us focus on the counterplanning process itself. Consider some examples which illustrate counterplanning situations.

EVENT 4.1   Johnny and Bobby saw a ten dollar bill on the sidewalk. Bobby, running slightly ahead of Johnny, said "finders keepers!" However, Johnny tripped him and picked up the ten dollar bill for himself.

EVENT 4.2   Senator Jones wanted the anti-abortion bill passed. Suspecting a filibuster by liberal members of the senate, he set up the bill as an
amendment to HEW funding.

In the first event, Johnny thwarted Bobby's goal of taking the $10 bill.
This is an instance of a simple counterplanning situation. Bobby had the
goal of owning the ten dollars, and Johnny had the same goal. The same
object cannot be owned by two different people. Therefore, if Johnny was
to own the ten dollars, he had to prevent Bobby from doing so. This must
be why Johnny tripped Bobby. In order to say that we have understood
event 4.1 we must be able to answer the question "Why did Johnny trip
Bobby?" It is impossible to answer this question without determining the
goals of the actors, the conflict between these goals, and the reason why
Bobby's and Johnny's actions focus not only on the pursuit of their own
respective goals, but also on blocking each other's inferred goals.

The second event illustrates a more involved counterplanning situation. Senator Jones foresaw a probable counterplanning effort against
his plan to fulfill the goal of anti-abortion legislation. As a result, he
planned to circumvent the possible thwarting of his plan by the liberal
senators. Senator Jones based his counterplan on the inference that liberal
senators do not wish to block or delay HEW funding. We have understood
event 4.2 only if we can answer the question "Why did Senator Jones link
his bill to HEW funding?" In order to answer this question we need to
understand that Jones expected a conflict situation to arise and that the
expected filibuster was the counterplan which he wanted to circumvent.
(We also need some knowledge of parliamentary procedures.) Hence, it
is crucial to understand conflict situations and counterplanning processes
in order to model human understanding of many events similar to 4.1 and
4.2.

In this chapter we develop a model of counterplanning-based reasoning that can generate the inferences required to understand events
such as 4.1 in much the same manner as our discussion above. We develop
our model of counterplanning with the objective that it be context-inde-
pendent. Our process model of counterplanning should be equally
applicable to understanding events 4.1, 4.2, international political events,
such as those discussed in the preceding chapters, and most other domains
of human interaction. Counterplanning situations are characterized by
goal conflicts and subsequent schemes to resolve the conflicts in the best
interests of the counterplanning actors. Most of our work focuses on
interpreting conflicts and counterplanning actions described in various
events. There are many kinds of events, such as the two presented above,
which cannot be understood without a notion of intentional counterplanning. The counterplanning methods discussed in this and subsequent

chapters are also applied to the generation of possible counterplans in well-defined situations.

In order to understand the counterplanning actions taken by actors in an event, we must understand the conflict situation that necessitated the counterplanning efforts. For instance, in understanding event 4.1, we first realize that both Bobby and Johnny want the same $10 bill. This leads to a conflict situation that allows us to interpret Johhny's tripping of Bobby as a counterplan to stop Bobby from reaching the $10 bill first. In event 4.2, we have to realize that Senator Jones's goals conflict with the goals of the liberal senators before we understand why Jones feared a filibuster and why he chose his counterplanning actions. In the following section we turn our attention to conflict situations. Understanding the nature of a conflict often suggests various appropriate counterplanning methods which the actors may pursue.

4.2 A Characterization of Goal Conflicts

There are many types of conflicts that can arise between individuals, groups of people, social institutions, companies, and governments. A conflict is a situation in which there are two or more actors whose goals differ and interfere with each other. In this section we classify different types of conflict situations. Conflict situations are analyzed in terms of the goals of the actors and the strategies they employ in trying to resolve their conflicts so as to achieve their respective goals. Counterplanning strategies are presented concurrently with our discussion of different types of goal conflicts.

The conflict situations that we analyze arise when an actor cannot achieve his goal simply by formulating a plan that ignores the actions and goals of other actors. A plan thus formulated in a conflict situation is prone to failure because of accidental interference or, in the more interesting case, intentional blocking on the part of another actor. Wilensky [1978] analyzes goal conflicts internal to one actor. It is necessary to analyze internal conflicts in order to determine why an actor chooses to pursue one goal while abandoning other plausible goals. Here, we are primarily interested in external conflicts between two or more actors. Consider two such examples; one event is an accidental interference situation and the other is an intentionally generated goal conflict.

EVENT 4.3   John wanted to drive to the bowling alley, but Mary took the car to go shopping.

EVENT 4.4   Ethiopia and Somalia are fighting for military control of the Ogaden Desert.

Event 4.3 is an instance of accidental goal conflict. Mary did not necessarily intend to keep John from going bowling, but, nevertheless, John's plans were thwarted by Mary's action. Ethiopia and Somalia are intentionally trying to prevent each other from achieving their respective goals of gaining military control over the Ogaden. It is clear that neither country is likely to achieve military control if it totally ignores the actions and plans of its opponent. In both cases the counterplanner (i.e. the actor whose goal stands to be blocked as a result of the goal conflict) must intentionally plan or re-plan his strategy for achieving his goal by taking the goals and actions of the other parties into account.

Goal conflicts can be categorized according to different criteria and along various dimensions. We present a classification of goal conflicts that is useful in understanding the application of counterplanning strategies. The primary distinction in a taxonomy of goal conflicts is the nature of the conflict itself. The goals of the two political actors in event 4.4 represent mutually exclusive states. Only one nation can have sovereignty over a region; therefore, only one of the two political actors can achieve its goal. The goals of the actors in event 4.3 do not exclude each other. There is nothing inherent in Mary's wanting to go shopping and John's wanting to go bowling which should cause one goal to preclude the fulfillment of the other. It is the particular plan (i.e., driving) chosen by John and Mary which causes the conflict, since both plans require use of a single resource, their car. If either actor could modify his/her plan (e.g., take the bus), both goals would be fulfilled.

Here we analyze intentional goal conflicts and counterplanning actions typical of each type of conflict. Plan interferences, such as event 4.3, are discussed in the following chapters. Most goal conflicts arise from mutually exclusive goal states desired by two or more actors. For instance, a mutual-exclusion goal conflict arises when both actors in event 4.1 want the same ten dollar bill. Somali sovereignty over the Ogaden desert is mutually exclusive with Ethiopian sovereignty, as exemplified in event 4.4.

Many, but not all, mutual-exclusion goal conflicts call for counterplanning actions. Event 4.5 is an example of a goal conflict with mutually exclusive goal states where no counterplanning actions could possibly be appropriate.

EVENT 4.5   John wants it to snow, but Mary was hoping for an Indian summer.

Once given the goal-conflict state and any necessary situational information, we need some rules to determine whether to expect counterplanning actions. Furthermore, if we are to understand the events we need to know who will do the counterplanning and what types of actions may be appropriate.

We first consider some strategies to determine the applicability of counterplanning methods to mutual-exclusion goal conflicts. Later we analyze various counterplanning strategies that suggest courses of action to promote the best interests of an actor in a goal conflict situation.

4.3 When to Expect Counterplanning

There are several factors that determine whether counterplanning strategies are applicable in a situation. These factors include the degree to which the goals come into conflict, the relative importance of the goals in conflict, the time constraints on the goals, and the ability of each actor to successfully thwart the efforts of the opposing actor. If an actor is completely unable to thwart his opponent's goal, then he may choose to abandon his own mutually exclusive goal. If a goal is of very high importance, then the counterplanning effort will be pursued more strongly when that goal is blocked. Certain types of goals such as preservation goals are inherently more important than other goals such as experience goals. Schank and Abelson [1977] and Wilensky [1978] discuss the goal taxonomy and the process of understanding plans to pursue the various types of goals. We discuss the subjective importance of goals, defined by the goal trees presented in the preceding chapter, as a crucial means of guiding and focusing the counterplanning process.

Let us consider some strategies to determine whether counterplanning is applicable in a mutual-exclusion goal conflict between two actors, X and Y. Since mutual-exclusion situations are inherently symmetrical, we will focus on the strategies that an actor X can apply in order to achieve his goal G(X) taking into account Y's pursuit of G(Y), when G(X) and G(Y) are mutually exclusive goal states. The following counterplanning strategies may be applied by X in order to resolve the goal conflict in his favor:

STRATEGY 4.1   BLOCK COMPETING GOAL
   X may try to block G(Y) independent of his pusuit of G(X). If X
   succeeds, the mutual-exclusion state no longer applies.

STRATEGY 4.1'   EXPECTED BLOCKING
   Y should be prepared for the eventuality that X may try to
   block G(Y) and take steps to prevent the goal blockage.

STRATEGY 4.2   PRIORITY SCHEDULING

IF X can achieve G(X) before Y can achieve G(Y),

THEN X should plan to pursue G(X) at the earliest possible opportunity.

STRATEGY 4.2'   GOAL SCHEDULE INTERFERENCE

IF X can achieve G(X) before Y can achieve G(Y),

THEN Y should try to delay X's pursuit of G(X) simultaneously with Y's pursuit of G(Y).

These strategies specify when to expect counterplanning efforts in mutual-exclusion goal conflicts, and they suggest what type of counterplanning effort to expect. The need for such strategies in understanding goal-conflict events is illustrated by the following example:

EVENT 4.6   Luigi is expected to testify against the Chicago underworld boss. The police are keeping Luigi's whereabouts secret.

Q - 4.6.1   Who are the police hiding Luigi from?

Q - 4.6.2   Why are they hiding him?

In order to answer these questions we first need to realize that the goal of the police (obtaining Luigi's testimony) and the goal of the underworld boss (not being convicted of any crime) are mutually exclusive states. Applying strategy 4.1 to this goal conflict generates the expectation that the underworld boss may do something to stop Luigi from testifying. The second sentence in event 4.6 needs to be interpreted in light of strategy 4.1'. The police are preparing for a possible counterplanning attempt on the part of the Chicago underworld boss, the other party in the mutually exclusive goal-conflict state. Hence, the police are counterplanning to block a precondition of whatever plan the underworld boss may invoke (e.g., kill Luigi, bribe him, or threaten him. All these plans require as preconditions that the underworld know where Luigi is located.)

Having understood 4.6 as an application of counterplanning strategies 4.1 and 4.1' enables us to see how questions 4.6.1 and 4.6.2 may be answered. Question 4.6.1 presupposes a counterplanning effort on the part of the police. This effort is matched to the application of strategy 4.1'. Hence, the blocked precondition to the underworld plan is keeping Luigi's whereabouts unknown to the underworld. This answers our question: The police are hiding Luigi from the underworld. The answer to the second question comes for free. Given that strategy 4.1' was invoked, the question becomes one of why this strategy was invoked. Checking the test clause of strategy 4.1' tells us that it was invoked in response to an expected counterplanning on the part of the underworld. What was this counterplan? The underworld might want to silence Luigi.

It is crucial to understand event 4.6 in terms of the counterplanning strategies, otherwise the causal connection between the two sentences in event 4.6 cannot be understood. Furthermore, without understanding this causal relation, questions such as 4.6.1 and 4.6.2 cannot be answered.

Consider some examples where counterplanning strategies 4.2 and 4.2' are necessary to understand an event. We start with event 4.1 discussed earlier:

EVENT 4.1 Johnny and Bobby saw a ten dollar bill on the sidewalk. Bobby, running slightly ahead of Johnny, said "finders keepers!" However, Johnny tripped him and picked up the ten dollar bill for himself.

QUESTION 4.1.1 Why did Johnny trip Bobby?

ANSWER 4.1.1 Because Johnny realized that Bobby would reach the $10 sooner unless he stopped him.

EVENT 4.7 The general said, "We have to reach the mountain pass before the enemy." The scout replied, "But sir, the enemy is much closer than we are to the pass." "Then I shall delay them with a cavalry attack on their right flank!"

The actors in events 4.1 and 4.7 must have invoked some version of strategies 4.2 and 4.2' in order to decide what type of counterplanning action was appropriate. A person interpreting these events must be able to reconstruct the relevant aspects of the counterplanning process. We claim that in the understanding process strategies 4.2 and 4.2' are brought to the attention of the understander by the goal-conflict situation and the temporal considerations of stories such as 4.1 and 4.7. Hence, in example 4.1, counterplanning strategy 2 should be brought to the focus of the understander by the fact that both Johnny and Bobby want the $10 and the fact that Bobby asserts that whoever reaches the ten dollar bill sooner gets to keep it. Counterplanning strategy 4.2' should be activated when understanding Johnny's viewpoint; i.e., Bobby will succeed in fulfilling his goal (consequently blocking Johnny's goal of possessing the $10) by applying strategy 4.2 unless Johnny intervenes.

The generality of the counterplanning strategies makes them applicable to the interpretation of events in many different situations where the actors may pursue different types of goals. The primary reason why this is possible is that counterplanning depends on the *type of interaction* among the goals of the primary actors, rather than the precise nature of these goals or the situational details. The fact that these strategies are quite general requires the understanding process to make use of situational information (e.g., scripts) and to relate information to the goal hierarchies of the actors by performing goal-directed inference. Hence, counterplanning is an integral part of our subjective understanding paradigm; it functions in conjunction with other inference and memory processes.

There are goal-conflict situations in which several counterplanning strategies must be applied in order to understand the course of action taken by one of the actors. For instance, in understanding event 4.7 we need to know not only that according to strategy 4.2' the general needed to delay the enemy's advance on the pass, but somehow we must interpret the diversionary flank attack as an appropriate means to achieve this end. The interpretation of actions as part of the counterplanning process is characterized by other, more specific counterplanning strategies discussed in this chapter. Some counterplanning strategies such as 4.2' can be recursive. For instance, in event 4.7, the enemy may realize that the flank attack was meant to allow the general's army to reach the pass sooner; therefore, strategy 4.2' may once again be applied to somehow delay the general's army while they disengage from the attacking cavalry.

The POLITICS system applies counterplanning strategies to resolve the goal conflicts that often arise from the ideological goals of the participants. We saw some examples of how counterplanning strategies direct the understanding process in the POLITICS examples presented in the previous chapter. Here we discuss part of a question-answer dialog in which POLITICS applies the four strategies we discussed. (A fully annotated computer run for this example is presented in Chapter 7.)

(INTERPRET U.S.-CONSERVATIVE)

INPUT TEXT: The United States Congress voted to fund the Trident submarine project.

Q: What did the U.S. Congress do this for?

A: THE UNITED STATES CONGRESS WANTS THE UNITED STATES ARMED FORCES TO BE STRONGER.

Q: What should the U.S. do if Russia also builds nuclear submarines?

A: THE UNITED STATES SHOULD BUILD MORE SUBMARINES.

The first question to U.S.-conservative POLITICS confirms that the goal of the U.S. Congress (therefore the U.S. goal) has been properly established. The second question presupposes a Russian action of the same type as the strengthening of the U.S. military. POLITICS infers the Russian goal of military strength from the ideological goal tree. Increasing military strength in both U.S. and Russian goal trees is a subgoal to being stronger than one's opponents. Clearly, only one country can be stronger than the other; therefore, we have a mutual-exclusion goal conflict. POLITICS detects the conflict and interprets the Russian action as a possible counterplan to the U.S. action by applying Strategy 4.1. Strategy 4.2 is tested and found applicable as a possible counterplanning measure by the U.S. against Russia. POLITICS believes the U.S. to be better able to build military hardware; therefore, the U.S. can achieve superior military strength faster than Russia. This fulfills the test clause of strategy 4.2; hence POLITICS answers with the appropriately instantiated action clause of this counterplanning strategy.

4.4 Diversionary Counterplanning Strategies

We turn to some of the more specific counterplanning strategies applicable to a mutual-exclusion goal conflict. A frequently encountered set of strategies operate on the principle of diverting the efforts of an actor in the goal conflict away from direct pursuit of his goal. There are essentially three classes of diversionary strategies, all relying on the fact that if an actor has to divert his efforts to other matters, he is less likely to succeed at his original task. We group the diversionary strategies into the three categories listed below:

1. Threaten higher level goals of one's opponent.

2. Dissipation of effort—Threaten other goals.

3. Trick option—Convince one's counterplanning opponent that other important goals are threatened.

4.4.1 Threatening higher level goals

As we investigated in the previous chapter, a partial ordering of the goals of an actor with respect to their inherent importance is useful knowledge for the understander. We previously discussed how this ordering can focus the goal-directed inference process; now we investigate its significance in understanding counterplans. Consider the process of understanding the following two examples:

EVENT 4.8   John and Bill were playing tennis and got into an argument over whether the last volley was in-bounds. Bill threatened to quit the game, but John yielded.

EVENT 4.9   The United States supported Israel in the 1973 Middle-East war. Subsequently the Arabs imposed an oil embargo on the United States and its allies.

The first sentence in event 4.8 states that there was a mutual-exclusion goal conflict between John and Bill: only one player can be the winner of a point in a competitive sports event. From the second sentence we infer that playing the game is more important for John than winning a particular point. The opposite appears to be the case for Bill. We claim that the same counterplanning strategy is applicable to making these inferences and to understanding why the Arabs imposed an oil embargo in event 4.9. This counterplanning strategy is presented below. The understander checks on the applicability of the strategy to the goals and actions of the actors if the trigger condition matches the currently relevant situation. Thus, in our process model of goal-focused understanding, only some of the counterplanning strategies are actively considered at a given stage of the interpretation process.

STRATEGY 4.3   THREATEN HIGHER LEVEL GOAL

TRIGGER   Mutual-exclusion goal-conflict situation between G(Y) and G(X).

IF   X can find a goal G'(Y) to block, where G'(Y) is a goal of higher importance to Y than G(Y),

THEN   X should try to block G'(Y). X can expect Y to pursue G'(Y) and abandon G(Y).

REFINEMENT   G'(Y) should be chosen such that:
1. Y cannot pursue both G'(Y) and G(Y) simultaneously, or
2. Y can accomplish G'(Y) only if X stops his blocking action.

Strategy 4.3 means that in a mutual-exclusion goal-conflict situation, one actor (X) may threaten a higher level goal of the second actor (Y), in order to make Y preserve that higher level goal. Since an actor's attention, time, and material resources are limited, Y may not be able simultaneously to protect his higher level goal and pursue his goal that conflicts with X's goal. Thus, X will be in a better position to win the conflict situation and achieve his own goal. The "refinement" part of the rule gives some advice to help X make his choice on which one of Y's higher importance goals to threaten. X knows which goals Y may consider more important by querying Y's goal tree. Our model assumes that the various actors know about each other's primary motivations. X should threaten a goal that requires Y's full attention, time, or material resources to protect. Alternatively, X can threaten an important goal that Y cannot protect. This gives X a bargaining position to tell Y that he will stop his threat only if Y abandons the (presumably less important) goal that conflicts with X's goal. Bargaining strategies are discussed in greater detail later in this chapter.

How does strategy 4.3 help us understand event 4.8? Let us substitute John for Y and Bill for X. John's goal in the dispute, G(Y), is winning the argument over the close line call. G(X) is Bill's mutually exclusive goal of also winning the argument. The fact that John abandoned G(Y) as a result of a threat made by Bill tells the understander that Bill applied counterplanning strategy 4.3. Strategy 4.3 tells us that in order for Bill's threat to be effective, he must have threatened a goal that John holds as more important than winning the point in dispute. Since Bill threatened to end the game, we conclude that playing the tennis game is John's more important goal.

Each counterplanning strategy described in this chapter can be interpreted from the perspective of either actor in the goal conflict. Thus, strategies 4.2 and 4.2' are essentially dual interpretations of the same counterplanning principle. Whether the original or primed version of the strategy is applied in the interpretation process depends on the identification of the understander with one of the actors. Most counterplanning strategies, such as strategy 4.3, are symmetrical with respect to the courses of action that can be taken by X or Y. Therefore, these strategies can be applied by either actor in a conflict situation.

Strategy 4.3 can be used in a predictive framework or in an explanatory manner. In understanding event 4.9 we need to pose and answer the question "Why did the Arabs impose an oil embargo?" Using knowledge about the goals of the Arabs and the goal of the United States to help Israel, the understander can establish the goal conflict between the Arabs and the United States. The mutual-exclusion goal conflict is between the U.S. goal of aiding Israel and the Arab goal of preventing U.S. aid to Israel.

Having interpreted the situation thus far, an understander can proceed in two different manners. The first manner is to predict all the possible counterplanning actions the Arabs might take to make the U.S. end aid to Israel. If, in interpreting the rest of the event, the understander matches an action with one of the previously predicted counterplanning actions, the understander can conclude that indeed the Arabs were counterplanning against the U.S. and that their counterplan was the predicted course of action. Such a process would require the understander to generate vast numbers of hypotheses and subsequently test each hypothesis as a possible explanation of the situation. There is no evidence to suggest that people generate all possible inference paths in a given interpretation in order to discard all but one path that matches reality. From our discussion in Chapter 1 and an analysis of event 4.9, it appears much more plausible that people only pursue a small number of relevant inference paths. Therefore, generating all possible plans of action is not a reasonable psychological model of human thinking; nor does it lend itself to reasonable constraints on the computational time that the system may require in order to generate and test all alternative actions on the part of the Arabs.

A more reasonable alternative to the generate and test process is the following: Given the existence of the mutual-exclusion goal conflict, strategies 4.1 and 4.1' predict that the two actors may counterplan against each other. No further predictive inferences are generated at this point. The rest of the event should be interpreted in light of the expectation that the two actors may counterplan to resolve their goal conflict. Recall event 4.9:

> EVENT 4.9   The United States supported Israel in the 1973 Middle-East war. Subsequently the Arabs imposed an oil embargo on the United States and its allies.
>
> QUESTION   Why did the Arabs impose the oil embargo?

When the understander learns of the Arab oil embargo, he tries to see if this is a reasonable course of action to take as a counterplan against the U.S. goal of aiding Israel. Counterplanning strategy 4.3 (refinement 2) matches the type of interaction between the Arab plan and the U.S. goal. The Arabs are threatening a higher level U.S. preservation goal by cutting off oil supplies, and the U.S. cannot do anything to directly remedy the situation. Now the Arabs can bargain to end the embargo in return for the end of U.S. aid to Israel. Therefore, the understander can establish the Arab counterplanning actions by applying strategy 4.3 in an explanatory manner. The result of the Arab actions is matched to the action part of the strategy. This match, suggested by our previous expectation that a counterplanning action was likely, allows the understander to infer that the Arabs were invoking counterplanning strategy 4.3.

The explanatory mode of reasoning is superior to the predictive mode because it does not require the generation and subsequent testing of an arbitrarily large set of possible courses of action. It is also a more reasonable model of human thought. Before and during the 1973 Arab-Israeli war, few people foresaw an Arab oil embargo. When the embargo came, however, the reasons for the Arab action became apparent.

4.4.2 The structure of the counterplanning strategies

Our model of counterplanning is essentially a goal-directed rule-based system. Each strategy is a rule that tests the goal-conflict state between the two actors, the goal trees of each actor, and occasionally the plan that each actor is pursuing. If the test of a rule is true, the action part of the rule suggests a counterplanning method that is likely to succeed. The action part of the rule may have additional conditions or refinements. The structure of a counterplanning strategy is illustrated in figure 4.1:

Figure 4.1. The structure of a counterplanning strategy

STRATEGY   <rule#k>   <title>

   TRIGGER   Conjunction of <test1, test2, . . . , testn>

       IF   Conjunction of <testn+1, testn+2, . . .>

    THEN   Sequence of <action1, action2, . . .>

REFINEMENT   <subrule#k1, subrule#k2, . . .>

The test part of each rule is divided into the "trigger" clause and an additional "if" clause. In order for a rule to apply, both clauses must be true in the counterplanning situation. The reason for our division of the test clause in such a manner is to reduce the time that the process model must spend searching for an applicable strategy. All the trigger conditions are "inexpensive" tests: that is, they are tests that can be applied directly to the situation without requiring further inference or complicated matching. Furthermore, the trigger conditions are compiled into a discrimination network. This organization allows the addition of new strategies without a corresponding linear increase in the search time required to test all the applicable counterplanning strategies.

Once the trigger conditions for a rule have been met, the additional tests are performed. These tests may be arbitrarily complex, requiring further inference and possibly requiring other counterplanning strategies to be invoked. However, the trigger conditions usually restrict the set of applicable counterplanning strategies to a small number in any given situation (typically three or four). Furthermore, counterplanning strategies reflect common-sense reasoning about how to deal with adverse situations. As such, each strategy is sufficiently general to apply across most reasonable human conflict domains. This means that the total number of counterplanning strategies is relatively small compared to the total number of rules and information contained in the situation-specific scripts. We have found approximately forty counterplanning strategies suffice to model counterplanning actions in most situations and most goal conflicts. (The strategies are presented throughout in Chapters 4, 5, and 6.)

The action part of each strategy (denoted by the word THEN) is a sequence of counterplanning methods to be applied in the current context by one of the actors. If a strategy is applied, the "refinement" field is checked before the sequence of actions is performed. The refinement contains one or more additional rules which usually provide further detail to the counterplanning situation. These rules are truly subrules to the counterplanning strategies because they are invoked only in the case that all the tests of the strategy are true, and, in addition, the test clause of each subrule is also true. In structure, our strategies are much closer to the rules in expert systems (such as PECOS, Barstow [1977]) than to more constrained production systems (e.g., Newell's [1973] PSG system).

We continue our discussion of diversionary counterplanning strategies.

4.4.3 Trick options and dissipation of effort

Consider another diversionary counterplanning strategy:

> STRATEGY 4.4   DISSIPATION OF EFFORT
>
> TRIGGER   Mutual-exclusion goal-conflict situation between G(Y) and G(X).
>
> IF   Y cannot simultaneously pursue many goals,
>
> THEN   X should try to block many of Y's other goals in order to focus Y's efforts away from G(Y).

Strategy 4.4 is necessary to understand event 4.7. We previously discussed the application of strategies 4.2 and 4.2' to understand *why* the army general was counterplanning in event 4.7. Strategy 4.4 tells us *what* his counterplanning effort consists of. We reiterate event 4.7 below:

> EVENT 4.7   The general said, "We have to reach the mountain pass before the enemy." The scout replied, "But sir, the enemy is much closer than

we are to the pass." "Then I shall delay them with a cavalry attack
on their right flank!"

The reader of event 4.7 has the expectation that the attack may enable
the general to achieve his goal of reaching the pass first. This expectation
can only come from a realization that the general is invoking strategy 4.4
or some variant thereof. The reader, not being a military expert, cannot
evaluate the relative merits and importance of defending against cavalry
attacks in contrast with advancing on the mountain pass. Therefore, the
causal connections of the general's action can be interpreted as a counterplan only because the understander expects the general to formulate
a counterplan (strategy 4.2') and because the general's action under the
situation is an instance of counterplanning strategy 4.4.

The understanding process for event 4.7, including recognition of an
instance of strategy 4, proceeds in an explanatory rather than in a predictive manner. That is, we do not believe that the reader generates a host
of possible counterplanning actions that the general could take and subsequently recognizes the action taken by the general as one of the
alternatives. As we mentioned before, this process would require the
understander to have substantial military knowledge. In a sense, the
counterplanning strategies are used to hypothesize that the decision process in the general's mind focuses on the resolution of the goal-conflict
situation. Hence, the general's flank attack is interpreted as a counterplanning action because some (as yet unspecified) counterplanning actions
were predicted by strategy 4.2'. This is another instance of using counterplanning strategies in an explanatory manner, much like the reasoning
process used to understand event 4.9.

Counterplanning strategies 4.3 and 4.4 differ in the certainty of their
expectations and the necessity of repeated application. In strategy 4.3 the
expectation that the higher level goal, G'(Y), will be pursued is almost
certain. The uncertainty, if any, comes in whether pursuit of G'(Y) will
necessarily preclude the achievement of the conflict goal, G(Y). There is
no such guarantee when other goals of unknown relative importance to
G(Y) are threatened. For instance, the understander would not be very
surprised if event 4.7 continued with "The enemy gained the pass after
the ineffectual cavalry attack." On the other hand, consider the following
event:

EVENT 4.10   John broke into the liquor store looking for the cash register. The
owner met him with a loaded shotgun and said, "Get lost before
I pull the trigger." John proceeded to open the cash register and
take the money.

The owner of the liquor store invoked strategy 4.3. He threatened John's self-preservation goal, a higher level goal than acquisition of money. The reason why the last sentence in event 4.10 strikes us as rather absurd is that John violated the expectation that he would give higher priority to the more important goal, staying alive. Hence, a failure of an expectation from strategy 4.3 is considered anomalous behavior, but failure of strategy 4.4 expectations can and often do occur in various types of events.

Strategy 4.4 may be applied to several of Y's goals; the more goals X threatens, the better his chances of diverting Y from pursuit of G(Y). In strategy 4.3 it suffices to threaten one goal. Both strategies presuppose that Y cannot ignore the threatened goals, achieve G(Y), and only then worry about goals that X threatened to block. Hence, there is an additional constraint on X's choice of which of Y's goals to threaten: the goals must be such that X can block them before Y can achieve G(Y).

Let us turn our attention to a diversionary strategy that is not directed at other goals of the opponent.

STRATEGY 4.5   DIVERTING FOCUS OF ATTENTION

TRIGGER   Mutual-exclusion goal-conflict situation between G(Y) and G(X).

IF   Y needs his full attention to pursue G(Y),

THEN   X should cause other events to take place that divert X's attentions from his plan to pursue of G(Y).

Strategy 4.5 is based on the same principle as the two previous diversionary strategies: An actor cannot simultaneously pursue multiple courses of action. Awareness of this simple principle applied to other actors (as well as the counterplanner) guides our formulation of the diversionary counterplanning strategies. Each strategy is based on a different method of causing an actor to simultaneously have more than one goal to worry about. There are various kinds of limitations that restrict the ability of an actor to pursue multiple courses of action. We classify these limitations on the simultaneous pursuit of multiple courses of action into the following categories:

1. Limitations on available time.
2. Mental and physical limitations on the number of actions that can be performed simultaneously.
3. Limitations of material resources.
4. Limitations of ability.

5. Goal of avoiding certain consequences of one's actions.
6. Interactions between different courses of actions.

All of the counterplanning strategies are based on these limitations of time, resources, and effort in pursuing multiple goals. The strategies that we have investigated thus far fall into the first two limitation categories. The same is true for strategy 4.5, as illustrated by event 4.11:

> EVENT 4.11 John and Bill were engaged in a chess game. During Bill's move John kept talking about his hot date the previous night. Eventually, Bill lost a rook and resigned the game.

Bill cannot simultaneously focus his attention on John's story and on playing chess, an instance of limitation category 2. Hence, assuming intentionality on John's part, event 4.11 can be understood as an instance of John's applying strategy 4.5 to resolve the goal conflict of both players.

The third type of diversionary strategy involves deception. If an actor Y believes that there is some reason why he should divert his attention or his efforts away from his goal G(Y), then X may more easily pursue G(X). When the belief is not founded in reality but caused by some act on X's part, it is an instance of deception used as a counterplanning strategy. Both strategies 4.3 and 4.4 have their "trick-option" counterparts. A trick option (Schank and Abelson [1977]) means that one actor appears to follow a particular course of action while in reality he follows a different course. We label trick-option strategies with an asterisk as follows:

STRATEGY 4.3*   TRICK OPTION: FALSE THREAT

> Same as strategy 4.3 but either
> 1. X only appears to threaten the higher level goal G'(Y), or
> 2. X threatens to block G'(Y) but has falsely convinced Y that G'(Y) should be one of Y's high level goals.

STRATEGY 4.4*   TRICK OPTION: FALSE DIVERSION

> Same as strategy 4.4 but X need only appear to threaten Y's goals G1(Y), G2(Y), etc.

Strategy 4.3* is rather ubiquitous in everyday life. Bluffing and making threats with no intent to carry them out are some common applications of counterplanning by means of invoking the trick option. Strategy 4.3* is also useful in understanding some novel situations such as the following story:

EVENT 4.12   John and Bill were competing for Mary's attentions at a party. John, noticing that Bill was more successful, went to the telephone next door and called the host to tell him that Bill's house was on fire. Regretably, Bill had to leave the party in great haste.

In our society, John's and Bill's goals of courting Mary are mutually exclusive; therefore, the counterplanning strategies, including strategy 4.3*, are applicable. Bill's higher level goal of preserving his house, belongings, and possibly his family overrides any further immediate consideration of his previous goal. The fact that Bill's house was not on fire is relevant only to the likelihood of success of 4.3*. It is possible, for instance, that Bill may see through the ruse by calling his house or calling his neighbors.

The second part of strategy 4.3* is illustrated by a used-car salesman convincing his potential customer that he really wants a Cadillac Seville instead of the economy car he intended to buy. The customer has the goal of preserving as much of his money as possible while purchasing a car. The car dealer has the mutually exclusive goal of parting the customer from as much money as possible. The high pressure sales technique used by the car dealer may proceed as follows: He convinces the customer that a luxury car is much more desirable than an economy car. The customer is led to believe that his goal of owning a Cadillac is of higher importance than his goal of preserving money. The customer sees his goal of achieving higher status by owning a luxury car threatened if he buys an inexpensive economy car. Therefore, the dealer has convinced the customer to abandon his original goal of preserving his money. Most counterplanning strategies described in the following sections have their own trick-option alternatives.

4.5 Counterplanning Strategies Based on Goal Compromise

A significant class of counterplanning strategies in mutual-exclusion goal conflicts is the set of bargaining strategies. These strategies are characterized by a willingness to compromise on the part of the disputing actors. Willingness to compromise is mediated by many factors such as whether compromise is possible, necessary, or desirable on the part of both disputing actors.

There are two basic classes of bargaining strategies; each class is characterized by the type of compromise that the counterplanning actors are willing to accept. Let G(X) be X's goal, and G(Y) by Y's goal. As before, these two goals define a mutual-exclusion conflict.

BARGAINING STRATEGIES

1. Partial fulfillment of G(X) and/or G(Y).

2. Goal substitution of G(X) and/or G(Y) by another goal not involved in the conflict.

The first class of strategies assumes the possibility of either goal in the goal conflict being partially fulfilled. Let us define "partial fulfillment" of a goal with the aid of some illustrative examples:

EVENT 4.13   John was a very ambitious salesman. He wanted to become president of General Petroleum corporation.

Case (a)   John was fired and blacklisted for unethical business practices.

Case (b)   John tried very hard and was eventually appointed vice-president of General Petroleum.

Case (c)   John's meteoric rise in the corporate structure culminated in the presidency of the company.

In case (a), John failed to achieve his goal. In case (c), John clearly achieved his goal. What can we say about case (b)? Strictly speaking, John did not achieve his goal of becoming president. However, John did not totally fail in fulfilling his ambition. We classify case (b) as partial fulfillment of his goal. John achieved something less than the presidency of the company, but by any reasonable measure of success, he succeeded in obtaining some of the power, prestige, and wealth associated with the presidency of a company.

The following examples are instances where there can be no partial fulfillment of a goal:

EVENT 4.14   The New York Yankees wanted to beat the Boston Red Sox. The Yankees were leading until the bottom of the ninth when Rice won the game for Boston with a grand slam.

EVENT 4.15   Hubert Humphrey came very close to winning the 1968 presidential elections, but lost to Nixon.

In Event 4.14 the Yankees failed to fulfill their goal. The fact that they almost won cannot be considered partial fulfillment, as there are no intermediate states between winning and losing a baseball game. The same argument applies to event 4.15. There was no real partial fulfillment of Humphrey's goal, no matter how close he came to winning the election.

What is the crucial difference between examples 4.13 and the two latter examples? Becoming president of a company is a complex goal subsuming several simpler goals such as achieving social respect, power, and wealth. (Wilensky [1978] discusses the phenomenon of goal subsumption.) Success on each one of these simpler goals is measured on a continuum rather than on an all-or-nothing outcome. Therefore, there are two measures of partial success in achieving a goal.

The first measure applies to a complex goal that subsumes several other goals. We define success to be the case where all the subsumed goals are fulfilled, and failure to be the case where none of the subsumed goals are fulfilled. Partial fulfillment is defined in the obvious manner; the goal is partially fulfilled if some of the subsumed goals are fulfilled. For instance consider the following case:

EVENT 4.16   John wanted to marry Susan. They decided to live together instead.

Did John achieve his goal? Strictly speaking the answer is "no". But, if we understand that marriage is a goal subsumption state, we realize that for all intents and purposes John fulfilled most of the goals subsumed by marriage, such as achieving companionship, periodic satisfaction of the sex drive, etc. Since marriage also involves a change in social and legal status not necessarily associated with living together, we say that John partially fulfilled his goal. By this measure, partial fulfillment of a goal is a case in which the specific goal sought is not fulfilled, but a significant fraction of the underlying reasons for pursuing the goal are fulfilled.

The second way in which partial goal fulfillment is measured applies to goal states that can take a continuum of values. Acquisition of money and achievement of social stature are examples of continuum-valued goals; there are virtually infinite degrees of social stature and of the amount of money that a person can acquire. We define success differently for preservation goals than for achievement goals (called "P-goals" and "A-goals" respectively—Schank and Abelson [1977] define the goal taxonomy.) Let us call the *initial* value of the goal state "I", the *desired* value of the goal state "D", and its *resultant* value at the time when we must decide whether the goal succeeded "R". For P-goals it is usually the case that I = D, and for A-goals I < D. The success and failure conditions of continuum-valued goals are given by the following table:

Table 4.1.   Partial Fulfillment of Goal States

	Failure	Partial Success	Success
A-GOAL	I = R < D	I < R < D	I < R = D
P-GOAL	R < I = D	R slightly < I = D	R = I = D

Let us consider how the success table applies to an example of related A-goals and P-goals:

EVENT 4.17   Somalia wanted to conquer the Ogaden region in Ethiopia. The Somalis launched an invasion.

Case 1.   The Somalis conquered the entire Ogaden.

Case 2.   The Ethiopian army checked the Somali invasion, yielding only a border sector and several villages.

Case 3.   Ethiopia beat back the Somali attack, defeating the invading army.

From a Somali perspective, event 4.17 is an attempt to fulfill an A-goal, achieving military control of the Ogaden region which was previously under Ethiopian control. Hence, the present state: I = no control over the Ogaden, and the desired state: D = controlling the entire Ogaden region. In case (1) the Somalis achieved a state of military control over the Ogaden, resulting in state $R = D > I$. Therefore, the Somalis fully succeeded. In case (2) the Somalis achieved military control of a (probably small) part of the Ogaden region. Thus, $I < R < D$; the Somalis partially succeeded. In case (3) the Somalis achieved nothing relevant to their goal. Therefore $I = R < D$, total failure.

We can interpret event 4.17 from an Ethiopian perspective. The primary Ethiopian goal is to preserve their sovereignty over the Ogaden region, a P-goal with $I = D$ = Ethiopian control of the Ogaden. In case (1) the Somalis control the Ogaden, a state mutually exclusive with Ethiopian control of the same region. Thus, $R < I = D$, meaning that the Ethiopian P-goal failed. In case (2) Ethiopia controls most but not all of the Ogaden; therefore, R is slightly less than I and D, our condition for partial success. In case (3) Ethiopia fulfills its goal of maintaining sovereignty over the Ogaden; $R = I = D$.

There are different types of goal-conflict situations, depending on the nature of goals in conflict. These differences are reflected in the counterplanning strategies applicable to each type of goal conflict. The three types of conflicts are P-goal vs. P-goal, A-goal vs. A-goal, and P-goal vs. A-goal conflicts. Let us analyze each class of conflict situation in terms of the possible resolutions.

P-goal vs. P-goal conflicts are never mutual-exclusion goal conflicts. If X's goal and Y's goal consist of maintaining the status-quo of two different goal states, these two states have to already co-exist in the world. Therefore, by definition, the goal states cannot be mutually exclusive.

Conflicts of this nature arise only when X's plan to preserve G(X) interferes with Y's plan to preserve G(Y). Plan-interference conflicts of this general nature are analyzed in the following chapters. Event 4.6, presented earlier in this chapter, is an instance of a mutually exclusive P-goal vs. P-goal conflict.

A-goal vs. A-goal are among the most commonly occurring goal conflicts in everyday life. For instance, events 4.1, 4.7, 4.11, 4.12, 4.14 and 4.15 are all A-goal vs. A-goal conflicts. All of the counterplanning strategies discussed thus far are applicable to this class of goal conflicts. Counterplanning strategies based on compromise and goal substitution, discussed below, apply primarily to A-goals. People are much less willing to compromise the preservation of something which they already have; they are more likely to compromise the acquisition of some new goal state. Therefore, satisfaction with the partial fulfillment of a goal is more likely to occur in A-goal conflicts. The counterplanning strategies based on substituting one of the goals in the conflict for a new, non-conflict goal also apply primarily to A-goals. For instance, if Somalia invades Ethiopia, it is very unlikely that Ethiopia would be willing to substitute its goal of preserving sovereignty over the Ogaden for any other conceivable goal.

The asymmetrical goal-conflict state is the P-goal vs. A-goal conflict. Events 4.9, 4.10 and 4.17 are examples of this type of conflict, as is the Arab-Israeli dispute from an Arab viewpoint. The counterplanning strategies characterizing this type of conflict include the compromise strategies and goal substitution, whereby the P-goal actor may induce the A-goal actor to pursue an alternate, non-conflicting goal. The latter, in turn may try to get as much as he can in return for abandoning his original A-goal.

Let us turn our attention to partial goal-fulfillment and goal-substitution bargaining strategies to determine how the nature of the goal conflict affects their application.

STRATEGY 4.6   GOAL COMPROMISE

TRIGGER   G(X) and G(Y) are mutually exclusive and may be partially fulfilled.

IF   X cannot achieve G(X) by other counterplanning strategies,

THEN   X should try to partially fulfill G(X) by bargaining with Y to compromise mutually on partially fulfilling their respective goals.

Metaphorically, strategy 4.6 states that if one cannot have the entire pie then one should try to bargain for at least a slice. The following example illustrates partial fulfillment of goals as a result of compromise:

EVENT 4.18 Professors Smith and Jones kept blocking each other's efforts to become chairman of their department. Eventually Smith agreed to support Jones in the next election, with the stipulation that Jones support Smith in the following election.

Strategy 4.6 is invoked when other measures fail; one does not compromise if one can totally fulfill one's goal. In order to understand event 4.18, one must realize that the very existence of a goal conflict prevents either actor from making further progress toward his goal. In this case, the understander should expect compromise as the only reasonable course of action. The compromise in event 4.18 is that each actor fulfills his acquisition of the power/prestige goal, but only for a limited time.

Strategy 7 is more cooperative in nature than strategy 4.6, but involves the same principle of compromise on partially attainable goals:

STRATEGY 4.7 COOPERATION BY MUTUAL NEED

TRIGGER G(X) and G(Y) are mutually exclusive and may be partially fulfilled.

IF neither X nor Y can independently achieve their respective goals, but can succeed only by pooling their efforts,

THEN X and Y should compromise on partially fulfilling G(X) and G(Y) and plan jointly for their fulfillment.

Strategy 4.7 states that cooperation may be a necessary course of action in spite of conflicting goals. Event 4.19 illustrates this point:

EVENT 4.19 Jesse James and Bill Morgan joined forces to heist the payroll train.

We infer that both actors had the A-goal of acquiring the money in the payroll train. These goals are mutually exclusive but may be partially fulfilled. Suppose we had to answer the question: "Why did Jesse James and Bill Morgan join forces?" The most reasonable answer is: "Probably because neither could heist the train by himself." This answer cannot be inferred from the goal conflict itself; the existence of a goal conflict would predict competitive rather than cooperative actions. Therefore, the understander has to be aware of strategy 4.7—cooperation between actors with conflicting goals is reasonable if neither actor can otherwise fulfill his goal. Strategy 4.7 predicts that Jesse and Bill will partially fulfill their A-goals; i.e., they will split the take. This prediction accords with our intuition of what normally happens in this type of situation.

The following event is another example of forced cooperation. Without the compromise of sharing government power, neither party would achieve its goal of governing Italy.

> EVENT 4.20   In Italy neither the Christian Democrats nor the Communist Party was able to form a majority government. They formed an unprecedented coalition to govern the country.

Strategies 4.6 and 4.7 have their trick options, defined similarly to the trick options of strategies 4.3 and 4.4:

> STRATEGY 4.6*   TRICK OPTION: FALSE COMPROMISE
>
> Same as strategy 4.6, but X can pretend to agree on compromise (to divert Y's efforts) while pursuing some other means of counterplanning.

> STRATEGY 4.7*   TRICK OPTION: FALSE COOPERATION
>
> Same as strategy 4.7, but after X and Y have mutually fulfilled their common goal, X can counterplan against Y with the purpose of blocking G(Y) and totally fulfilling G(X).

The trick option can be applied to events 4.18 and 4.19 as follows:

> EVENT 4.18   (possible continuation):
> Jones supported Smith's successful bid for the chairmanship, but in the next election Smith badmouthed Jones.

> EVENT 4.19   (possible continuation):
> After the successful train heist, Jesse James shot Bill Morgan and took the entire loot.

The understanding process for event 4.18 assumes that both Jones and Smith invoke strategy 4.6. The use of the word "but" in the continuation of event 4.18 suggests that an expectation has been violated. (Schank [1975] describes the "but test", a heuristic method to determine what is inferred in understanding a text.) Since badmouthing Jones violates Smith's part of the bargain, the violated expectation can be interpreted as a signal to the understander that Smith has invoked strategy 4.6*. The bargain was only a ruse to prevent Jones from blocking Smith's A-goal.

Understanding the continuation of event 4.19 also requires one to realize that the trick option has been invoked. Cooperation between Jesse and Bill resulted in partial fulfillment of their respective goals, but then Jesse counterplanned (unbeknown to Bill) and totally fulfilled his A-money goal at Bill's expense. It is interesting to note that if the understander of event 4.19 knows about Jesse James's goals and subgoals (i.e., has a reasonably detailed goal-subgoal importance hierarchy of the type discussed in the preceding chapter), then the understander may expect treachery on Jesse's part. Hence, the goal hierarchies of the actors help to determine which counterplanning strategy is more likely to be invoked by the actors in a goal-conflict situation.

4.6 Counterplanning Strategies Based on Goal Substitution

In some goal-conflict situations, a useful class of bargaining strategies is based on goal substitution. There are different types of goal substitution, as discussed in Schank and Abelson [1977]. Here we are concerned with how goal substitution is invoked in bargaining strategies. Let us consider an example of goal substitution:

> EVENT 4.21   Johnny and Billy were arguing over who would get to ride their new bicycle. Johnny said, "If you let me ride it, I'll give you my candy bar." Billy promptly agreed.

In event 4.21 Billy substituted his goal of riding the bicycle with the goal of eating a candy bar. Moreover, Johnny was aware that Billy might be amenable to this goal substitution. Johnny used his knowledge of Billy's goals to propose the bargain that ended their goal conflict. The general bargaining strategy invoked by Johnny is the following:

> STRATEGY 4.8   GOAL SUBSTITUTION
>
> > TRIGGER   G(X) and G(Y) are competing goals and X knows about Y's other goals.
> >
> > IF   X can bring about G'(Y), one of Y's goals that is at least as important as G(Y),
> >
> > THEN   X should bargain with Y to substitute G'(Y) for G(Y) as Y's actively pursued goal. (This leaves X free to pursue G(X).)
> >
> > REFINEMENT   Apply this strategy only if G(Y) is not a P-goal.

Strategy 4.8 is usually more applicable if Y's goal in the conflict is an A-goal, rather than a P-goal, for two reasons: First, P-goals are usually more important, thereby making X's task of finding a G'(Y) of at least equal importance more difficult. Second, people rarely compromise on P-goals, regardless of their importance. It is more difficult for one to sacrifice something one already has achieved than to abandon an A-goal, even in the case where the latter may be of more importance. For instance, it is usually not the case that a person will abandon his job in order to spend his time applying for another, possibly higher paying job. It is more likely that he will retain his current job (P-goal), and, as time permits, apply for a better job (A-goal).

Strategy 4.8, being asymmetrical, has two trick options:

STRATEGY 4.8*a   Trick option: FALSE SUBSTITUTION

> Same as strategy 4.8, but X does not bring about G'(Y) after Y abandons G(Y).

STRATEGY 4.8*b   Trick option: FALSE ACCEPTANCE

> Same as strategy 4.8, but Y re-establishes G(Y) (thereby blocking G(X)) after X brings about G'(Y).

Another type of goal-substitution bargaining strategy involves mutual abandonment of both G(X) and G(Y). This strategy is invoked in the case that the continued goal conflict itself violates more important goals for both X and Y than the original conflict goals.

STRATEGY 4.9   MUTUAL GOAL ABANDONMENT

> TRIGGER   G(X) and G(Y) are mutually exclusive and other counterplanning efforts may violate higher level goals than G(X) and G(Y).
>
> IF   X also has the goal of NOT(G(Y)),
>
> THEN   he should negotiate with Y to mutually abandon G(X) and G(Y). (Otherwise X may simply choose to abandon pursuit of G(X).)

Strategy 4.9 plays an important role in the POLITICS domain. For instance, consider the following event processed by POLITICS from a U.S.-liberal perspective:

EVENT 4.22   The United States Congress voted to fund the Trident submarine project.

QUESTION 4.22.1   What might Russia do next?

ANSWER 4.22.1   RUSSIA WILL PROBABLY BUILD MORE SUBMARINES.

QUESTION 4.22.2   What should the U.S. do if Russia also builds nuclear submarines?

ANSWER 4.22.2 THE UNITED STATES SHOULD NEGOTIATE WITH RUS-
SIA TO STOP THE ARMS RACE.

Strategy 4.9 is invoked to answer the second question. From a U.S.-
liberal perspective both the United States and the Soviet Union have the
high-importance goal of preserving world peace. Continued goal conflict
over which country is militarily stronger (i.e., the arms race) could violate
the higher level P-goal of preserving peace. Since each country also has
the goal of preventing the other country from being the dominating world
power, strategy 4.9 suggests negotiation to mutually abandon the goals of
attaining military superiority.

Strategy 4.9 also explains many instances of goal abandonment
such as:

> EVENT 4.23 Smith and Jones both wanted to move into the one-person office
> overlooking the front garden. Their dispute irritated their co-work-
> ers. Smith decided to yield his claim on the desired office.

Why did Smith abandon his goal? He was in a goal-conflict situation with
Jones in which their counterplanning efforts had the effect of violating
Smith's goal of preserving social relations with his co-workers. Strategy
4.9 is applicable to this scenario because a higher level goal is violated by
the continued conflict. Since it does not make any difference to Smith's
goals whether he alone abandons his goal or Jones does likewise, Smith
chooses the path of least resistance, simple goal abandonment, as suggested by strategy 4.9.

There are other reasons for abandoning goals in conflict situations.
These reasons are considered in the following chapters, as they depend
on the type of plan being pursued and whether or not the goals are instrumental in nature.

4.7 Conclusion

The counterplanning process is focused and guided by the goals of the
counterplanning actors. An understander of an event involving counterplanning strategies must know or infer the goals of the actors in order to
understand the counterplans. To this purpose, the understander applies
his subjective beliefs as to the motivations of the counterplanning actors.
Thus, he subjectively analyzes their actions by focusing the counterplanning inferences in the directions that are most relevant to his goals and
the goals he attributes to the event actors.

The goal trees of the actors determine when to counterplan, when to temporarily suppress a goal, and when to abandon the goal. In summary, *the counterplanning strategies in themselves are independent of any subjective point of view, but their application to any conflict situation depends upon the goals and subjective beliefs of the counterplanning actors*.

5

Plan Conflicts in Counterplanning

5.1 Why Investigate Plan Conflicts?

Two actors pursuing different plans may intentionally or accidentally interfere with each other's plan. In the previous chapter we analyzed intentional counterplanning in mutual-exclusion goal conflicts. Here we investigate other sources of conflict among people, countries, and institutions. Consider the following conflict situations:

EVENT 5.1 John was going to drive to the bowling alley, but his wife wanted the car to go shopping.

EVENT 5.2 The public works department was installing a new sewer main. John did not want them to dig up his front lawn. He made an appointment with the town planning board.

EVENT 5.3 The Seabrook nuclear power plant construction was repeatedly delayed by the anti-nuclear Clamshell alliance.

EVENT 5.4 The two gladiators were thrown in the arena. Cassius tried for a quick victory with a surprise double feint, but his Nubian opponent parried and counterattacked.

EVENT 5.5 John organized a volleyball team for the people in his company. They decided to practice during lunch hours. This upset Bill, who wanted to start a lunch-hour poker game. John, who intensely disliked Bill, was very happy.

How do we understand events such as the five listed above? All the events involve a conflict situation between two or more people, but the conflicts cannot be categorized as well-defined mutual-exclusion goal conflicts. The first event is an accidental plan interference situation. There is an element of accidental interference in the second event, but one that should have been foreseen by the planners of the new sewer line. People, in general, do not like having their lawns ruined. A more salient feature of the second

conflict event is the fact that John cannot resolve the conflict by interacting directly with the public works crew on the scene. If he wants them
to change their actions, he has to deal with the people who planned the
installation of the sewer. Only they can reverse or modify their decision.

The first two events have one important aspect in common that
differentiates them from the conflict events discussed in the previous
chapter: the conflict situations result from the plan that an actor is pursuing. There is no reason to assume an underlying mutual-exclusion goal
conflict. John may well be in favor of a sewage system, but not the side
effect of a ruined lawn if the sewer passes through it. In the first event,
John need not have any reason to oppose the shopping trip of his wife;
nor does his wife need to object to John's going bowling. It is only the
particular plans they chose that accidentally conflict with each other.

Understanding plan-conflict situations requires a detection of the
conflict situation and a subjective interpretation of the action in the event
as a counterplanning effort. The understander usually identifies with one
of the actors in the conflict event, depending upon how closely in accord
with his own goals are the goals he believes that actor to have. After
determining the existence of a conflict situation, the understander focuses
on the aspects of the situation that are relevant to the counterplanning
process from his subjective perspective. In general, only some aspects of
a situation are relevant to the plan conflict; many other aspects are, at
best, tangential. The less relevant aspects can lead the inferencer to consider many subjectively unimportant facts, creating many useless inference
paths. We need to distinguish between the aspects of a conflict that must
be considered in the formulation of a counterplan by one of the actors,
and the set of all possible descriptions of a situation. The former is a very
restricted subset of the latter. To illustrate the necessity of isolating the
relevant information from a conflict situation, consider a set of descriptions of the situation in event 5.2:

1. John's front garden consisted of lawn rather than shrubbery or flowers.

*2. John wants to preserve his lawn but does not necessarily oppose the con-
    struction of a new sewer line.

3. The public works department was installing a sewer line but not a fresh water
    pipe.

4. John made an appointment with the planning board rather than walking in on
    their discussions.

*5. The public works department operates under the direction of the town plan-
    ning board.

6. The sewer main is a new one, not an old one being rerouted.

7. John probably lives in his house and either owns it or rents it.

Only the starred facts describing (or inferred from) the conflict situation are necessary to understand the type of conflict and possible counterplanning measures. Consider some plausible continuations to event 5.2:

EVENT 5.2   (continuation 1):
John tried to convince the planning board to find an alternate location for the sewer main, where less damage to private property would be incurred.

EVENT 5.2   (continuation 2):
John asked the board to re-landscape his lawn after laying the sewer main.

It is clear the non-starred facts are irrelevant in understanding either continuation. The starred facts, however, are quite necessary. An understander must not only be aware of John's goal of preserving his lawn and the Department of Public Works' goal of laying the sewer main; one must also be aware that the conflict is accidental (it was not the intention of the planning board nor of the public works department to damage John's lawn), that the public works crews have no authority to resolve the situation, that the planning board does have the authority, and that John is willing to try for an amicable solution (as opposed to initiating a law suit or shooting at the public works crew).

If we are to model the understanding process necessary to interpret event 5.2 and its continuations, we must know ahead of time what types of knowledge are important to consider in a plan-conflict situation. For event 5.2, the types of knowledge required are information about who initiated the conflict situation (therefore who has the power to change it), whether the conflict was intentionally or accidentally caused, and the likely predisposition of the actors to settle the conflict amicably. It is also necessary to know that the plan conflict is not rooted on a mutual-exclusion goal conflict (therefore, the counterplanning strategies of the previous chapter are inapplicable).

These categories of information are also useful in interpreting event 5.1 and plausible continuations, such as "John took the bus." or "John drove his wife to the store on his way to the bowling alley." Once again, the understander has to be aware of the accidental nature of the conflict, the expected cooperative predisposition between spouses, and the fact that there is no serious goal conflict underlying the plan interference.

It is also necessary to consider the degree to which the actors in a conflict situation are predisposed to cooperate, whether a plan interference can escalate to a serious goal conflict, and the degree to which a conflict is really accidental. For instance, John and his wife are very likely to cooperate; we would be very surprised to hear that John beat up his wife and took the car, after failing to agree on a compromise solution. On the other hand, it is quite reasonable to expect John to sue the planning board if his appeals are ignored. The dichotomy in the possible types of counterplanning actions following events 5.1 and 5.2 arises because in the second event John is less predisposed to cooperate, and, since his goal is of higher importance, he is more willing to escalate the conflict.

5.2 A Dimensional Analysis of Plan Conflicts

Let us categorize the knowledge that an understander should look for in a plan-conflict situation in order to suggest or understand possible counterplanning measures. There are essentially six significant aspects that apply across most plan conflicts. These aspects are best encoded as scales along orthogonal dimensions, since we require a measure of comparison among the level of cooperation between actors in different circumstances and the relative importance of goals underlying a conflict. We propose ranking plan-conflict situations along the following six dimensions:

1. Accidental vs. intentional plan conflict.

2. Competitive vs. cooperative predispositions toward resolving the conflict.

3. Interference as a mere inconvenience vs. total goal blockage.

4. Mutual-exclusion goal conflict underlies the plan conflict vs. ultimate goal agreement but conflict on the means used to bring about the goal.

5. Externally imposed conflicts vs. internally motivated ones.

6. Very important goal threatened as a result of the plan conflict vs. insignificant goal threatened.

The classification of plan-interference conflicts along these dimensions has a twofold effect on the understanding process. First, our classification facilitates the selection of counterplanning strategies applicable to understanding a given conflict event. Second, the effectiveness of a given counterplanning strategy can be evaluated by the understander if the conflict situation has been ranked along the above dimensions. Thus, the understander is better able to predict the probable outcome of a counterplanning srategy.

Let us see how event 5.1 may be classified in terms of our dimensions. The classification should help the understander to determine reasonable counterplanning strategies and evaluate their expected outcome. The conflict in event 5.1 is accidental. Both actors are predisposed toward cooperating with each other. The plan interference is more of a nuisance than a true goal blockage. There is no mutual-exclusion goal conflict underlying the plan conflict. There is no external cause for the conflict; i.e., no third party initiated the conflict situation. The importance of the goals threatened by the plan interference is relatively low. (Going bowling and going to the store are usually not high importance goals to people.)

All of these facts tell us that the resolution to the conflict will be by cooperative means. Neither actor is likely to apply mutual-exclusion goal-conflict counterplanning strategies. Either actor may abandon his/her goal to resolve the conflict. Probably no third party will be involved in the conflict resolution process. Both actors may still fulfill their goals if one or both of them modify their plans to circumvent the interference. Hence, information relating to our six dimensions gives us a coherent analysis of the conflict situation in event 5.1. This analysis is complemented by the counterplanning methods encoded in the various counterplanning strategies.

We rate the five events on our conflict classification dimensions using a numerical scale ranging from -10 to $+10$ for each dimension. -10 signifies the leftmost end of the scale; 0 denotes ambivalence; and $+10$ denotes the rightmost end of the scale. For instance, -5 on the cooperative predispostion vs. competitive predisposition scale means that both actors are willing to try cooperative means to resolve their conflict, but are not totally committed to such means in the event a mutually acceptable solution is not found. The precise numbers along the scales are not very crucial; we are quantifying approximate measures primarily for reasons of relative comparisons.

All the dimensions are subject to the point of view of the counterplanning actor. In some cases, the two actors perceive the conflict situation in the same terms with respect to our dimensions, but this is not necessarily the case. Recall event 5.3.

EVENT 5.3   The Seabrook nuclear power plant construction was repeatedly delayed by the anti-nuclear Clamshell alliance.

The Clamshell alliance views the situation in event 5.3 as stemming from a very high importance mutual-exclusion goal conflict. Clamshell believes that nuclear power is wrong and evil; its primary goal is to eliminate the use and proliferation of all forms of nuclear power. This directly conflicts with the goal of the Seabrook builders to build a new nuclear power plant. The Seabrook builders, on the other hand, view the actions of the Clamshell group as a nuisance, a plan interference that must be overcome in order for Seabrook to proceed with the construction. This difference manifests itself in the different strategies that the two groups will use against each other. For instance, Clamshell tries to convince the public and Seabrook builders of the danger and immorality of nuclear power, but the Seabrook workers focus their counterplanning efforts on applying legal means to stop the Clamshell interference.

We present a dimensional analysis of events 5.1 through 5.4. In the case that both parties have the same subjective interpretation of the conflict situation only the common set of values along the dimensions is given. Where each party differs in its perception of the conflict, we give the values corresponding to each interpretation.

Table 5.1.   Dimensional Analysis of Plan Conflicts

Dimension		Event 1	Event 2		Event 3		Event 4
(Negative)	(Positive)	both sides	Pub. works	John	Sea-brook	Clam-shell	both sides
Accidental	Intentional	−10	0	−5	+10	+10	+10
Competitive	Cooperative	+10	0	0	−10	−10	−10
Inconvenience	Total Blockage	−8	−8	5	−5	+10	+10
Means Conflict	Goal Conflict	−8	−5	−5	−5	+10	+10
External Cause	Internal Cause	+5	−8	−8	0	+5	−10
Low Imp. Goals	High Imp. Goals	−5	−8	+2	+10	+10	+10

We read the table as follows for event 1: The conflict situation was purely accidental (−10 on the accidental vs. intentional dimension). Both John and his wife are totally predisposed to cooperate (+10 on the competitive vs. cooperative dimension). Both parties consider the conflict to be much more of an inconvenience than a mutual-exclusion goal blockage. The −8 on the means vs. goal conflict suggests a true plan conflict rather than hidden goal conflict. Rather than paraphrasing the information contained in the table, let us analyze each dimension and what it can tell us about conflict situations that is useful in guiding the understanding process.

5.3 Accidentally vs. Intentionally Caused Conflicts

Let us consider what the dimension-rating table tells us about appropriate counterplanning strategies in each of the four events. We start by analyzing what counterplanning expectations are generated from the values along the first dimension. If the plans of two actors interfere accidentally, it is often the case that low-order strategies are inappropriate. A low-order strategy is a plan of action that takes very little effort to carry out, and usually has no adverse consequences or side effects. For instance, a low-order strategy for obtaining information is to simply ask for it. A higher order strategy, applied to the same situation, is to threaten the person who is withholding the desired information. (Schank and Abelson [1977] and Meehan [1976] discuss the ranking of planning units, called planboxes, such as ASK and THREATEN.)

If a conflict between two actors has been intentionally brought about by one actor, the other party is not likely to succeed by applying low-order strategies. For instance, the Seabrook builders will not succeed in ending the Clamshell interference by simply asking, "Could you please let us continue building our nuclear power plant?". The strategies below suggest appropriate courses of action based on the accidental-intentional dimension. Let N be the value along this dimension, X be the counterplanning party, and Y be the other party in the conflict.

STRATEGY 5.1   ACCIDENTAL CONFLICT

  TRIGGER The source of the conflict is known (or can be inferred) by the understander.

    IF the conflict is purely accidental (N = −10),

  THEN X should try first:
INFORM-REASON(conflict, Y), followed by ASK(end of conflict, Y), or possibly INVOKE-THEME(end of conflict, Y, theme).

STRATEGY 5.2   INTENTIONAL CONFLICT

  TRIGGER The source of the conflict is known (or can be inferred) by the understander.

    IF the conflict is purely intentional (N = +10),
  THEN X should abandon low-order counterplanning.

We apply these strategies to the dimensional rating of the four events. In event 5.1, $N = -10$; the conflict situation between John and his wife is purely accidental. Strategy 5.1 tells us that John or his wife may need only to inform each other of the plan interference in order for the other party to help rectify the conflict situation. If awareness of the conflict is insufficient, John can ask his wife if it is all right with her for him to take the car. Alternatively, one spouse can draw upon their mutual relationship in order to request a favor; e.g., "Please drop me off at the mall on your way to the bowling alley." Schank and Abelson call this type of planning unit INVOKE-THEME. The existence of a social relationship, such as marriage, allows a person to request a favor and expect the other party to comply, within the scope of behavior defined by the social relationship.

In event 5.2, John views his conflict with the public works department as accidental in nature. He does not blame them with willful intent to destroy his front lawn. Therefore, it is likely that he may apply strategy 5.1, informing or asking the planning board to reconsider their decision of installing the sewer line under his front lawn. There is less of an expectation that John can succeed in event 5.2 than in event 5.1. The reason for the diminished expectation is twofold: It is possible that the planning board already considered the side effect of their plan (harming lawns) in making their decision; thus, the conflict is not totally accidental. This is why the accidental vs. intentional scale has the value -5 as compared with -10 for the previous event. The second reason for the decreased likelihood that strategy 5.1 can succeed in event 5.2 is that John cannot apply INVOKE-THEME as he could in the conflict situation with his wife. There is no well-established relationship between John and the planning board.

The parties in event 5.3 perceive the event as an intentionally premeditated conflict situation. Both the Clamshell Alliance and the Seabrook builders know that they will not succeed by applying low-order strategies against each other. In essence, this is what strategy 5.2 tells the understander: Do not interpret the actions of either party as possible low-order strategies, because it is unlikely that either party will bother to attempt such strategies. Strategy 5.2 makes similar predictions about event 5.4, repeated below:

EVENT 5.4   The two gladiators were thrown in the arena. Cassius tried for a quick victory with a surprise double feint, but his Nubian opponent parried and counterattacked.

Neither gladiator is likely to ask the other to allow himself to be killed. If the understander knows about ritualized combat situations, he can predict that the means used in the conflict will be violent in nature without recourse to strategy 5.2. (The resolution means will be some form of OVERPOWER, another of Schank and Abelson's planning units.) It is reassuring, however, that the more specific knowledge of ritualized combat situations agrees with the more general heuristic prediction of strategy 5.2.

Strategies 5.1 and 5.2 are meta-strategies, in the sense that they suggest other, more specific strategies to pursue or abandon. In the event that the intentions of the actors are not known we cannot apply either strategy. If the actors intended the conflict to come about as a side effect to their primary objectives ($-5 < N < +5$), but the conflict was not their primary intention, our two strategies provide no help to the counterplanning process. In such cases, the counterplanner must rely on strategies indexed from values along other dimensions, or indexed by the classification of the nature of the plan conflict (discussed in the following chapter).

5.4 Competitive vs. Cooperative Predispositions

Our second dimension describes the predispositions of the actors in an event prior to the inception of the conflict situation. A cooperative predispositon tells the understander that the conflict will probably be solved and that amicable means will probably be tried first. A competitive predisposition suggests that either side is less likely to compromise, thus making low-order strategies and bargaining strategies less effective. It may also be the case that one or both sides want the conflict situation to perpetuate itself, suggesting that no strategies may be effective. (When we use the word "competitive" we mean only a lack of willingness to compromise in order to resolve the conflict situation.)

Consider some concrete examples. In event 5.1 John and his wife, by virture of their relationship, are probably predisposed to mutual cooperation regardless of the nature of their plan interference. This suggests that they may work together toward a solution of the conflict situation. Furthermore, some type of compromise is likely. We cannot reasonably infer the predisposition of the parties in event 5.2; therefore, this dimension does not help the understander to interpret or suggest counterplanning solution.

Neither the Clamshell alliance, nor the Seabrook builders, are predisposed to cooperate. In order to make this judgment an understander would require information about the previous actions and counteractions between the nuclear industry and anti-nuclear demonstrators. It is often the case that, in order to rank a conflict situation along the competitive vs. cooperative dimension, an understander needs background information about the actors and their relationship. Given the competitive nature of the relationship between Seabrook and Clamshell, we can infer that one side may want the conflict to perpetuate itself, and that strategies requiring mutual interaction, such as bargaining strategies, are likely to fail. Indeed, Clamshell wants to focus public attention on the anti-nuclear movement by perpetuating the conflict. Some attempts at reconciliation initiated by Seabrook failed to produce any compromise.

Let us make explicit the strategies we discussed informally above:

STRATEGY 5.3   COOPERATIVE PREDISPOSITION

TRIGGER   The predisposition of the actors in the conflict towards each other is known.

IF   both actors have cooperative predispositions,

THEN   X should communicate with Y to arrive at a mutually acceptable solution.

REFINEMENT   If necessary, X should negotiate a compromise solution with Y.

STRATEGY 5.4   COMPETITIVE PREDISPOSITION

TRIGGER   The predisposition of the actors in the conflict towards each other is known.

IF   Y has a competitive predisposition,

THEN   X should not expect negotiations to work. X should expect Y possibly to perpetuate the conflict.

The competitive vs. cooperative dimension is somewhat correlated with the accidental vs. intentional dimension. Accidental conflicts often result in cooperative dispositions towards resolving the conflict, and intentional conflicts result from competitive dispositions. There are many cases, however, where competitive does not imply intentional or vice versa. Similarly, accidental conflicts often do not imply cooperative predispositions. This prevents us from collapsing the two scales into a single dimension. Recall event 5.5:

EVENT 5.5   John organized a volleyball team for the people in his company. They decided to practice during lunch hours. This upset Bill, who wanted to start a lunch-hour poker game. John, who intensely disliked Bill, was very happy.

The conflict between lunch-hour volleyball and poker resulted from accidentally scheduling the two events in the same time slot. John, however, is not predisposed to cooperate with Bill, for reasons outside the conflict situation. According to strategy 5.4, John is likely to want the conflict situation to continue, rather than cooperating to find a mutually acceptable solution. We need strategy 5.4 if we are to answer the question "Why was John happy?". It was not the volleyball game or the poker game that made him happy. It is his competitive attitude toward Bill, and his opportunity to express that attitude by prolonging the conflict, that makes John happy.

5.5 Inconvenience Vs. Total Goal Blockage

The inconvenience vs. total goal-blockage dimension helps us to determine the focus of the actions taken by each actor in response to the plan conflict. Strategies 5.4 and 5.5 determine when an actor should focus his attention on counterplanning actions, and when he should reformulate his existing plan. These strategies are triggered on the basis of the value along our third dimension. This dimension tells us whether the plan interference leads to an inevitable goal blockage, or whether there are other means of achieving the actor's goal. In the latter case the plan interference is more of an inconvenience than a real goal blockage. Strategy 5.5 applies if the value along the goal blockage dimension is high (e.g., N > +5); otherwise strategy 5.6 is applicable. We use the following notational conventions: G(X) is X's goal, and P/G(X) is X's plan to fulfill G(X).

STRATEGY 5.5   PLAN INTERFERENCE MEANS GOAL BLOCKAGE

TRIGGER   Y is blocking X's plan P/G(X).

IF   P/G(X) is the only means for X to achieve G(X) (N > +5),

THEN   X should counterplan to thwart Y's efforts at blocking P/G(X).

STRATEGY 5.6   ALTERNATE MEANS METHOD

TRIGGER   Y is blocking X's plan P/G(X).

IF   There are other means of achieving G(X) (N < +5),

THEN   X should either:

1. Ignore Y's interference and either modify or totally formulate a new plan P'/G(X), or

2. If the new plan proves to be more costly to carry out than
the old one plus the counterplanning actions against Y, X
should counterplan to thwart Y's interference.

REFINEMENT   If the blocked goals are of high importance (e.g., the value
along the sixth dimension is > +5), both alternatives 1 and 2
may be pursued simultaneously.

Consider how these strategies apply to our example events. In event 5.1,
N = −8. Therefore, if John or his wife have alternate means of transportation, strategy 5.6 suggests that one or the other should choose this
option. In event 5.3, the Seabrook builders perceive the Clamshell alliance
as more of a nuisance than a real threat. Strategy 5.6 predicts that they
will choose the least-cost option of either modifying their plan to circumvent the Clamshell's efforts, or counterplan directly against Clamshell to
stop its blocking actions. Since building the nuclear power plant is a high
importance goal, the refinement in strategy 5.6 tells us that both reformulating the construction plans and counterplanning against Clamshell
should be expected. (Seabrook has, indeed, altered their construction
plans in an attempt to placate environmentalists, while pursuing legal
actions against the Clamshell alliance.)

From the subjective viewpoint of the Clamshell alliance, event 5.3
signifies total goal blockage. Clamshell cannot fulfill its goal of stopping
nuclear power if Seabrook builds the power plant. Therefore, strategy
5.5 predicts that it will focus its efforts entirely on counterplanning against
the Seabrook builders. In event 5.2, John views the actions of the public
works department as blocking his goal of preserving his lawn. He has no
alternative plans to fulfill the preservation goal other than counterplanning
against the threatened action by the public works department. Strategy
5.5 predicts that he will try to block their actions. His visit to the planning
board must be interpreted in this light. Upon reading event 5.2, we infer
that his visit to the planning board must be related to a means of stopping
or altering the sewer construction plan of the public works department.
Strategy 5.5 applies also to event 5.4. The goal of each gladiator is to
preserve his own life. The goal of one gladiator can only be achieved by
preventing the other gladiator from carrying out his combat plan. Thus,
we understand why they focus their efforts on countering each other's
plans in the fight.

The "cost" measure mentioned in alternative 2 of strategy 5.6 is
difficult to define precisely. We define a plan as being costly if it violates
any of the goals on the importance goal tree of the actor; the higher the
violated goal is in the goal tree, the more costly is the plan. For instance,

if John has a prolonged argument with his wife, this may partially violate his goal of preserving a good marital relationship. By this measure, counterplanning may be costly, but finding alternative transportation is the least-cost plan. (i.e., It has no goal-violation cost associated with it.) Another measure of cost associated with carrying out a specific plan is the consumption of resources necessary to carry out other plans. (Resource limitations in counterplanning is discussed in the following chapter, see also Wilensky [1978]). Thus, the true cost of pursuing a plan is a combination of both measures.

5.6 Underlying Goal Conflict vs. Pure Plan Interference

Some plan conflicts are based on underlying goal conflicts; usually the goal conflicts are reducible to mutual-exclusion goal states. Other plan conflicts, such as the one illustrated by events 1 and 2 are truly conflicts about the means used by two actors to accomplish their respective goals. The reason why we differentiate the two classes of plan conflict is that all the goal-conflict strategies discussed in the previous chapter can be brought to bear in the former class but would be quite inappropriate in the latter class of plan interference situations. The degree to which a plan conflict reflects an underlying goal conflict determines the likelihood that the goal-conflict counterplanning strategies will be invoked. Goal conflicts can give rise to multiple plan conflicts. For instance, the Clamshell alliance is interfering with the plans of Seabrook; but if Clamshell found a more effective way to stop nuclear power, it would probably change tactics without much hesitation. The understander should realize that if this situation comes about it can be explained in terms of the fact that Clamshell perceives its plan interference to be based on a mutual-exclusion goal conflict between the two sides. The Clamshell actions that interfered with Seabrook were part of its counterplanning effort in direct service to resolving a high-importance goal conflict.

It is equally important to analyze the case where a mutual-exclusion goal conflict does not underlie a plan interference situation. If the public works department, in event 5.2, had a more effective way of destroying John's lawn, we do not expect them to pursue such a course of action. The destruction of John's front lawn was not a goal, but a true plan interference, from the perspective of the public works department. It is, therefore, just as important *not* to apply the goal-conflict strategies to understand this event, as it is to apply those strategies in understanding any actions by the Clamshell alliance in event 5.3. We formalize this distinction in the following strategies:

STRATEGY 5.7   UNDERLYING GOAL CONFLICT

TRIGGER   The source of the plan conflict between X and Y is known.

IF   there is a mutual-exclusion goal conflict between G(X) and G(Y) underlying the plan conflict between P/G(X) and P/G(Y),

THEN   X may apply the mutual-exclusion strategies to counterplan against G(Y).

STRATEGY 5.8   Veto strategy: NO GOAL CONFLICT

TRIGGER   The source of the plan conflict between X and Y is known.

IF   the plan conflict is only an interference, not arising from an existing goal conflict,

THEN   X will not apply any goal-conflict strategies.

In our counterplanning model, strategies are only applied if they are expected, i.e., if their trigger conditions are fulfilled or if they are invoked from another strategy, such as 5.7. The reason for having a veto strategy such as 5.8 is that some other strategy or mechanism may have activated the goal-conflict strategies. We explicitly wish to block the application of these strategies in pure plan interference situations. For instance, if in the process of negotiating the SALT treaty (i.e., applying mutual-exclusion goal-compromise strategy 4.6), Cyrus Vance discovers that he and Andrei Gromyko disagree on where to conduct their negotiations, we do not want to apply the goal-conflict rules activated by the SALT issues to understand this rather minor plan interference. In a large rule-based system it is not always possible to foresee all interactions among the rules at the time that the system is created. Veto rules, such as strategy 5.8, are useful when we want some rules to be specifically deactivated for certain classes of situations.

Internally vs. Externally Imposed Conflict Situations

The internally vs. externally imposed dimension is very useful in constraining the type of counterplanning options open to each actor. The plan conflict in event 4 was caused by an external agency. Roman gladiators were slaves who were forced to fight in the arena. They could accomplish nothing by trying to bargain with each other, since gladiators did not have the option of not fighting. In event 1, however, there was no outside agency causing the plan conflict. Therefore, John and his wife were free to find a mutually acceptable solution to their conflict. The following counterplanning strategy suggests appropriate courses of action for externally imposed plan conflicts:

STRATEGY 5.9   EXTERNALLY IMPOSED CONFLICT

TRIGGER   Plan conflict between P/G(X) and P/G(Y).

IF   a plan conflict is caused by Z, an external agency,

THEN   X has the following alternatives:

1.   Abandon P/G(X).

2.   Bargain with Z to end the plan conflict.

3.   Counterplan directly against P/G(Y), without the recourse of bargaining strategies.

4.   Counterplan against the plan used by Z that imposed the plan conflict.

REFINEMENT   If G(X) and G(Y) match, then X should join forces with Y against Z on alternatives 2 and 4.

Let us see how strategy 5.9 applies to the two events in which an external cause has brought about the plan conflict. In event 2, the planning board decided where the public works department should construct its sewer line. The plan conflict between John and the public works department, therefore, was caused by an external agency. What are John's counterplanning options? He can abandon the plan to preserve his lawn, bargain with the planning board, try directly to stop the construction of the sewer line, or attack the entire plan of building new sewer lines. Strategy 5.9 rules out options such as bargaining directly with the public works crew (they do not have the authority). The focus of the counterplanning effort is shifted from the other party in the plan conflict to the causative agency. Similarly, the gladiators can only continue to fight against each other, try to convince their masters to end the combats, or rebel against their masters. (In ancient Roman history, the gladiator-initiated revolt led by Spartacus is an instance of the third alternative.)

The last dimension measures whether low importance or high importance goals were blocked as a result of the plan conflict. This dimension does not index any counterplanning strategies directly, but plays an important part in determining the applicability of other strategies and refinements, such as the refinement to strategy 5.6.

5.8 How POLITICS Uses Counterplanning Strategies

In most conflict events interpreted by POLITICS, many different counterplanning strategies may apply to the active goals, goal conflicts, and
plan interferences. It is the interaction among the various strategies and
their application to varied scenarios that makes POLITICS an interesting
tool to test our hypotheses of subjectively-oriented reasoning. In order to
illustrate strategy 5.9, we discuss how POLITICS interprets an event
about the Angolan civil war. Strategy 5.9 interacts with four other counterplanning strategies to understand event 5.6 and to suggest appropriate
U.S.-conservative policy. First, we present strategies 5.10 and 5.11, both
invoked in understanding event 5.6. Conjunctive-goal strategy 5.12, and
strategy 6.11, discussed in Chapter 6, are also applied in the understanding process. We list these four strategies below.

STRATEGY 5.10   MULTI-GOAL STRATEGY

TRIGGER   Plan conflict between P/G(X) and P/G(Y),

IF   Y's plan can fulfill more than one high level goal,

THEN   X should:

1. Abandon any strategy whose purpose is to convince Y to
   change his plan or otherwise compromise, unless all other
   strategies fail.

2. Expect Y to concentrate more effort in the pursuit of
   P/G(Y) than normally expected.

STRATEGY 5.11   GOAL BLOCKAGE OPTION

TRIGGER   Plan conflict between P/G(X) and P/G(Y), and X cannot
   directly block P/G(Y).

IF   X cannot easily pursue a different P'/G(X),

THEN   he should counterplan to make Y abandon G(Y). (Thus, Y is
   left with no reason to pursue P/G(Y).)

STRATEGY 5.12   FOCUS ON MOST IMPORTANT GOAL FIRST

IF   Y is pursuing more than one goal that X wants to block,

THEN   X should rank these goals in terms of importance to Y, and
   block the most important G(Y) first. (Thus, X has the greatest
   leverage to apply to Y in a bargaining or confrontation
   situation.)

STRATEGY 6.11   UNBLOCKING A MEDIATING PRECONDITION

IF   Y is blocking a mediating precondition for P/G(X),

THEN   X should choose the least cost alternative among:

1. Establish the goal G1(X) = Bring about the mediating precondition by some means independent of Y's actions. Suspend P/G(X) until G1(X) is achieved.

2. Choose a new plan P', such that P'/G(X) does not require this mediating precondition.

3. Set up the mutual-exclusion goal conflict G(X) = "Y is not blocking the mediating precondition to P/G(X)." Invoke the mutual-exclusion counterplanning strategies.

EVENT 5.6   *(INTERPRET U.S.-CONSERVATIVE)

INPUT STORY: Cuba sent troops to aid the MPLA faction in Angola.

Q1: Why did Cuba send troops to Angola?

A1: BECAUSE RUSSIA PROBABLY TOLD CUBA TO SEND TROOPS, AND CUBA WANTS COUNTRIES TO BE COMMUNIST.

Q2: What should the U.S. do about it?

A2: THE U.S. SHOULD MAKE RUSSIA WITHDRAW THE CUBAN TROOPS.

In order to interpret event 5.6, POLITICS used the military-aid script, information about the Angolan conflict, and the U.S. goal trees. The following plan interference scenario was inferred: The U.S. should have been planning a military victory for UNITA, the non-Communist faction. (The U.S. goal of having UNITA in control of Angola was already in POLITICS's memory from the interpretation of a previous event.) Cuba's military aid plan blocks a mediating precondition for the U.S. plan; namely, that UNITA be stronger than the MPLA. Therefore, there is a plan-conflict situation between the U.S. and Cuba. The mediating precondition triggers counterplanning rule 6.11 as a possible explanation for future U.S. actions. In establishing how Cuba's plan interacts with Cuba's goal trees, POLITICS discovers that Cuba could have been servicing two goals, the spread of communism and acting as an agency to pursue Soviet goals.

The latter goal is a subgoal for Cuba's getting Soviet aid, which is in turn a subgoal to all Cuban preservation goals. Cuba needs Soviet aid to survive. Having understood this much, POLITICS, working in an explanatory mode, is satisfied with its interpretation of event 5.6. If there were more actions in event 5.6, they would be interpreted in light of the expected counterplanning which arises from the plan conflict.

Question 2 forces POLITICS to function in a predictive mode, that is, to generate a plausible counterplan from a United States perspective. Because the Cuban plan services multiple goals, strategy 5.10 constrains POLITICS from attempting to negotiate directly with Cuba, except as a last resort. Strategy 6.11 generates three possible counterplans: re-establish the mediating precondition (i.e., make UNITA stronger), choose a new plan to fulfill the U.S. goal (i.e., put UNITA in control of Angola), or block the Cuban plan (i.e., recall the Cuban troops). The alternatives in the counterplanning strategy are ordered best-first on the basis of previous experience. The course of action that has succeeded most often in the past is tried first. In a predictive mode, POLITICS processes each alternative until one course of action is found which fulfills the U.S. goals. Making a country or a political faction stronger is the goal of the military-aid script. At this point an earlier version of U.S.-conservative POLITICS simply suggested sending troops to aid UNITA.

POLITICS checks the preconditions of suggested plans of action. There are different types of preconditions that help to focus the counterplanning process, as discussed in Chapter 6. One mediating precondition for military aid on the part of the United States is congressional approval. This precondition cannot be met, because there is a situational rule that Congress will veto any action involving the U.S. in a foreign civil war. Therefore, this counterplanning alternative is abandoned; the next one (generating a new plan) also fails; and the third alternative is tried.

How does POLITICS counterplan to block Cuba's troop buildups? Strategy 5.10 states that since the Cuban plan is multi-purposed, Cuba is unlikely to compromise or negotiate. Strategy 5.11 is invoked since there are no applicable strategies to directly counterplan against Cuba's plan. Strategy 5.11 suggests direct counterplanning against Cuba's goals. This is refined by strategy 5.12 as counterplanning against Cuba's most important goal. The Soviet-agency goal is judged to be the more important one because it is a necessary subgoal to the highest level P-goals (an application of the importance determination rules discussed in Chapter 3). Hence, POLITICS decides that the U.S. should counterplan to block Cuba's goal of being a Soviet agency. Strategy 5.9 is triggered at this point (the Soviet Union is considered an external cause of the U.S.-Cuban conflict) and POLITICS generates the application of strategy 5.9 as an answer to the second question. That is, POLITICS suggests focusing the U.S. counterplanning effort against the Soviet Union in order to remove the most important cause of the Cuban troop buildup.

5.9 Concluding Remarks

As we can see from the counterplanning rules used in the POLITICS example, not all strategies are indexed by the values on our dimensional analysis. The exact nature of the plan conflict itself plays an important role in determining counterplanning strategies and in vetoing certain courses of action. The next chapter discusses the plan-conflict counterplanning strategies indexed by our knowledge of the way in which two plans can come into conflict.

We have focused our discussion on how to use the dimensional analysis to choose the appropriate counterplanning strategies in order to understand conflict events. However, we have said little about how a conflict situation is rated along the five dimensions. The analysis of a conflict situation is heavily dependent on the knowledge and beliefs of the understander. If an understander's perception of a husband-wife relation is a cooperative one, he assumes a cooperative predisposition in understanding plan conflicts arising between husbands and wives. On the other hand, if the understander's marital experiences negate the cooperative assumption, he may project his own beliefs and interpret the conflict situation between them quite differently. A more competitive rating would suggest different counterplanning strategies; hence, the understander would not expect John and his wife to settle their plan interference by amicable compromise.

Similarly, the understander's beliefs about the goals of the actors determines his rating along the means vs. goals conflict scale and the nuisance vs. total blockage scale. Thus, the subjective interpretation of the understander deeply influences the dimensional analysis of the conflict situation, which in turn affects the understanding of the ensuing counterplanning actions.

6

The Structure of a Plan Conflict

6.1 A Classification of Plan Conflicts

Understanding plan conflicts and subsequent counterplanning actions may require a deeper analysis of the plan than we presumed thus far. The dimensional ranking of plan conflicts provides us with one useful method of indexing plan-based counterplanning strategies. There is another productive source of information that can be tapped to help an understander discover applicable counterplanning strategies. The manner in which the plan-conflict state affects an actor's plan often suggests ways to nullify effects of the conflict. These ways of nullifying the effects of a conflict situation can be encoded as counterplanning strategies. In order to illustrate the necessity of analyzing the way in which the conflict situation blocks an actor's plan, consider the following event:

> EVENT 6.1 Bill was standing in line for the shuttle flight to New York. The woman in front of him bought the last ticket. Bill offered to buy her ticket for $20 more than she paid for it.

In order to understand the conflict situation in event 6.1, we need to use the following information: Bill planned to take a plane to New York. Buying a ticket is a necessary precondition for Bill's plan. The woman who bought the last ticket prevented Bill from fulfilling the necessary precondition. Furthermore, we need to infer that Bill's offer to buy the ticket is an attempt to rectify the blocked precondition by means of a bargaining strategy. This reasoning process requires a more detailed analysis of Bill's plan and knowledge of exactly how the plan was blocked than the strategies presented in the previous chapter can give us. Therefore, in some cases the counterplanner should investigate the nature of the conflict situation with respect to the specific plan being pursued, in order to formulate an effective counterplan. An understanding of the exact nature of the conflict complements the dimensional analysis of the circumstances surrounding the conflict situation that we discussed in Chapter 5. For instance, consider the following modification to event 6.1:

> EVENT 6.2   Bill was standing in line for the shuttle flight to New York. Pete, who intensely disliked Bill, bought the last ticket for the flight. Bill sought out another passenger and tried to purchase his ticket.

Understanding event 6.2 proceeds in much the same way as understanding event 6.1: We must realize that Bill is counterplanning to fulfill the blocked necessary precondition to his plan. However, in order to answer the question "Why did Bill seek out another passenger?", we must use information about Bill's and Pete's predispositions towards each other. Bill did not think that Pete would sell him the ticket. Why? Counterplanning strategy 5.4, discussed in the previous chapter, tells us that if the actors have a hostile or competitive predisposition toward each other, bargaining strategies are likely to fail. Thus, in order to understand event 6.2, we need to use information about the predisposition of the actors, encoded as one of our dimensions, as well as information about the precise nature of the plan interference.

Consider another event that requires a deeper understanding of the nature of the conflict situation than the dimensional analysis gives us.

> EVENT 6.3   John was spraying DDT around the basement to kill roaches, but Mary was afraid their cat would be poisoned as well. Mary told John about her fears, and John immediately stopped spraying.

What exactly is the conflict in event 6.3? John's plan threatens to block one of Mary's goals. Furthermore, it is possible that John also has the goal of preserving the cat's life, but he is unaware of the side effect of his plan. We know much more about the conflict situation than merely its accidental nature. The conflict situation occurs when one person's plan threatens the other person's goal and the former is unaware of the consequences of his action, but possibly willing to abandon his plan upon understanding these consequences. Mary's appeal to John is based on a goal that John may share with Mary, and that John should have taken into consideration in formulating his ill-conceived plan. The understander cannot answer a question such as "Why did John immediately stop spraying?", unless it has been inferred that John was unaware of the consequence of his act and that John does not want these consequences to come about. This discussion suggests that the understander should take into account the state of an actor's knowledge about his actions, their consequences, and the possible conflicts that may be caused by incomplete knowledge of the situation. In the following sections we discuss a classification of plan conflicts based on the nature of the conflict and its effects on both counterplanning actors.

6.2 A Taxonomy of Plan-conflict Situations

This section examines a plan-conflict taxonomy much like the classification of mutual-exclusion goal conflicts discussed in Chapter 4. Since our classification is based on the nature of the plan conflict, each type of conflict situation suggests certain counterplanning strategies. There are two general types of plan conflicts. The first type is characterized by the execution of a plan blocking another actor's goal. In the second type the execution of a plan by an actor directly interferes with the actions of a second actor who is pursuing his own plan. There are three classes of direct plan interference. In the first class the execution of a plan consumes or occupies a resource necessary for the other actor's plan. In the second type of direct interference the first actor's plan violates a necessary precondition for the second actor's plan. In the third type one actor's plan makes it more costly for the second actor to execute his plan. (E.g., when the city repairs a street, it forces motorists into detours.) We present an outline of our plan interference classification. Subsequently, we discuss each type of plan interference and the counterplanning strategies they suggest. Recall our notational conventions: G(X) is X's goal, and P/G(X) is the plan X pursues to fulfill G(X).

    I. P/G(X) blocks G(Y).

        A. Unintentional goal blockage.

        B. P/G(X) intentionally chosen to block G(Y).

    II. P/G(X) and P/G(Y) directly interfere.

        A. Limited common resource is necessary for both plans.

            1. The resource is time dependent.

            2. The resource is consumable and irreplacable.

            3. The resource is help from a third party.

        B. Executing P/G(Y) changes the state of the world so as to:

            1. Block a mediating precondition for P/G(X).

2. Block an uncontrollable precondition for P/G(X).

3. Block a controllable precondition for P/G(X).

C. P/G(Y) makes executing P/G(X) more troublesome (costly).

The dimensional analysis discussed in the previous chapter applied equally to these types of plan-conflict situations. However, each general type of plan interference suggests a different set of appropriate counterplanning strategies when analyzed in terms of the nature of the conflict situation. First, we analyze plans that block goal states (type I conflicts).

6.3 Counterplanning Against Non-intentional Goal Blockage

Consider some conflict events where one actor's plan unintentionally blocks a second actor's goal state. Plans that are pursued for the sole purpose of blocking goal states come as a result of goal conflicts; therefore, the goal-conflict counterplanning strategies discussed in Chapter 4 apply to these situations. Here we devote our attention to situations where goal blockage is either unintentional, or, at worst, tangential to the primary purpose of the plan. We reiterate event 6.1 for our discussion.

EVENT 6.1 John was spraying DDT around the basement to kill roaches, but Mary was afraid their cat would be poisoned as well. Mary told John about her fears, and John immediately stopped spraying DDT.

EVENT 6.4 John bought an expensive moose-head trophy that Mary detested. The following summer the Salvation Army came asking for donations. Mary generously gave them some used clothing and the moose-head trophy.

EVENT 6.5 It was the last play of the football game. Bill made a brutal flying tackle on John, the opposing quarterback, fracturing one of his ribs. John accused Bill of unnecessary violence and of holding a personal grudge against him. Bill countered that his tackle was just a normal part of the game.

Event 6.1 is an instance of a plan having side effects that threaten to block someone else's goal; this type of conflict corresponds to class I-A in our plan-conflict taxonomy. As we mentioned earlier, Mary's P-goal of keeping her cat alive and healthy was threatened as a (presumably unintentional) side effect of John's plan to exterminate the roaches. It is probable that John shared Mary's P-goal but was unaware of the fact that his plan could have threatened the cat's health. This scenario suggests the following counterplanning strategies:

STRATEGY 6.1   UNINTENTIONAL GOAL BLOCKAGE

   TRIGGER   P/G(Y) threatens G(X), but G(X) and G(Y) are not in conflict.

         IF   X believes that Y is unaware of the fact that carrying out
                P/G(Y) threatens to block G(X).

      THEN   X Should try the following in sequence:

                1. If Y shares X's goal, INFORM Y about the side effect
                    of his plan.
                2. Otherwise, ASK Y to stop P/G(Y) and INFORM Y of the
                    conflict as the reason for abandoning P/G(Y).
                3. Invoke the rest of the PERSUADE planboxes in their usual
                    progression.

STRATEGY 6.2   INCIDENTAL GOAL BLOCKAGE

   TRIGGER   P/G(Y) threatens G(X), but G(X) and G(Y) are not in conflict.

         If   X can devise a new plan for Y, P'/G(Y) that does not threaten
                G(X).

      THEN   X should ASK Y to pursue P' instead of P. (Also INFORM Y
                that P blocks G(X) and P' does not.)

REFINEMENT   If P' is more costly to pursue than P, X may offer to help Y
                pursue P' as added inducement.

STRATEGY 6.3   LAST-RECOURSE DEFAULT

   TRIGGER   P/G(Y) threatens G(X), but G(X) and G(Y) are not in conflict.

         IF   strategies 6.1 and 6.2 do not succeed,

      THEN   X should counterplan to block a necessary precondition of
                P/G(Y).

NOTE: The PERSUADE package (Schank and Abelson [1977]) is a set of plan-
         ning strategies, called planboxes, that describe how an actor X can
         convince Y to follow a given course of action. The planboxes are ranked
         in terms of the severity of the actions they propose. For instance, ASK is
         ranked low and OVERPOWER is ranked high.

Strategy 6.1 is invoked in understanding event 6.1. When we see that
Mary's INFORM-REASON sufficed to make John abandon his plan to
spray DDT, we conclude that he also probably wanted the cat alive and

healthy. That is, since we know the course of action taken by Mary, we use strategy 6.1 to conclude the conditions under which that course of action makes sense. This is another instance of an explanatory (rather than predictive) usage of a counterplanning strategy.

6.4 Premeditated Plan Interference and Multi-purpose Plans

Event 6.4 is an example of plan-conflict class I-B, where X chooses the plan P/G(X) to intentionally block G(Y). This kind of goal blockage is opportunistic in nature. X needs to formulate a plan P to achieve his goal G(X). He also wants to block G(Y), but may not be willing to spend the effort to counterplan against G(Y). If, in the process of deciding what plan to use, X realizes that one of the alternatives blocks G(Y) as well as fulfilling G(X), he chooses this multi-purpose plan. In event 6.4, Mary wanted to fulfill her goal of giving a charitable contribution. She also wanted to get rid of their moose-head trophy (i.e., block John's P-goal for the trophy), although she had done nothing to this effect until the opportunity arose. When the Salvation Army asked for contributions, Mary formulated her plan to block John's P-goal while fulfilling her "good citizen" goal. Our discussion is summarized in the following strategy:

>STRATEGY 6.4   OPPORTUNISTIC COUNTERPLANNING

>TRIGGER   X needs to formulate a plan for G(X), and he also wants to block G(Y).

>IF   G(X) is more important to X than blocking G(Y),

>THEN   X should formulate and pursue a plan P/G(X). If possible P should be chosen such that, as a side effect, P blocks G(Y).

>ELSE   (i.e., If blocking G(Y) is more important) X should try to fulfill G(X) as a side effect of his counterplan to block G(Y).

Strategy 6.9 is actually implemented as two strategies, one for the "THEN" clause, another for the "ELSE" clause. This strategy provides us with another rationalization to explain why John is happy in event 5.5. We repeat this event discussed in the preceding chapter:

>EVENT 5.5   John organized a volleyball team for the people in his company. They decided to practice during lunch hours. This upset Bill, who wanted to start a lunch-hour poker game. John, who intensely disliked Bill, was very happy.

Applying strategy 6.4 to event 5.5 requires the understander to postulate that John had the goal of causing trouble for Bill. Given that John intensely disliked Bill, this is a reasonable hypothesis.

We present a POLITICS computer run to illustrate the second part of strategy 6.4. The multi-plan strategy 6.5, listed below, is also invoked in the POLITICS processing of event 6.6. (Once again, the "THEN" and "ELSE" clauses are implemented as separate strategies.)

> STRATEGY 6.5   OPTIMIZE CHOICE OF PLAN
>
> > TRIGGER   X can pursue more than one plan to block G(Y).
> >
> > IF   X has other active goals,
> >
> > THEN   apply Strategy 6.4.
> >
> > ELSE   IF X has no other important goals or if 6.4 fails, choose the least-cost plan.

Start of POLITICS Interpretations and QA Dialogs

PTYCON LOG FILE   12-Feb-78 3:11:29

PTYCON> CONNECT (TO SUBJOB) 1
[CONNECTED TO SUBJOB POL(1)]

Politics Run	Annotation

EVENT 6.6
    *(INTERPRET US-CONSERVATIVE)

INPUT STORY:

Iran wanted to buy US F-15 fighter airplanes. Congress approved the sale.	We skip over the application of the $ARMSALE script used to extract the meaning of the sentence.

$ARMSALE GOAL PREDICTED:
  US GOAL:
  ((ACTOR *IRAN*
    TOWARD (*STRENGTH* VAL X)
    LEAVING (*STRENGTH* VAL
                PREV)
    INC (*ORDERLARGE*)))

PREVIOUS GOAL CONFLICT
ACTIVATED:
(#CONFLICT
  TOK: GOALCON7
  ACTOR1: *U.S.*
  ACTOR2: *RUSSIA*
  GOAL1: ((ACTOR   *US*
      TOWARD (*SCONT*
          VAL REGION12)

      INC (*POS*)))
  GOAL2: ((ACTOR   *RUSSIA*
      TOWARD (*SCONT*
          VAL REGION12)
      INC (*POS*))))

POLITICS monitors all goal conflicts involving the main ideological actor (the U.S.). This results in matching an $ARMSALE goal (increasing political influence) with the existing goal conflict between the U.S. and Russia over establishing their political influence in the Middle East (REGION12).

INFERENCE:
  CON3 IS US STRATEGY
  FOR CONFLICT GOALCON7
$ARMSALE GOAL EXPLAINED

CON3 is the main concept of the $ARMSALE script, i.e., the expected sale of F-15's to Iran.

PROCESSING

((ACTOR *US*
  <=>   (*MBUILD*)
  OBJECT ((ACTOR *US*
      <=> ($ARMSALE)))))

The second sentence is processed. POLITICS tries to explain the U.S. decision to sell arms to Iran in light of the U.S.-Soviet conflict.

EXPLAINING US CHOICE OF PLAN . . .
COUNTERPLANNING STRATEGY
CS-MULTI-PLAN2 ACTIVATED.

CS-MULTI-PLAN2 is strategy 6.5.

(CS-DUAL-PURPOSE1 INVOKED
FROM CS-MULTI-PLAN2)

COUNTERPLANNING STRATEGY
CS-DUAL-PURPOSE1 ACTIVATED.

CS-DUAL-PURPOSE1 is
strategy 6.4.

SEARCHING US-CONSERVATIVE
GOAL TREES . . . MATCH FOUND.

USGOAL9 MATCHES PATHSPEC
(FUNCTION: RESULT) OF
(GOAL2 TYPE: SECONDARY
  FUNCTION:
  ((CON ((ACTOR *US*
      <=> ($ARMSALES)))
    RESULT ((ACTOR ECON8
      TOWARD (*STATE*
      VAL (NORM)))))))))

Why $ARMSALES? POLITICS finds that this script fulfills a second U.S. goal: selling things abroad helps the U.S. balance of payments.

EXPECTATION:
CS-DUAL-PURPOSE1 TO SUCCEED.
$ARMSALE PLAN EXPLAINED

EXPECTATION:
GOALCON7 TOWARD *US* GOAL
SUCCEED.

EXPECTATION: USGOAL9
TO SUCCEED.

INTERPRETATION COMPLETED,
READY TO ACCEPT QUESTIONS.

The above computer run is the bulk of the POLITICS interpretation process for event 6.6. We start analyzing the inference process when POLITICS infers that ATRANSing (transferring) weapons to a pro-U.S. (therefore anti-Soviet) country in the Middle East can be explained as a U.S. counterplan in a continuing U.S.-Soviet goal conflict over political power in the Middle East. At this point, POLITICS has explained the U.S. goal (in terms of the pre-existing dispute) but not the U.S. choice of a plan. Essentially, POLITICS asks itself: "Why did the U.S. sell arms, when there are other ways to accomplish the same goal (such as military aid)?" Strategy 6.5 is applied. Since under the U.S.-conservative ideology the U.S. has many active goals, the first alternative of strategy 6.5 is tried. POLITICS knows the chosen plan; therefore, strategy 6.4 is applied "in reverse" to determine if the arms-sale plan can fulfill at least one other U.S. goal. This proves to be the case, since the arms-sale script has the secondary goal of improving the U.S. balance of payments, a goal also found in the U.S.-conservative goal tree. Therefore POLITICS has explained the U.S. choice of plan by finding a counterplanning strategy that suggests this plan to be superior to other candidates.

Let us turn to event 6.5, reiterated below, and see how the counterplanning strategies are crucial in understanding the dispute.

EVENT 6.5   It was the last play of the football game. Bill made a brutal flying tackle on John, the opposing quarterback, fracturing one of his ribs. John accused Bill of unnecessary violence and of holding a personal grudge against him. Bill countered that his tackle was just a normal part of the game.

The dispute ensuing from Bill's tackle consists of John's and Bill's argument over whether the side effect of the tackle was intentional or accidental. John claimed that Bill invoked strategy 6.4; that is, he claimed that Bill had the goal of harming John, and therefore chose an unnecessarily brutal tackle. Bill claimed that the execution of his plan accidentally interfered with John's goal of staying healthy. The latter alternative is acceptable as permissible (but not desired) in a football game scenario. Intentional blocking of goals that are irrelevant to the game do not constitute acceptable courses of action. In order to understand the argument in event 6.7 we need to know the classification of the plan-intereference situation from the perspective of each actor. This allows the understander to interpret Bill's tackle as an application of different counterplanning strategies depending on the point of view of the understander.

Some scenarios constrain the class of goal conflicts to which counterplanning strategies may be applied. There are also situations that constrain the class of strategies that can be applied. For instance, the U.S. and Japan are military allies. This prevents counterplanning against each other's P-goals and political-control goals, but not against each other's economic A-goals. The class of goal-conflict strategies that depend on threatening higher level goals are not generally applicable by the U.S. and Japan in mutual counterplanning efforts. The use of situationally forbidden strategies or the application of counterplanning strategies to forbidden types of goal conflicts may alter the situation and the relationship between the two actors. For instance, if the U.S. were to threaten Japan with an invasion unless Japan stopped economic competition with the U.S., the U.S.-Japanese alliance would quickly collapse to be replaced with a relationship of a different nature. It is, therefore, important to consider the constraints of the situation and the relationship between the actors in the process of counterplanning.

6.5 Plan Conflicts Based on Resource Limitations

We define a direct plan interference between X and Y to be a situation in which both actors cannot execute their plans simultaneously because of some limiting factor. Plan interferences can be classified by the nature of the limiting factor. The limiting actors are analyzed from three distinct perspectives; each perspective suggests applicable counterplanning strategies: The three methods of analyzing a plan conflict are: (1) Determine whether a common resource is required by both X and Y to pursue their respective plans. If a limiting resource is found, direct the counterplanning effort toward controlling the resource. (2) Analyze the preconditions of each plan. If the execution of one actor's plan blocks a necessary precondition for the other actor's plan, use this interaction as the basis for selecting counterplanning strategies. Control of a resource may be a necessary precondition for a particular plan. In this case, the counterplanning strategies suggested by both modes of analysis may be applicable. (3) Determine if the execution of one actor's plan changes the state of the world, making it more difficult for the second actor to pursue his plan. In this case consider the extent to which the plans interfere with each other. If the interference is minimal, consider the possibility that no counterplanning action may be required.

6.6 Resource-limitation strategies

There are three types of situations that define resource limitations. They depend on the resource and its use in the actor's plan. Each type of resource limitation suggests different counterplanning strategies. Resource limitations also account for why an actor cannot simultaneously pursue certain types of plans (Wilensky, [1978]). Our analysis focuses on the use of resource limitations as a means of classifying counterplanning strategies. The scenario where counterplanning strategies and resource-limited planning meet is characterized by the existence of a single resource available to two or more actors who require its use. We divide resource limitations into three general classes:

> III-A A limited common resource is necessary for both plans.
> 1. The resource is time dependent.
> 2. The resource is consumable and irreplacable.
> 3. The "resource" is help from a third party.

6.6.1 Time-dependent resource limitations

Consider some examples of counterplanning based on time-dependent resources.

> EVENT 6.7   John wanted to drive to the bowling alley, but Mary took the car to go shopping.

> EVENT 6.8   John was driving to Mary's house. As he approached the Main street intersection, he saw that the Thanksgiving parade was in full swing. John had to drive several miles out of his way.

> EVENT 6.9   Bill and John shared an apartment near the campus. John was planning on having his girlfriend stay over that night, but he was reminded that Bill's mother was flying in to visit them. After a short argument with Bill, John decided to convince his girlfriend to come over the following night instead.

Event 6.7 is our familiar example from previous chapters. The plan interference, however, can also be characterized as two actors needing to use
the same resource, their car. Earlier, we discussed several possible counterplanning strategies for this situation, including plan abandonment by
one actor, and cooperative planning (such as one actor driving the other
to his/her destination). Two additional courses of action that either actor
can pursue are resource substitution and resource scheduling. Essentially,
John can substitute for the car a resource that serves the same function
of providing a means of transportation (e.g., ride his bicycle). Alternatively, John can reschedule the execution of his plan (e.g., wait until Mary
returns). Each of these two courses of action corresponds to a counterplanning strategy (6.7 and 6.8 respectively) based on the need for a shared
time-dependent resource.

STRATEGY 6.6   CONTROL-RESOURCE SUBGOAL

TRIGGER   P/G(X) and P/G(Y) need resource R, where R cannot be used
in more than one plan at a time.

IF   G(X) and G(Y) are in a mutual-exclusion conflict, or if strategies
6.7 and 6.8 have failed,

THEN   X should create and pursue the high-priority goal G' (X) =
DCONTROL (X,R).

STRATEGY 6.7   RESOURCE SUBSTITUTION

TRIGGER   P/G(X) and P/G(Y) need resource R, where R cannot be used
in more than one plan at a time.

IF   X can find an alternative resource R' such that P/G(X) can use
R' instead of R (possibly with minor modifications to P),

THEN   He should substitute R' for R and pursue his previous plan.

STRATEGY 6.8   RESOURCE SCHEDULING

TRIGGER   P/G(X) and P/G(Y) need resource R, where R cannot be used
in more than one plan at a time.

IF   R is a time-dependent resource, X should agree with Y to have
X pursue P/G(X) at time T1, and Y pursue P/G(Y) at time
T2, where T1 does not equal T2.

REFINEMENT   If one plan has to be rescheduled, it should be the one that
causes the least cost problems for both actors.

Strategies 6.7 and 6.8 are applicable when the two actors are cooperatively predisposed and there is no underlying goal conflict to their plan interference. Strategy 6.6 should only be applied if X and Y cannot (or will not) cooperate. Hence, we see that the dimensional analysis discussed in Chapter 5 proves useful in deciding the appropriateness of counterplanning strategies indexed by other means.

Event 6.8 can be understood in terms of strategy 6.7, if one considers the street to be a public resource. Main Street could not be used simultaneously by motorists and the Thanksgiving Day parade. Therefore, John chose an alternate resource: he used different roads to pursue the same general plan of driving to Mary's house.

Understanding event 6.9 requires strategy 6.8. John's girlfriend and Bill's mother could not occupy the apartment the same night. The multiple use of the apartment as a resource to both John's and Bill's plan is not physically impossible, but it is socially forbidden. Thus, we have time-dependent resource conflict. The fact that John agreed to delay his girlfriend's visit constitutes a rescheduling of his plan as it was competing for the same time-dependent resource. This tells the understander that strategy 6.8 was successfully invoked to resolve the plan interference. At this point the understander can answer the question "Why did John agree to delay his girlfriend's visit?" by stating the conditions under which strategy 6.8 succeeds in scheduling the interfering plans in the manner specified in event 6.9. Namely, the answer should be: "John's girlfriend and Bill's mother could not be at the apartment at the same time. It must have been easier to reschedule the visit by John's girlfriend."

6.6.2 Consumable resource limitations

Two plans can interfere when both require a common, consumable resource. Let us look at some events where this type of resource limitation causes a plan conflict. In some cases control of a consumable resource becomes an important goal. If there is competition for control, then mutual-exclusion goal conflicts occur (triggered by strategy 6.6), and the counterplanning strategies in Chapter 4 become applicable. For instance, a consumable resource that is in much demand at present is petroleum. Since this resource enables countries, companies, and individuals to pursue many different plans, the acquisition and control of this resource has become an important goal to virtually every country in the world. This situation is essentially a goal-subsumption state, discussed in Wilensky [1978] under different circumstances. Let us consider some cases where an actor has a definite plan requiring a consumable resource.

EVENT 6.10   Mary was proud of the life savings she and John accumulated. She had enrolled their son at an expensive private University. One day John emptied the bank account and headed for Las Vegas.

EVENT 6.11   Billy took some cookies from the cookie jar. Johnny took them away from him and began to eat them. Billy took some more cookies.

EVENT 6.12   Billy was about to eat the last candy bar, but Johnny took it away and began to munch on it. Billy started crying, and Mom stepped in, telling them to share the candy bar.   .

EVENT 6.13   John was trying to type his term paper. He asked Bill if he could borrow the typewriter. Bill said he had only one carbon ribbon, which he needed for his own term paper. John agreed to buy him a new ribbon in the morning, and proceeded to use Bill's typewriter.

Strategies 6.6 and 6.7 are applicable not just to time-limited resource conflicts, but also apply to conflicts based on consumable resources. For instance, event 6.11 illustrates strategy 6.7: Billy substituted the unavailable resource (the cookies Johnny took away) with a new resource (another handful of cookies from the cookie jar), allowing his plan to proceed.

Strategy 6.8, however, is only applicable to non-consumable resources. Plan scheduling only makes sense if the resource still exists after the execution of the first plan. Therefore, the methods suggested in strategy 6.8 takes a different form for consumable resources, in the following strategy:

STRATEGY 6.9   RESOURCE PRIORITY

TRIGGER   P/G(X) and P/G(Y) need resource R, where R cannot be used in more than one plan at a time.

IF   R is a consumable resource, and G(X) and G(Y) are not in conflict,

THEN   X should pursue one of the following courses of action:
1. Divide R between X and Y if it suffices for both P/G(X) and P/G(Y).
   REFINEMENT   Both actors may need to slightly modify their plans to accommodate the reduced amount of resource.
2. If more R can be obtained in the future, the present R should be used for the more urgent plan with the stipulation that the other actor gets the future R for his plan.
3. Failing 1 and 2, X should try to carry out P/G(X) before Y consumes R.

Strategy 6.9 is necessary to understand events 6.12 and 6.13. In event 6.12, one needs to understand that Mom was imposing the first alternative of strategy 6.9 on Johnny and Billy, forcing them to modify their plans, i.e., eating part of a candy bar rather than the whole thing. The fact that Mom chose this strategy tells the understander that she thought that as a result of her action the plan conflict should be terminated. Thus, strategy 6.9 would answer the question: "Why did Mom make them share the candy bar?"

The second alternative of strategy 6.8 helps us understand event 6.13. Both Bill and John needed the carbon ribbon, a consumable resource. Applying alternative 2 to the facts that the ribbon can be replaced, and that Bill agreed to let John have the currently available ribbon, tells the understander that John's need must have been the more urgent one. (E.g., his paper may have been due sooner.)

6.6.3 Human resource: help from a third party

Sometimes, two actors require assistance from the same third party. Some types of assistance, such as advice, can be given to many actors simultaneously, but other types of assistance require that the third party focus its attention on the needs of one actor to the exclusion of helping others. We classify this type of assistance in the same category as physical resources because it shares a large fraction of the counterplanning strategies with resource limitations. Consider the following event for which some of our previous resource-limitation counterplanning strategies are applicable.

> EVENT 6.14   John and Bill wanted to take flying lessons. The flying instructor told them that his schedule was almost full. He could only accommodate one of them.

> CONTINUATION 6.14.1   John signed up and Bill decided to wait until the next set of lessons.

> CONTINUATION 6.14.2   John signed up and Bill went to another flying school.

> CONTINUATION 6.14.3   John signed up immediately, before Bill could make up his mind on what to do.

> CONTINUATION 6.14.4   John slipped a $50 bill to the flying instructor. His lessons started that afternoon.

Event 6.14 describes a resource-limitation conflict, where the resource is human assistance. Neither actor can carry out his plan of taking flying lessons without the active cooperation of the flying instructor. Since flying lessons require the full attention of the instructor on teaching a single student, John and Bill cannot simultaneously carry out their respective plans. Continuation 6.14.1 is an application by John and Bill of strategy 6.6, resource scheduling. Bill applies resource substitution (strategy 6.4) in continuation 6.14.2. John invokes strategy 6.11, discussed in the following section, and the more general goal-oriented strategy (strategy 4.2 discussed in Chapter 4 and reiterated below) to achieve the controllable-precondition subgoal of enrolling for the class. Incidentally, he blocked Bill's mutually exclusive subgoal of doing the same thing.

STRATEGY 4.2   PRIORITY SCHEDULING

IF   X can achieve G(X) before Y can achieve G(Y),

THEN   X should plan to pursue G(X) at the earliest possible opportunity.

The last continuation to event 6.14 illustrates a resource-limitation strategy that is only applicable if the resource is human assistance. Bill bargains with the instructor to secure his assistance over John's mutually exclusive wishes. The general strategy is presented below:

STRATEGY 6.10:   SECURING HUMAN ASSISTANCE

TRIGGER   P/G(X) and P/G(Y) need resource R, where R cannot be used in more than one plan at a time.

IF   R is human assistance,

THEN   X has the following alternatives:

1.   X should use the PERSUADE package to convince R to help X instead of helping Y.

2.   If R is time limited, X should use the PERSUADE package to convince R to create more time (e.g., sacrifice other activities) so that R can assist both X and Y.

3.   X may ASK R if there is an R' who can perform the same function. If such an R' exists, either X or Y should invoke strategy 6.7 (resource substitution) on R'.

The first alternative of the above strategy was invoked by John in continuation 6.14.4. If the understander is not aware that one of John's options is to persuade the instructor to accommodate him, it is very difficult to understand why John gave him $50. Therefore, some rule like strategy

6.10 (as well as knowledge about the different means of social persuasion) is necessary to understand event 6.14 followed by its fourth continuation. The second and third alternatives of strategy 6.10 are illustrated in the following two possible continuations of event 6.14:

> CONTINUATION 6.14.5   John offered to let the instructor use his yacht if he gave John lessons on Saturday.

> CONTINUATION 6.14.6   John asked to be referred to some other flying instructor, and was told of a pilot who gives private lessons. Bill went to see this pilot.

6.6.4 Resources as measures of cost

We discussed in a previous section that the cost associated with a plan was a combination of two factors: 1) other goals that may be violated by carrying out the plan, and 2) the consumption of resources not available for use in other plans. The second measure of cost applies also to time-dependent resources and human-assistance resources. In the former case, an actor precludes the pursuit of another plan he wished to pursue if the second plan required the same resource (Wilensky [1978]). In the latter case the same problem may exist, but, more importantly, the person may not be willing to be of assistance more than a few times (or may require compensation in the form of another useful resource). Thus, cost is measured in terms of what cannot be done in the future as a result of an actor's present actions.

The acquisition of some resources, such as money for people, and energy-producing substances for countries, becomes an important subsumption goal in itself. In a similar manner, cultivating friendships and having people owe favors become goal states, as these can be considered to be resources useful in future plans. For instance, having political connections is a useful resource-subsumption state for many different types of plans. Severing political or interpersonal ties, therefore, can have a high cost because it wastes human resources.

6.7 Counterplanning Against Blocked Preconditions

In order to successfully execute a plan, there are usually some preconditions that must hold true. Schank and Abelson [1977] classify preconditions into three categories: controllable, uncontrollable, and mediating preconditions. For instance, if John's plan is to ask Mary where the bank is located, the following preconditions must be met: (1) John must establish a communications link with Mary, such as telephoning her, or being in physical proximity. (2) Mary must know where the bank is located. (3) Mary must be willing to convey the information to John.

The first precondition is a controllable precondition, because we assume that John can achieve it at will. The second is an uncontrollable precondition; John cannot bring this precondition about by any action on his part. The third precondition is called a mediating precondition. "Mediating" means that the planner can try to bring this condition about, but its final outcome rests on the actions of another party. For instance, John can use the persuade package to convince Mary that she should tell him where the bank is, but there is no guarantee that John will succeed.

In a plan-interference situation it is often the case that the interference is caused by one actor's plan blocking a necessary precondition of the other actor's plan. We analyze the general type of counterplanning strategies applicable to each type of precondition violation as listed below:

II-B Executing P/G(Y) changes the state of the world so as to:

  1. Block a mediating precondition for P/G(X).

  2. Block an uncontrollable precondition for P/G(X).

  3. Block a controllable precondition for P/G(X).

Consider an event where one actor's plan blocks a mediating precondition of another actor's plan:

EVENT 6.15   Johnny needed his father's permission to go to the baseball game. His brother Billy was playing with Dad's tools, something which Johnny knew would make his father angry.

CONTINUATION 6.15.1   Johnny decided to put away the tools before asking his father's permission to go to the game.

COMMUNICATION 6.15.2   Johnny told Billy that he would punch him in the nose unless he put away Dad's tools.

In order to understand event 6.15 with either continuation we need to know strategy 6.11, and we need to have a rule to the effect that when parents get angry at their children, they are unlikely to allow them new privileges. The first continuation corresponds to the first alternative of strategy 6.11, and the second continuation corresponds to the third alternative. We need strategy 6.11 to understand why Johnny first put away the tools and then asked his father's permission. We need the third alternative of 6.11 to understand the causal relation between Johnny's threat to Billy and the pursuit of his plan to go to the baseball game. Here is strategy 6.11:

STRATEGY 6.11   UNBLOCKING A MEDIATING PRECONDITION

IF   Y is blocking a mediating precondition for P/G(X),

THEN   X should choose the least cost alternative among:

1. Establish the goal G1(X) = Bring about the mediating precondition by some means independent of Y's actions. Suspend P/G(X) until G1(X) is achieved.

2. Choose a new plan P', such that P'/G(X) does not require this mediating precondition.

3. Set up the mutual-exclusion goal conflict G(X) = "Y is not blocking the mediating precondition to P/G(X)." Invoke the mutual-exclusion counterplanning strategies.

Consider the case where one actor's plan blocks an uncontrollable precondition of another actor's plan. We cannot apply the first alternative of strategy 6.11 because, by definition, an actor cannot bring about uncontrollable preconditions. The second and third alternatives are applicable to both mediating and uncontrollable preconditions. Another possibility suggests itself if the blockage is temporary: wait until the uncontrollable precondition is no longer blocked. For blocked mediating preconditions, the waiting option is subsumed under alternative 1 in strategy 6.11 if a more active means to re-establish the blocked mediating precondition cannot be applied. (For instance, in event 6.10, Johnny could have waited until his father was no longer angry, assuming the baseball game was sufficiently far in the future.) Here is the blocked uncontrollable-precondition counterplanning strategy:

STRATEGY 6.12   UNBLOCKING AN UNCONTROLLABLE
PRECONDITION

IF   Y is blocking an uncontrollable precondition for P/G(X),

THEN   X should choose the least cost alternative among:

1. Choose a new plan P' such that P'/G(X) does not require this uncontrollable precondition.

2. Invoke the mutual-exclusion counterplanning strategies to thwart Y's continued blocking of the uncontrollable precondition.

3. If Y's blockage of an uncontrollable precondition for P/G(X) is temporary, X should suspend P until Y no longer blocks this precondition. Then, X should resume the pursuit of P/G(X).

To illustrate the third alternative of strategy 6.12, consider the following event:

EVENT 6.16   Smith wanted to be elected chairman of the department. The elections were cancelled that year by the dean. Smith bided his time until the following year.

QUESTION 6.16.1   What was Smith waiting for?

If the understander realizes that event 6.16 is an instance of the third alternative of strategy 6.12, it is clear how the question should be answered. Smith has not given up his goal; he merely suspended it until the temporary blockage of the uncontrollable precondition was removed in the following year. Hence, an appropriate answer is: "Smith was waiting until the following year to run for chairman."

Counterplanning against blocked controllable preconditions is much simpler. Indeed, in many cases the actor whose plan's controllable precondition was blocked re-establishes the precondition without recourse to other counterplanning measures. The following is the blocked controllable precondition strategy:

STRATEGY 6.13:   UNBLOCKING A CONTROLLABLE PRECONDITION

IF   Y is blocking a controllable precondition for P/G(X),

THEN   X should choose the least cost alternative among:

1. Re-establish the blocked controllable precondition.
   REFINEMENT   X should choose the method for re-establishing this precondition in such a way that it will not be blocked once again by P/G(Y).

2. Use the PERSUADE package to convince Y to abandon or change his plan in order that the controllable precondition to P/G(X) is no longer blocked.

6.8 Partial Plan Interference

One way to characterize plan interference is the degree to which two plans interfere. Consider the following two examples:

> EVENT 6.17   Texaco was drilling for oil in the Gulf coast. Mobil had an active oil well on an adjacent tract. Both companies complained that they were decreasing each other's output by tapping the same oil deposit.

> EVENT 6.18   German Chancellor Schmidt was upset because President Carter's remarks on human rights were making it more difficult for him to negotiate with East Germany and Russia.

In both of the above events there was a dispute over partially blocked plans. Texaco and Mobil were partially blocking each other's uncontrollable precondition to the plan of drilling oil; there has to be sufficient oil in the ground for economically feasible exploitation. Carter was partially blocking a mediating precondition for Schmidt's plan of negotiating with the Communists; all parties in a negotiation have to be willing to negotiate. In neither case did the partial precondition blockage prevent the plan from being carried out, but in both cases it made it more difficult for the respective parties.

The same counterplanning rules apply to partial plan conflicts and to total blockage situations. There is, however, one additional parameter of significance: the degree to which the partial interference blocks the normal execution of a plan. In general, we apply the following heuristic strategies:

> STRATEGY 6.14   MINOR PLAN INTERFERENCE
>
> TRIGGER   P/G(Y) is partially blocking X's pursuit of P/G(X).
>
> IF   the interference is very minor,
>
> THEN   X should continue to pursue P/G(X), ignoring Y's actions.

> STRATEGY 6.15   SEVERE PLAN INTERFERENCE
>
> TRIGGER   P/G(Y) is partially blocking X's pursuit of P/G(X).
>
> IF   P/G(Y) makes P/G(X) almost impossible to carry out,
>
> THEN   X should invoke the same counterplanning strategies as in total blockage.

STRATEGY 6.16   COSTLY-BUT-LIVABLE PLAN INTERFERENCE

TRIGGER   P/G(Y) is partially blocking X's pursuit of P/G(X).

IF   the interference increases the cost of doing P/G(X), without totally blocking P,

THEN   X should simultaneously pursue P/G(X) and counterplan against Y to stop his blocking actions.

REFINEMENT   The cost of the counterplanning should not exceed the cost of executing the partially blocked P without recourse to counterplanning actions.

Event 6.18, for instance, illustrates an application of strategy 6.16. Chancellor Schmidt pursued his plan of negotiating with the Communists while publicly indicating his displeasure against Carter's policy. Indicating one's displeasure is a relatively low-cost counterplan, since it uses no tangible resources and does not directly violate any goals.

6.9 A Note on the Subjective Beliefs of the Understander

Many of the strategies discussed in this chapter are modulated by the beliefs of the understander. For instance, some strategies require the counterplanner to estimate the cost of his actions in light of what other significant goals he may not be able to accomplish. Knowing what other goals each actor has and the relative importance of these goals is the purpose of the goal trees. The understander's beliefs about the goal trees of the actors in the plan conflict determine his understanding of the cost of their action to them. This, in turn, helps the understander infer the counterplanning actions they are likely to pursue. If the understander's beliefs about the motivations of the actors is inaccurate, his understanding will suffer because he will try to interpret their actions in terms of the wrong counterplanning strategies.

7

An Annotated Example of the POLITICS System

7.1 Introduction

In this chapter we present an annotated protocol of the POLITICS system interpreting an event and answering questions about its interpretation. The event is first interpreted from a conservative ideology and then from a liberal ideology. We have not previously discussed the parsing, script application, situational inference, and question-answering processes for POLITICS. Here, these processes are analyzed by investigating a detailed example of their application in a POLITICS event interpretation and question-answer dialog. We also discuss the role of the ideology goal trees and the counterplanning strategies as a crucial part of the overall understanding process.

The first stage in interpreting most events consists of an integrated process of parsing the English input and instantiating appropriate scripts to derive a minimal understanding of the situation. Scripts, described in Schank and Abelson [1977] and Cullingford [1977], serve two important purposes in understanding events that require access to large amounts of world knowledge. Scripts contain sequences of events describing stereotypical and/or mundane situations frequently encountered (possibly with variations) by the understander. Scripts are also a useful mechanism for grouping inferences, since the activation of a script defines the context in which an event is to be interpreted. It is primarily the latter feature that helps POLITICS understand the Trident submarine event. The application of scriptal inferences is illustrated in the interpretation of the Trident submarine event presented below.

7.2 A Detailed U.S.-conservative Interpretation

Start of U.S.-conservative POLITICS Interpretation

PTYCON LOG FILE   1-Mar-78 2:44:20

PTYCON> CONNECT (TO SUBJOB) 1
[CONNECTED TO SUBJOB POL(1)]

Computer Processing	Annotation

*(INTERPRET US-CONSERVATIVE)
 	
INCORPORATING US-CONSERVATIVE
IDEOLOGY GOAL TREES . . .
(*US* TOP-GOAL: G0)
(*RUSSIA* TOP-GOAL: G27)
 	
(TXPN G27)
((ACTOR (#POLITY REF (DEF)
            MEM (*RUSSIA*))
TOWARD (*CONTROL* VAL (+ 10))
OBJECT (*WORLD*))
    MODE (*INTENTIONAL*))
INITIATING PARSER . . . DONE
	Before processing any events, POLI-TICS incorporates goal trees encoding a political ideology.
	
	The most important U.S. goal in the conservative ideology is Communist containment (G0)
	
	The most important Soviet goal is taking over the entire world (G27). Goals are encoded as desired changes to the present state of the world.

Let us see how the goals in the ideological goal trees, discussed in Chapter 3, are encoded in POLITICS. Each goal is either a preservation goal (P-goal) or an achievement goal (A-goal). P-goals are encoded as a representation of an existing state of the world that must be maintained, and A-goals are represented as a desired state change to the present state of the world. If a P-goal is violated by an event, then that goal is replaced by an A-goal to re-achieve the violated state. The U.S.-conservative goal of Communist containment and its subgoal of increased U.S. military strength are encoded as follows:

```
[GOAL PART (*US*)
    GOALSTATE
        ((ACTOR (#POLITY GOVTYP (*COMMUNIST*))
            IS (*PCONT* VAL (0))
            OBJECT (#GROUP NUMBER (*INDEF*)
                MEMBER (#POLITY
                        GOVTYP (*COMMUNIST*
                        MODE (NEG))))))
        TOK G0
        GOALTYPE *PGOAL*
        SUPERGOALS (NIL)
        SUBGOALS (G1 G4 G5)
        GREATER-IMPORTANCE (NIL)
        LESSER-IMPORTANCE (G2 G3)]
```

```
[GOAL PART (*US*)
    GOALSTATE
        ((ACTOR   (*US*)
        TOWARD (*STRENGTH*
            TYPE (*MILIT*).
            INC (*POSVAL*)
            VAL (*SPEC* GREATER
                (*STRENGTH*PART (*RUSSIA*)
                    TYPE (*MILIT*))))))
    TOK G1
    GOALTYPE *AGOAL*
    SUPERGOALS (G0)
    SUBGOALS (G8 G9)
    GREATER-IMPORTANCE (NIL)
    LESSER-IMPORTANCE (G12 G19)]
```

Each goal in the ideology encodes the desired goal state or state transition and its relationships to other goals in the ideology. The first goal above is the U.S.-conservative goal of Communist containment. We may read the goal state as follows: "The United States wants to keep all non-Communist countries free from Communist domination." Since Communist containment is the most important U.S. goal, it is not a subgoal to other goals (i.e., it has no "supergoals"), and it has no greater importance goals. There are, however, subgoals to Communist containment, such as military strength (goal G1). There also are less important goals in the U.S.-conservative goal tree (goals G2 and G3). For instance, goal G2 is the preservation of free enterprise in the U.S.

The military strength goal state reads: "The United States should increase its military strength to be greater than Russian military strength." The relation between this goal and other goals in the U.S. conservative goal tree is defined by the subgoal, supergoal, greater importance, and lesser importance links.

7.2.1 The initial interpretation phase

POLITICS starts interpreting a story after incorporating the ideological goals into its working memory.

Computer Processing	Annotation
INPUT STORY: The United States Congress voted to fund the Trident submarine project.	The input event is typed in English to the POLITICS parser. Parsing in POLITICS is part of an integrated memory process—there is no separate module that can be labeled "the parser".

PARSING . . .

CREATING ORG0
(#ORG TYPE (*GOVT*)
    NAME (CONGRESS)
    PART (*US*)
    REF (DEF))

FOUND ACTION FRAME:
((<=> ($VOTE ACTOR ORG0)))

MEMORY INTEGRATING PARTIAL
PARSE . . .
    ($PARLIAMENT-PROC
    ACTOR ORG0
    TRACK ($VOTE))

ACTIVE MEMORY REQUEST
PATH SPECIFICATION:
    ($PARLIAMENT-PROC
        $VOTE ISSUE)

FOUND ACTION FRAME:
((ACTOR NIL
    <=> (*ATRANS*)
    OBJECT (*MONEY* AMOUNT
                (SUFF))
        TO NIL
        FROM NIL
        INSTR NIL))

SEARCHING ACTOR OF:
((<=> (*ATRANS*)
    OBJECT (*MONEY* AMOUNT
                (SUFF))))

FOUND: ORG0

MATCHED MEMORY REQUEST

ATRANS IS
($PARLIAMENT-PROC
    $VOTE ISSUE)

Parsing and memory integration of new events is a single, unified process.

Processing from left to right, the parser analyzes the phrase "The United States Congress" and finds the memory referent for this concept.

Next, "voted" is processed and found to be an action frame. Action frames are structures that can predict other structures. For instance "vote" can predict that the parser should find a group of people voting and an issue being decided.

Memory uses its knowledge of how the U.S. Congress works (encoded in the $PARLIAMENTORY-PROC script) to conclude that the $VOTE is part of the parliamentary procedure that Congress normally engages in.

The most important part of a congressional vote is its performative aspect: the issue voted on and the outcome of the vote. This information is encoded in the $PARLIAMENT-PROC script. The parser uses this information to create an expectation focusing on the issue of the vote. This process is significant because once the important information is identified, the parser can afford to ignore other parts of the input that it does not understand. For instance, POLITICS cannot understand: "the lobbying effort was intense." If this phrase was part of the above input it could be safely ignored.

The parser looks for an object of the vote. It finds that the transfer of money implicit in the phrase "to fund . . ." is an appropriate issue for Congress to vote on. Every script role has a set of constraints that must be satisfied by the entity that fills them. The object of a $VOTE must be a Congressional action or a bill.

MEMORY ASSERTS $FUND
PRIMARY ACTION: ($FUND)
 INSTR ($PARLIAMENT-PROC)
 INSTR ($VOTE)
 IMBEDDED (*ATRANS*)

Now, the $FUND script is activated because the *ATRANS* of money is the most important event in $FUND. The relation of the other actions with respect to $FUND are established.

ACTIVE MEMORY REQUEST

PATH SPECIFICATION:

 ($FUND &FUNDER)
MATCHED ((&FUNDER ORG0)

ACTIVE MEMORY REQUEST
PATH SPECIFICATION:
 ($FUND &FUND-CON)

$FUND became the focus of attention because $PARLIAMENTARY-PROC is what Congress does every day, and therefore is not as interesting as the new event. The parser tries to match the script roles with items in the input. A script role stands for someone or something that always performs the same function in the context of the script.

ACTIVE MEMORY REQUEST
PATH SPECIFICATION:
 ($FUND &FUNDEE)

The parser also tries to find who is being funded (&FUNDEE) and what is being funded (&FUND-CON). The agency instigating the funding (&FUNDEE) is the U.S. Congress.

ACTIVE MEMORY REQUEST
PATH SPECIFICATION:
 ($FUND &MONEY)

MATCHED ((&MONEY
 (MONEY AMOUNT (SUFF))))

Not surprisingly, the ATRANSed money is the &MONEY that $FUND knows about.

CREATING WEAPON0
 (#WEAPON TYPE (*SUBMARINE*)
  NAME (TRIDENT))

"The Trident Submarine Project"

——END OF INPUT REACHED——

UNFULFILLED MEMORY REQUESTS
 (($FUND & FUNDEE)
 ($FUND &FUND-CON))

POLITICS reached the end of the input without establishing referents for &FUNDEE and &FUND-CON.

DEFAULT SPECIFICATIONS:
&FUNDEE ISA *INSTITUTION*
CREATING ORG1
 (#ORG INVOLVING WEAPON0)

POLITICS extracts from $FUND the information it has on &FUNDEE, but it can only conclude that it is an organization having something to do with the Trident submarines.

&FUND-CON ISA ★ACT★
CREATING CON3
((ACTOR ORG1
    <=> (★DO★)
  INSTR (★MONEY★))
INVOLVING WEAPON0)

&FUND-CON has to be some event. Since the syntactic object of the verb "to fund" is the Trident submarines (WEAPON0), the parser asserts that the &FUND-CON event has something to do with WEAPON0.

——PAUSE IN PROCESSING——

$FUND says that $FUNDEE will use the money for doing &FUND-CON.

★(TXPN (GET '$FUND 'MAINCON))

((ACTOR (#ORG TYPE (★GOVT★)
              NAME (CONGRESS)
              PART (★US★)
              REF (DEF)
              TOK ORG0)
  <=> (★ATRANS★)
OBJECT (★MONEY★ AMOUNT
                 (SUFF))
TO (#ORG INVOLVING
        (#WEAPON
         TYPE (★SUBMARINE★)
         NAME (TRIDENT)
         REF (INDEF)
         TOK WEAPON0))
  TOK ORG1)
FROM (★UNSPEC★ REL ORG0)
INSTR ($PARLIAMENT-PROC
       TRACK ($VOTE))
TIME ((AFTER NOW X))
MODE (★INTENTIONAL★))
TOK CON9)

The main event of the $FUND script is an ATRANS of &MONEY from the &FUNDER to the &FUNDEE. The memory representation of the fully instantiated event is the structure on the left.

The role specifications in a script frame are similar to Wilks's [1975] preferences in his templates and paraplates, but the scripts encode much more detailed situational knowledge.

The vote and parliamentary process scripts are instrumental to the funding event.

★P

COMPLETED.

INTERPRETING EVENT FROM A
U.S.-CONSERVATIVE IDEOLOGY.

The parser finishes when it has done its best to interpret the input event.

The representation of the main event in $FUND script may be paraphrased as follows: An agency of the U.S. government, called the Congress, has the intention of transferring money (from an unspecified source) to another agency which has something to do with weapons whose category is submarines and whose name is Trident. There is a note that the amount of money transferred is sufficient for its (as yet unspecified) purpose. This last fact comes from the dictionary definition of the word "fund". One should note that the word "fund" in the input event was not necessary to identify the $FUND script. The $FUND script was activated because the input event was an intentional transfer of money by a government agency. The following two events are also recognized as instances of the $FUND script by POLITICS:

1. President Carter decided to allocate money for the jobs program.

2. The Senate budget provides for production of the cruise missile.

7.2.2 The ideological interpretation phase

Since we are understanding the event as an instance of the $FUND script, we need to instantiate all the roles in the fund script. Instantiating these roles is essentially equivalent to answering the first four questions below. The fifth question is always asked in an ideological interpretation, as discussed in previous chapters. As the following questions are answered by POLITICS, it uses the answers to integrate the event representation into its memory model.

1. What agency will receive the money?

2. What will the money be used for?

3. Where did the money come from?
   [already answered by the input]

4. What is the connection between the Trident Submarines and the agency receiving the money?

5. What important implications (if any) does this action have on any high level US goal?

There are two types of inference in the event interpretation phase of POLITICS. The first is a specification inference that resolves references in the input event representation to entities in the POLITICS world model, or creates new entities if required. The reference problem has been studied in some detail (e.g., Charniak, [1972]). In the POLITICS system we do not attempt a comprehensive solution to the problem, but we have a rather intensive set of inferences to resolve references within our domain. Sometimes the reference specification includes the postulation of entities not specifically mentioned in the input, but which must exist in order for the political event to make sense. For example, the input sentence says nothing about an organization receiving the money. However, our knowledge of governmental funding tells us that there must be a recipient, and, furthermore, the recipient must have the necessary resources, abilities and legal authorization to carry out the project being funded.

The specification inferences are indexed by the scripts that define the situational context. These inferences focus on identifying the script roles with items mentioned in the input. For instance, the parser triggered the specification inferences that identified the FUNDER and narrowed down the possibilities for the FUND-CON and the FUNDEE. Thus, the specification inferences focus on the important situational aspects of an event. Each script indexes different sets of specification inferences, because each situation defines different items as being important. Parsing text by focusing on the important situational aspects, as defined by script-based expectations, characterizes the bulk of the POLITICS parsing process. A different form of script-driven parsing has been developed in parallel by DeJong [1979] for the FRUMP system, a program that skims lengthy newspaper stories over many different domains.

Some specification inferences apply only after the parser has completed its normal process. These are inferences that should be activated only if the input did not supply some necessary information needed to fulfill active script requests. For instance, the FUNDEE and the FUND-CON are not fully specified by the input, thereby triggering the inference rules below. $FUND contains 10 inference rules for inferring the nature of some script roles not fully specified in the input. These rules succeed if memory knows some crucial facts about other, already identified script roles. The script indexed inference rules are domain specific, and therefore inapplicable outside the $FUND domain. We list the specification inference rules that are triggered in processing the present funding event:

RULE-FUND F3

   IF &FUNDER is a government agency,
     AND &FUNDER delegates (AUTHORITY,
     RESPONSIBILITY, or MONEY) to &FUNDEE,

   THEN &FUNDEE is N levels below &FUNDER in the governmental structure

  REFINEMENT IF <that which is delegated> is of high (MILITARY, ECONOMIC or JUDICIAL) significance,

     THEN probably N = 1.

RULE-FUND F5

    IF   the GOAL of the funding is of a MILITARY nature,

    THEN   expect a MILITARY agency to receive the AUTHORITY to
spend the money (i.e., CONTROL of the money).

RULE-FUND F6

    IF   &FUND-CON involves an event or a physical object &X,
AND &FUNDER does not already have &X,
AND &MONEY is greater than or = the cost of &X,

    THEN   &FUND-CON is: &FUNDEE doing the necessary actions to
bring &X about.

RULE-FUND F8

    IF   &X (&X is the same variable as in RULE #6) has a physical
realization,
AND &FUNDEE controls the creation of objects of &X's
category,

    THEN   &FUND-CON = (&FUNDEE will build &X).

Throughout the initial analysis phase, the ideological goal trees were accessible to the parsing and script application process. This is because the ideological beliefs can bias any phase of the event interpretation process. In the process of applying script-indexed specification inferences, POLITICS sometimes needs to query the goals of a political actor, as is the case for RULE-FUND#5. Hence, the instantiation of a script in the initial interpretation of an event can be influenced by the goals of the ideology. The parser may also need to query the ideology when analyzing events that involve a possible ambiguity of motive. Consider a U.S.-conservative understanding of the following two events:

EVENT 7.1   Russia sent troops into Afghanistan.

EVENT 7.2   The United States sent an army division to South Korea.

A U.S.-conservative would understand event 7.2 as a military-aid scenario, but 7.1 would probably be understood as a military invasion. Why? Russia's goal of military and political expansion are furthered by invading Afghanistan, and the U.S. goal of containing Communist expansion (in this case North Korean aggression) is furthered by aiding South Korea. Furthermore, South Korea has the goal of receiving aid from anti-Communist nations, according to the conservative ideology, but Afghanistan has no similar goal of receiving Soviet military aid.

This type of event, the movement of a large country's military forces into a smaller country, can be interpreted as two different scenarios. This fact suggests that the parser must be able to use information from the ideology in order to apply the correct script. In a U.S.-conservative interpretation, event 7.1 is an instance of the $INVADE script, and event 7.2 is an instance of $MILITARY-AID. One way to solve this problem is to ignore goals, interpret both events as invasions (or both as military aid), and later apply goal analysis. In this paradigm, if an interpretation contradicts the goals, we would need to reinterpret that event and re-analyze the goals to see if the new interpretation is more reasonable. From an introspective viewpoint, it seems psychologically implausible to analyze each event first as the same type of scenario and later apply the ideological information to verify or contradict the interpretation. Such a process violates our theory of subjective understanding where the understander normally sees only one possible interpretation, namely the interpretation that is consistent with his ideology. Therefore, when the POLITICS parser notices that two different scripts may apply to one situation it checks with the ideology to see which script is consistent with the goals of the ideology.

The parser, therefore, cannot be separated from the rest of the memory and inference processes. Formulating a full representation of the input event is the first priority of the POLITICS interpretation phase. This process may be subjectively biased when there is more than one possible interpretation. After an event representation is formed, POLITICS determines how it affects the goals of the actors involved in greater detail. The following is the rest of the POLITICS interpretation of the Trident submarine event. We pick up the interpretation with the application of RULE-FUND#3 through RULE-FUND#8:

```
(APPLYING RULE-FUND#3 FROM
                $FUND)
```

Congress ATRANSed money to &FUNDEE. RULE-FUND#3 says that &FUNDEE must be a government agency whose authority is just below the authority of Congress.

```
INFERENCE: &FUNDEE =
(#ORG PART (*US*)
       RANK (LEV VAL (1))
       TYPE (*GOVT)
       TOK ORG1)
```

```
(APPLYING RULE-FUND#5 FROM
                $FUND)
INFERENCE: &FUNDEE =
```

Trident submarines are weapons, therefore used by the military. Thus,

```
(#ARMEDFORCES PART (*US*)
            RANK (COMMAND)
            TOK AF0)
```

&FUNDEE is probably a military
agency.

```
(APPLYING RULE-FUND#6 FROM
            $FUND)
```

```
INFERENCE: &FUND-CON =
((CON
  ((ACTOR (*MONEY* AMOUNT (SUFF))
   IS (CONTROL VAL
        (#ARMEDFORCES
            PART (*US*)
            RANK (COMMAND)
            TOK AF0))))
ENABLE
  ((ACTOR AF0
    <=> (*DO*)))
RESULT
  ((ACTOR (#WEAPON
            TYPE (*SUBMARINE*)
            NAME (TRIDENT))
        TOK WEAPON0)
   IS (CONTROL VAL AF0)))))
```

POLITICS searches for the necessary
actions enabling &FUNDEE to bring
about the Trident submarines, but
the script only states that money is a
necessary precondition.

```
(APPLYING RULE-FUND#8 FROM
            $FUND)
```

```
INFERENCE: &FUND-CON =
((<=>
  ($CONSTRUCT
   ACTOR (#ARMED FORCES
            PART (*US*)
            RANK (COMMAND)
            TOK AF0)
   ENABLEMENT (*MONEY*
            AMOUNT (SUFF))
   OBJECT (#WEAPON
            TYPE (*SUBMARINE*)
            NAME (TRIDENT)
            TOK WEAPON0)))
 MODE (*INTENTIONAL*)
 TIME ((AFTER NOW X)))
```

RULE-FUND#8 says that since
submarines are physical objects, the
way to bring them about is to construct them. (POLITICS does not
know about research and
development.)

```
INTERMEDIATE RESULT INFERENCES.
(APPLYING RULE-#4 FROM POLITICS)
((ACTOR (*US) ISTOWARD
        (*POWER*
            TYPE (*MILITARY*)
            VAL (N)
```

There is a small number of situational
inferences that apply to the entire
domain of international politics.

Rule-#4 is one such inference; it
states that if a country builds or

```
            INC (POS))
TOK CON13)
```

acquires weapons, it will be militarily stronger.

```
SEARCHING *US* GOAL TREE . . .

(GOAL G4 MATCHED)
G4 IS A SUBGOAL OF G0
*(TXPN G0)
   ((ACTOR (#POLITY
            TYPE (*COMMUNIST*)))
      TOWARD
   (*CONTROL*
      TYPE (OR (*POLITICAL*)
               (*MILITARY*)
               (*ECONOMIC*))
      OBJECT (#POLITY
              TYPE
              (*NONCOMMUNIST*))
      VAL (0)))
```

How does the construction of a new weapons system affect the goals of the U.S.? Increased military strength is found to be one of the goals in the U.S.-conservative goal tree. It is a subgoal of Communist containment, the highest level U.S.-conservative goal. Thus, POLITICS explains the U.S. decision to build the Trident submarines in terms of the increase in military strength. This increase in strength must have been the reason for the U.S. decision because it matches a subgoal of the most important U.S.-conservative goal: Communist containment

```
EXPLANATION PATH FOUND:
(($FUND &FUNDER ORG0
        &FUNDEE AF0
        &FUND-CON CON9
        &MONEY MONEY0)
   ENABLE
   ($CONSTRUCT &ACTOR AF0
               &OBJECT WEAPON0)
   RESULT
   CON13)
```

```
*(TXPN CON13)
   ((ACTOR (*US*) ISTOWARD
      (*POWER*
         TYPE (*MILITARY*)
         VAL (N)
         INC (POS))
TOK CON13)
```

CON13 is the resultant increase in U.S. military strength.

```
(CON13 MATCHES (*US* . G4))
((*US* . G4) SUBGOAL
 (*US* . G0))
```

U.S.-conservative POLITICS is satisfied with the explanation because it is consistent with its ideology.

```
INTERPRETATION COMPLETED,
READY TO ACCEPT QUESTIONS.
```

The goal directed inference process may be triggered from two sources of knowledge. The first source is contextual knowledge, encoded as scripts. For instance, in $FUND the &FUNDER gives the money to the &FUNDEE with the intention that the &FUNDEE will fulfill the purpose that the &FUNDER had in mind. This goal is usually well defined in terms of our full world knowledge, but it is poorly defined in terms of the linguistic realization of the Trident submarine event. The input event did not mention that the submarines would be built, nor did it mention why Congress may want the submarines. Building the submarines is a goal of the U.S. armed forces, a fact that POLITICS inferred by applying the inference rules grouped under $FUND and $CONSTRUCT. This goal is instrumental to the ultimate purpose of the U.S. Congress. Hence, the scripts tell us *how* Congress tends to make the Trident submarines come into existence, not *why* Congress chose to do so. The goals guiding the actions by Congress are inferred from the ideological U.S. goal tree. Thus, both contextual and ideological knowledge are necessary to model a person's interpretation of a political event.

7.2.3 The question-answering phase

Let us analyze a protocol of the question-answering process implemented for POLITICS. First, questions are categorized into classes of question types (Lehnert [1978]) as part of the parsing process. The question types tell us the nature of the information sought. Second, a discrimination network is used to test the question type and the body of the question in order to see where in memory to search for the answer (or, if nowhere, what further inferences or counterplanning strategies to apply). Finally, a memory search is performed or suggested inferences are applied. The first two questions in the question-answer dialog below are answered by searching the interpretation of the event. The third question requires counterplanning.

---

*What did the U.S. Congress do this for?

Parsing and question classification proceed simultaneously.

PARSING . . .
  (EVENT REL (*UNSPEC*))
STARTNP
  SUGGESTS QTYP: EVENTQ

The question type has been erroneously analyzed as a request to specify an under-specified event. POLITICS assumes that the question will be of the form "What did X do?"

ACTIVE REQUEST REQ-ACTOR
ACTIVE REQUEST REQ-EVENT

(#ORG TYPE (*GOVT*)
  NAME (CONGRESS)
  PART (*US*)

REF (DEF))
MATCHES PREVIOUS REFERENT:
ORG0

"The U.S. Congress" is a previously
encountered referent.

REQ-ACTOR FULFILLED: ORG0

This fulfills the question type request
for a specific actor.

UNDERSPECIFIED CD:
((ACTOR ORG0 <=> (*DO*)))

If the entire question was, "What did
the U.S. Congress do?", POLITICS
would have analyzed it successfully.

REQ-EVENT FULFILLED:
((ACTOR ORG0 <=> (*DO*)))

SUGGESTED MULTIPLE SEARCH

Now the word "this" comes in and
upsets the previous analysis.

(EVENT REL (*SPEC*)
  ACTIONSPEC (ACTION PREVIOUS)
  REF CON14)

REJECTING CURRENT QTYP:
EVENTQ

"This" in the present context stands
for a specific, previously mentioned
event.

SUGGESTED (*GOAL* REL CON14)

"For" usually starts a phrase, but
appearing as the last word in the
sentence, POLITICS can only make
sense of it if "for" is part of an
idiom. "what for" is matched as the
split idiom, meaning a request for the
purpose of a specified event.

PARSE FAILURE: (FOR)

EVAL (IDIOMATIC-MATCH
  (QUOTE (FOR)))

SUGGESTED QTYP: GOAL-EVENT

APPLYING QSEARCH D-NET TO:

(QSEARCH (QTYP GOAL-EVENT)
  (QBODY CON15))

*(TXPN CON15)
((ACTOR ORG0 <=> (*DO*))

  REL (*SPEC*)
  TOK CON15)

The purpose of an event suggests a
new question type. This and the
underspecified event (CON15) are
given to the discrimination net, which
tells POLITICS where to search for
the answer. (We show the application
of the D-net in greater detail when
we discuss the liberal interpretation.)

(MSEARCH
  (SOURCE !EXPLANATION)
  (PSPEC (LAST))
  (PATTERN
    EVAL (MSEARCH
      (SOURCE !EVENTMEM
      (PSPEC (*SELF*))
      (PATTERN CON15))))

MATCHED CON15

The D-net says that first one must
search for the specific event in question (in event memory). Then, the last
item in the POLITICS explanation of
that event is the actor's goal. (POLI-
TICS considers an event to be
explained only if it is related to a
goal.)

EXTRACTING (*SELF*)
(\$FUND &FUNDER ORG0
&FUNDEE AF0
&FUND-CON CON9
&MONEY MONEY0
TOK SCR2)

POLITICS finds the funding event by Congress as the main event in which Congress was the actor.

MATCHED SCR2
EXTRACTING (LAST)
CON13

The explanation yields CON13 as the purpose for the funding event. CON13 is the U.S. goal of increasing the military power of its armed forces.

THE ANSWER IS:
((CON CON13
IS (*GOAL* PART ORG0)))

*(TXPN CON13)
((ACTOR (*US*) ISTOWARD
(*POWER*
TYPE (*MILITARY*)
VAL (N)
INC (POS))
TOK CON13)

The answer is generated in English by a template-based generator.

THE UNITED STATES CONGRESS
WANTS THE UNITED STATES ARMED
FORCES TO BE STRONGER.

*Why should the US be
stronger?

The next question is easier to analyze. It involves only one search (for
a goal), and POLITICS finds the
correct question type on its first try.

PARSING . . .

ACTIVE REQUEST: CAUSAL-ANTE
ACTIVE REQUEST: GOAL-EVENT
ACTIVE REQUEST: GOAL-STATE

The three question types suggested by
"why".

(MODE (*INTENTIONAL*))
ASSERTED

The word "should" is ignored.

STARTNP
(#POLITY MEM (*US*)
NAME (US)
REF (DEF))
MATCHES PERMANENT TOKEN: *US*

There is no referent for "the U.S." in
the original input text, but there is
an entry for the U.S. in long term
memory.

((ACTOR (*US*) ISTOWARD
(*POWER*
TYPE (*MILITARY*)
VAL (N)
INC (POS))))
TOK CON16)

Once again we find "the U.S. be
stronger". This is a state description,
thus fulfilling one request activated
by "why".

REQUEST FULFILLED: GOAL-STATE
SUGGESTED QTYP: GOAL-STATE.

The question has been classified. Now we search for a goal that is fulfilled by bringing about this state (if there is any such goal).

APPLYING QSEARCH D-NET TO:
(QSEARCH (QTYP GOAL-STATE)
    (QBODY CON16))

(MSEARCH (SOURCE !IDEOLOGY)
    (PATH (SUPERGOAL))
    (PATTERN CON16))

The D-net suggests searching the ideology and extracting the supergoal (i.e., the goal to which CON16 is a subgoal). Searching the explanation would also have worked. In some cases the memory is redundant.

MATCHED CON16
CON16 MATCHES CON13
CON13 MATCHES G4

EXTRACTING (SUPERGOAL) OF G4
G0

CON16 matches CON13 built in the understanding phase and identified with G4—The U.S. military strength goal.

*(TXPN G0)
((ACTOR (#POLITY
      TYPE (*COMMUNIST*)))
    TOWARD
  (*CONTROL*
    TYPE (OR (*POLITICAL*)
        (*MILITARY*)
        (*ECONOMIC*))
    OBJECT (#POLITY
       TYPE
       (*NONCOMMUNIST*))
    VAL (0)))

The goal dominating military strength is Communist containment.

THE ANSWER IS:
  ((CON CON13 ENABLE G0))

The question type helps to formulate the linguistic realization of the answer.

THE UNITED STATES ARMED
FORCES SHOULD BE STRONG TO
STOP COMMUNIST EXPANSION.

Goal states are expressed using certain words such as "should", that may not be generated otherwise.

*What should the U.S. do if
Russia also builds nuclear
submarines?

The third question is more interesting; the answer is not to be found in the previous interpretation of the event. Counterplanning is required.

(EVENT VAL (*SPEC*))

(MODE (*INTENTIONAL*))
ASSERTED
SUGGESTED QTYP: GOAL-EVENT

This question type means: "search for an event that fulfills the specified goal".

STARTNP
(#POLITY MEM (*US*)
    NAME (US)
    REF (DEF))

Once again a referent for "the U.S. is found. This time it recalls the context of the last question.

MATCHES PERMANENT TOKEN:
  US
MATCHES ACTIVE-CONTEXT TOKEN:
  US

((ACTOR (*US*) < = > (*DO*)))

HYPOTHETICAL SCENARIO EXPECTED

STARTNP
(#POLITY MEM (*RUSSIA*)
  NAME (RUSSIA)
  REF (DEF))
MATCHES PERMANENT TOKEN:
  RUSSIA

(UNKNOWN WORD: ALSO)
(SYNTACTIC EXPECTATIONS
  (V ST-TR))
(SEMANTIC EXPECTATIONS
  NIL)

((< = >
($CONSTRUCT
  ACTOR (*RUSSIA*)
  OBJECT (#WEAPON
          TYPE (*SUBMARINE*)
          TOK WEAPON1))
TIME ((AFTER NOW X))
TOK CON19)
(NO SCRIPT INFERENCES
 TRIGGERED)

INTERMEDIATE RESULT
INFERENCES.
(APPLYING RULE-#4
 FROM POLITICS)
((ACTOR (*RUSSIA*) ISTOWARD
        (*POWER*
         TYPE (*MILITARY*)
         VAL (N)
         INC (POS))
TOK CON20)

SEARCHING *US* GOAL TREE . . .

(GOAL G37 MATCHED)
G37 IS A SUBGOAL OF G35
G35 IS A SUBGOAL OF G33

A query about an action followed by
the word "if" suggests that a hypothetical situation may follow.

Russian is also a permanent long term
memory entry.

The word "also" is unknown.

The POLITICS parser expected an
action or a state transition. If an
action appears later, "also" is
ignored. Otherwise the parser generates an error.

Russia building submarines fulfills the
action expectation. Since there are
no unfulfilled requests, the word
"also" is ignored.

The hypothetical situation of Russia
building submarines is interpreted by
POLITICS in the same manner as if it
were part of the original input event.

The general inferences conclude
that Russia will be stronger.

Building submarines fulfills the Russian goal of increasing their military
strength. This is a subgoal to being
stronger than all western nations,
which is in turn a subgoal of Soviet
world domination.

TWO ACTORS WITH ACTIVE GOALS

SEARCHING GOAL CONFLICTS . . .

(MUTUAL-EXCLUSION
　　((*US* . G3)
　　(*RUSSIA* . G35)))

POLITICS finds that G3 (The U.S. goal of being militarily stronger than Russia) is mutually exclusive with G35 (The Russian goal of being stronger than the U.S.).

QBODY REDEFINED
　　((CON CON19 DISABLE CON20))

APPLYING QSEARCH D-NET TO:
(QSEARCH (QTYP GOAL-EVENT)
　　　　(QBODY ((CON CON19
　　　　　　　　DISABLE
　　　　　　　　　CON20))
　　　))

POLITICS redefines the question to be, in essence, "What should the U.S. do to resolve the goal conflict?"

(MSEARCH
　　(SOURCE !EXPLANATION)
　　(PATH (DISABLE INSTR))
　　(PATTERN CON20))

The D-net suggests trying to see if the input event already suggests a resolution to the goal conflict.

SEARCH FAILURE . . .

The input only presents the conflict. No solution was suggested.

APPLYING QSEARCH D-NET TO:
(QSEARCH
　　(QTYP GOAL-EVENT FAIL)
　　(QBODY ((CON CON19
　　　　　　　DISABLE CON20))
　　　))

POLITICS tries again if there is another source of knowledge about solutions to conflicts. This is exactly what the counterplanning strategies (CRULES) were created for.

(MSEARCH
　　(SOURCE (APPLY: CRULES))
　　(PATH (DISABLE INSTR))
　　(PATTERN CON20))

TESTING CS-GOAL1 . . .
　　(INCONCLUSIVE)

TESTING CS-GOAL2 . . .

COUNTERPLANNING-STRATEGY
CS-GOAL2 ACTIVATED

POLITICS tries the counterplanning strategies applicable to mutual exclusion goal conflicts. First, it tries to see if the Russian goal can be blocked independently of the U.S. goal, but it does not know of any way to stop Russia from building submarines.

COUNTERPLANNING-STRATEGY
CS-RESOURCE-LIM4 ACTIVATE

$CONSTRUCT PRECONDITION

(*TECHNICAL* VAL (POS))

Next, POLITICS tries to see if the U.S. can achieve its goal before the Russians achieve theirs, and if the U.S. can preserve its goal. In order

(*ECONOMIC* VAL (POS))

SEARCHING *US* *TECHNICAL*
RESOURCES
((VAL (10)))

SEARCHING *US* *ECONOMIC*
RESOURCES
((VAL (10)))

SEARCHING *RUSSIA* *TECHNICAL*
RESOURCES
((VAL (8)))

SEARCHING *RUSSIA* *ECONOMIC*
((VAL (8)))

((< = >
($CONSTRUCT
  ACTOR (*US*)
  OBJECT (#WEAPON
          TYPE (*SUBMARINE*)
          NUMBER (*MANY*)
          TOK (WEAPON2)))
TIME ((AFTER NOW X))
MODE (*INTENTIONAL*)
TOK CON21)

THE UNITED STATES SHOULD
BUILD MORE SUBMARINES.

to construct submarines, technical
expertise and financial resources are
needed. The U.S. can outdo Russia
on both counts; therefore this strategy
succeeds.

U.S.-conservative POLITICS believes
that the U.S. can build submarines
faster than Russia and stay ahead in
military strength.

The counterplanning concludes by
extracting the means of accomplishing
the U.S. military strength goal: simply
build submarines faster than the
Russians.

The question-answering process is guided by the question type of each sentence. For instance, if a GOAL-EVENT question type is postulated, the parser is instructed to search for an event. If this, and nothing else, is found, the question type is confirmed. Both question type and the event (called QBODY) are given to a decision tree (implemented as a feature-based discrimination network) that outputs a search expression. This search expression is evaluated, and, if the search succeeds, the answer is retrieved from memory. If the search fails and if the decision tree knows what rules are applicable in inferring the types of information requested by the question type, then these inferences are applied to the QBODY.

The question-typing process and the idea of applying different search strategies to the QBODY were developed by Lehnert [1978]. The decision tree in the POLITICS system is more complex than the equivalent process in Lehnert's event-memory question-answering system because there are many types of memory that may potentially be searched (event memory, ideological goal trees, factual token memory, script body, goal-based explanation). Furthermore, the inference process can be re-activated by certain question types. We saw the third question activating script application (to understand Russia's $CONSTRUCTion of submarines) and the counterplanning process to infer the ideological U.S. response to the hypothetical Russian action.

Since question typing proceeds simultaneously with parsing and understanding of the question body, the entire process can function in a more strongly predictive fashion than would otherwise be possible. For instance, question words such as "why", "what for" and "what if" can suggest question types, which in turn generate predictions as to the content of the rest of the question. If these predictions are verified (as in the second and third questions), the question type is established. This facilitates the parser's job because the question type determines the type of structure that the parser must build (e.g., a goal specification, an event, or an action). If these predictions fail (as in the first question), the parser has to consider many more possiblities; but if it is able to build a structure incorporating the various parts of the sentence, the question type may then be established. In the first question, the parser needed to recognize the split idiom "what <PERFORMATIVE EVENT> for?", before establishing the appropriate question type.

Information about the goals of the actors is also used by the parser. In the third question the parser assumed that the submarines built by the Russians were for the same immediate purpose as the U.S. Trident submarines—increasing military strength. (We humans make the same assumption. For example, it does not occur to us that the Russian submarines might be research or rescue vehicles.) Hence, the parser is able to interpret the question "What should the U.S. do if Russia also builds submarines" as "What should the U.S. response be to the Russian's goal of increasing their military strength by building submarines", a much more concrete formulation of the task that counterplanning strategies should address.

7.3 A Detailed U.S.-liberal Interpretation

The initial phase of the U.S.-liberal interpretation of the Trident event proceeds in much the same manner as the conservative interpretation. However, after the script-based inferences and the general situational inferences are applied, U.S.-liberal POLITICS is unable to match the increase in military strength with any goal in the U.S.-liberal ideology. POLITICS assumes that all actions are done in service of a goal.

Constructing an explanation for an event, therefore, requires that the goal of the actor be inferred from his actions. Given this working definition of what constitutes an "explanation", POLITICS *assumes* that Congress wanted the U.S. to be militarily stronger and must establish *why* this is the case. After failing to match increased military strength with any U.S.-liberal ideological goal, POLITICS tries to see if any of the goals of the instantiated scripts matches an ideological goal. This process is based on the possibility that the goal of the actor of an event may be other than its functional purpose (e.g., Congress may have wanted to help financially a subcontracted company such as General Dynamics; increasing military strength would then be an incidental consequence of their action). POLITICS, however, equates the goals of the Congress with those of the U.S. as a whole. No U.S.-liberal goal directly matches possible scriptal goals of U.S.-liberal $FUND or $CONSTRUCT.

Finally, POLITICS tries to see if the functional purpose of the submarines (increase U.S. military strength) can be instrumental to another script rather than being a high-level U.S. goal. Here, POLITICS finds a match with the goal of a participant in the $ARMSRACE script. Both parties involved in an arms race have the goal of being militarily as strong as the other party. Hence, building submarines is interpreted as part of an undesirable, ongoing process (the arms race) rather than as a goal in itself. Scripts are organized hierarchically by the goals of the participants into a discrimination network. Hence, the process of accessing scripts given the goal of one of the participants is quite fast. In this manner, the search time to find a script increases at a sublinear rate with the number of scripts in the system. (The current implementation of POLITICS only contains 12 scripts, but potentially there are large numbers of scripts relevant to international politics. If we can make our discrimination network sufficiently bushy, the search time will, of course, be a logarithmic function of the total number of scripts in the system.)

7.3.1 The ideological interpretation phase

We discuss the liberal interpretation of the Trident submarine event, omitting that part of the initial segment in which the analysis proceeds in the same manner as the conservative interpretation.

Start of U.S.-liberal POLITICS Interpretation

PTYCON LOG FILE   1-Mar-78 3:36:51

PTYCON> CONNECT (TO SUBJOB) 1
[CONNECTED TO SUBJOB POL(1)]

Computer Processing	Annotation

*(INTERPRET US-LIBERAL)

INCORPORATING US-LIBERAL
IDEOLOGY GOAL TREES . . .
  (*US* TOP-GOAL: G0)
  (*RUSSIA* TOP-GOAL: G24)

INITIATING PARSER . . . DONE

INPUT STORY:
  The United States Congress
  voted to fund the Trident
  submarine project.

INTERMEDIATE RESULT INFERENCES
(APPLYING RULE-#4
  FROM POLITICS)

((ACTOR (*US*) ISTOWARD
  (*STRENGTH* TYPE (*MILITARY*)
              VAL (N)
              INC (POS))
  TOK CON13)

SEARCHING *US* GOAL TREE . . .

(G11 VIOLATED)
(G0 THREATENED)

NO GOAL MATCHED BY CON13

TRYING SCRIPTAL GOALS . . .
($FUND &FUND-CON)
SEARCHING *US* GOAL TREE . . .

($CONSTRUCT
  ((ACTOR &OBJECT
    IS (*POSS*
        VAL &ACTOR))))
SEARCHING *US* GOAL TREE . . .

NO GOAL MATCHED

SEARCHING SCRIPT-GOALS CON13

D-NET TESTS:

POLITICS incorporates the goals of
the liberal ideology.

The most important U.S. goal in the
liberal ideology is the same as the
most important Russian goal, the
preservation of peace in the world.
(G0 = G24)

The parsing and script-based inference phase is the same for both
ideological interpretations, therefore
we delete this part of the U.S.-liberal
interpretation.

The inference that increased military
strength results from building a weapons system is also made by U.S.-
liberal POLITICS.

Increased military strength is not an
important U.S. goal under the liberal
ideology, therefore no goal is
matched.

G11 is a reduction of the weapons in
the world, a subgoal of G0, world
peace.

POLITICS tries to see if the goals of
the instantiated scripts matched a
U.S. goal. Neither the funding event
nor possessing the constructed object
match U.S. goals.

Next, try to see if CON13 matches
the goal of a different script by applying the D-net that indexes scripts
according to the goals of the actors.

(ACTP CON13) NIL
(STATECHANGEP CON13) T
(MMQ (IS) !CONT) NIL
(EQP (IS) *STRENGTH*) T
(PROP (ACTOR *MEM*) *SMALL*)
NIL
(EQP (*STRENGTH* INC) POS) T

After some tests, the only script
where the goal of an actor matches
CON13 is $ARMSRACE.

$ARMSRACE

INSTANTIATING
  (&COUNTRY1 . *US*)
!EVALFORM
  (GET @*US* @ADVERSARY)
INSTANTIATING
  (&COUNTRY2 . *RUSSIA*)
INSTANTIATING
  (&BUILDUP1 . CON13)

The script roles of $ARMSRACE are
properly instantiated.

INFERENCE:
((ACTOR ORG0
    IS (*FEAR* VAL (8)
    OBJECT
      (*SPEC*
        VAL &COUNTRY2
        SOURCE *STRENGTH*)))

The arms race script states that the
two co-actors are afraid of each
other's military strength.

  TOK CON14)

((CON CON14 CAUSE CON13))

GOAL CONFLICT PREDICTION:
(&COUNTRY1 TOK *US*)
(&COUNTRY2 TOK *UNSPEC*)

The arms race situation, by definition,
involves a goal conflict.

EXPLANATION PATH FOUND:
(($FUND &FUNDEE ORG0
      &FUNDEE AF0
      &FUND-CON CON9
      &MONEY MONEY0)
ENABLE
($CONSTRUCT &ACTOR AF0
          &OBJECT WEAPON0)
RESULT
CON13)

This part of the explanation is the
same as in the conservative
interpretation.

(CON13 MATCHES
      ($ARMSRACE . &COUNTRY1))
((CON CON14 CAUSE CON13))

This is the new explanation coming
directly from the $ARMSRACE
script.

((G11 . *US*) VIOLATED)

((G0 . *US*) THREATENED)

INTERPRETATION COMPLETED,
READY TO ACCEPT QUESTIONS.

The ideological goal of world peace is still threatened. POLITICS generated an explanation for the Congressional action, but this explanation did not justify the action in terms of ideological goals.

POLITICS found an explanation for why Congress may have acted with the intention of increasing the United States' military strength: fear of some greater military strength. This explanation is encoded in the arms race script. Since the explanation does not lead to the fulfillment of a U.S. ideological goal, it is not treated as a justification for the action of the U.S. Congress. In the conservative interpretation, the explanation of why Congress wanted Trident submarines was equivalent to a justification of the congressional action. In the liberal interpretation, building submarines actually violates a U.S. goal (G11: there should be fewer weapons in the world) and threatens the most important U.S.-liberal goal (G0: world peace).

7.3.2 The question-answering phase

Let us analyze the question-answer dialog corresponding to the U.S.-liberal interpretation. The explanation above plays a key role in anwering the first two questions, and the counterplanning strategies pick up on the threatened and violated U.S. goals to answer the last question.

---

*What did the U.S. Congress do this for?

PARSING . . .
 (EVENT REL (*UNSPEC*))
STARTNP
  SUGGESTS QTYP: EVENTQ

ACTIVE REQUEST REQ-ACTOR
ACTIVE REQUEST REQ-EVENT

(#ORG TYPE (*GOVT*)
     NAME (CONGRESS)
       PART (*US*)
       REF (DEF))
MATCHES PREVIOUS REFERENT:
  ORG0

This is the same question that we asked U.S.-conservative POLITICS.

The question-typing and parsing processes proceed as before.

The requests triggered by the postulated question type help the parser narrow its focus of attention.

REQ-ACTOR FULFILLED: ORG0

UNDERSPECIFIED CD:
((ACTOR ORG0 < = > (*DO*)))

REQ-EVENT FULFILLED:
((ACTOR ORG0 < = > (*DO*)))

SUGGESTED MULTIPLE SEARCH
(EVENT REL (*SPEC*)
    ACTIONSPEC
        (ACTION PREVIOUS)
    REF CON14)

REJECTING CURRENT QTYP: EVENTQ

SUGGESTED (*GOAL* REL CON14)

SUGGESTED QTYP: GOAL-EVENT

The question type is reformulated as before because the parser contradicted the QTYP expectation that the question body would be only an event specification.

APPLYING QSEARCH D-NET TO:
    (QSEARCH (QTYP GOAL-EVENT)
             (QBODY CON15))
*(TXPN CON15)
((ACTOR ORG0 < = > (*DO*))
    REL (*SPEC*)
    TOK CON 15)

(MSEARCH
    (SOURCE !EXPLANATION)
    (PSPEC (LAST))
    (PATTERN
        (EVAL (MSEARCH
              (SOURCE !EVENTMEM
              (PSPEC (*SELF*)
              (PATTERN CON15))))

The D-net outputs a search pattern that looks at the explanation. The GOAL-EVENT question type asks for the immediate motivation of an event, not the eventual ideological justification.

MATCHED CON15
EXTRACTING (*SELF*)
($FUND &FUNDER ORG0
       &FUNDEE AF0
       &FUND-CON CON9
       &MONEY MONEY0
       TOK SCR2)

MATCHED SCR2
EXTRACTING (LAST)
((CON CON14 CAUSE CON13))

THE ANSWER IS:
    ((CON CON14 CAUSE CON13))

The explanation this time yields the reason for a military buildup extracted from the arms race script. In the conservative ideology, the military buildup itself was a justificational explanation because it was a goal in the U.S. ideological goal tree.

THE UNITED STATES CONGRESS
FEARED FALLING BEHIND IN THE
ARMS RACE.

*What might Russia do next?

PARSING . . .

SUGGESTED QTYP POS-EVENT

ACTIVE REQUEST REQ-EVENT

STARTNP
(#POLITY MEM (*RUSSIA*)
       NAME (RUSSIA)
       REF (DEF))

MATCHES PERMANENT TOKEN:
RUSSIA

(MODE (*UNCERTAIN*)) ASSERTED

((ACTOR (*RUSSIA*)
  <=> (*DO*)))

ACTIVE EXPECTATION: EVENT-SPEC

ACTIVE EXPECTATION: TIME-SPEC

ACTIVE EXPECTATION: HYPO-SPEC

(TIME ((AFTER (*LASTEVENT*
       INVOLVING *RUSSIA*))))

EXPECTATION FULFILLED:
TIME-SPEC

((ACTOR (*RUSSIA*)
  <=> (*DO*))
TIME ((AFTER (*LASTEVENT*
       INVOLVING *RUSSIA*)))
TOK CON18)

APPLYING QSEARCH D-NET TO:
(QSEARCH (QTYP POS-EVENT)
         (QBODY CON18))

(MSEARCH (SOURCE !SCRIPTS)
         (PATH (*NEXTEVENT*))
         (PATTERN

This question is different from the
one posed to U.S.-conservative POLI-
TICS. In that case, our question was
a followup of its answer to the first
question. Here, we are in a different
context. Our question should be
simple to answer because of the
active arms race script. This question
can also be answered by the more
general counterplanning process, but
POLITICS first tries to see if the
answer is part of its situational
understanding.

This is the only difference between
"might" and "will".

The parser is now sure of the QTYP
(possible events), and expects an
event description (e.g., "What will
Russia do in response to
<EVENT>"), a time specification, or
a hypothetical event situation (e.g.,
"What will Russia do if the
U.S. . . .."

This is the meaning of "next" in the
context of a POS-EVENT question.
The expectation for a time specification was satisfied.

```
                ((ACTOR (*RUSSIA*)
                  < = > (*DO*)))))

MATCHED ((ACTOR (*RUSSIA*)
              < = > (*DO*)))
IN $ARMSRACE
EXTRACTING (*NEXTEVENT*)
((ACTOR (*RUSSIA*)
  < = > &BUILDUP2))
```

POLITICS matches the event to the instantiated script mentioning Russia (i.e., $ARMSRACE), and extracts the temporally next event.

```
*(TXPN &BUILDUP2)
($CONSTRUCT
 ACTOR (*RUSSIA*)
 OBJECT (#WEAPON
           NUMBER (*MANY*)
           TOK (WEAPON1)))
MODE (*UNCERTAIN*)
TIME ((AFTER NOW X))
TOK CON19)
```

&BUILDUP2, a script role in $ARMSRACE, defaults to the construction of unspecified weapons unless otherwise determined in the input. The mode is uncertain because there is no direct causal connection between Russia finding out about the U.S. buildup and their own subsequent military buildup.

```
THE ANSWER IS:
 CON19
```

RUSSIA WILL PROBABLY BUILD
MORE WEAPONS.

*What should the U.S. do if Russia also builds nuclear submarines?

This is the same question asked of the U.S.-conservative interpretation. Once again counterplanning is required.

```
(EVENT VAL (*SPEC*))

(MODE (*INTENTIONAL*))
 ASSERTED
SUGGESTED QTYP: GOAL-EVENT

STARTNP
(#POLITY MEM (*US*)
         NAME (US)
          REF (DEF))
MATCHES PERMANENT TOKEN:
 *US*
MATCHES ACTIVE-CONTEXT TOKEN:
 *US*
```

The question analysis and parsing processes proceed in the same manner as described for the conservative question-answer dialog.

```
((ACTOR (*US*) < = > (*DO*)))

HYPOTHETICAL SCENARIO EXPECTED

STARTNP
(#POLITY MEM (*RUSSIA*)
         NAME (RUSSIA)
```

REF (DEF))
MATCHES PERMANENT TOKEN:
RUSSIA

(UNKNOWN WORD ALSO)
(SYNTACTIC EXPECTATIONS
 (V ST-TR))
(SEMANTIC EXPECTATIONS NIL)

((< =>
($CONSTRUCT
    ACTOR (*RUSSIA*)
    OBJECT (#WEAPON
            TYPE (*SUBMARINE*)
            TOK WEAPON2))
TIME ((AFTER NOW X))
TOK CON19)

Here the process diverges from the previous analysis. In the conservative interpretation no script inferences were triggered. Now, the Russian construction of submarines matches the predicted Russian construction of weapons in the $ARMSRACE script.

MATCHES ACTIVE SCRIPT:
$ARMSRACE
INSTANTIATING
(&BUILDUP2 . CON19)

SEARCHING *US* GOAL TREE . . .

The hypothetical scenario of Russia building submarines had already been foreseen by the arms race script. The question of the violated and threatened goal remains to be addressed.

CONFIRMING PREVIOUS GOAL
VIOLATIONS.
((G11 . *US*) VIOLATED)
((G0 . *US*) THREATENED)

SEARCHING *RUSSIA* GOAL TREE . . .
((G30 . *RUSSIA*) VIOLATED)
((G24 . *RUSSIA*) THREATENED)

SEARCHING GOAL CONFLICTS . . .

POLITICS finds that the U.S. and Russian scriptal armsrace goals are in conflict, as expected.

(MUTUAL-EXCLUSION
    ((*US* . CON13)
     (*RUSSIA* . CON19)

(PLAN-INTERFERENCE
    ((*RUSSIA* . G24)
     (#CONFLICT
        ACTOR1 *US*
        ACTOR2 *RUSSIA*))

The interesting point is that the existence of a goal conflict between the U.S. and Russia is itself a roadblock to plans for world peace. (Peace is defined as the absence of militarily-based conflicts.)

(PLAN-INTERFERENCE

    ((*US* . G0)
     (#CONFLICT
        ACTOR1 *US*

ACTOR2 *RUSSIA*))

APPLYING QSEARCH D-NET TO:
(QSEARCH
  (QTYP GOAL-EVENT)
  (QBODY ((CON *?*
          DISABLE
          !US-CONFLICTS)
)))

> Recall that the ideologies are U.S. centered; therefore, POLITICS tries to resolve the U.S. goal conflict only from the viewpoint of the U.S.

(MSEARCH
  (SOURCE (APPLY: CRULES))
  (PATH (DISABLE INSTR))
  (PATTERN !US-CONFLICTS))

> The counterplanning strategies, CRULES, are tried immediately.

TESTING CS-GOAL9 . . .

COUNTERPLANNING-STRATEGY
CS-GOAL9 ACTIVATED

> Strategy CS-GOAL9 (see Chapter (4)) states that if X and Y are in a goal conflict, and that conflict prevents both from achieving a higher level goal, X should negotiate with Y to end the conflict.

SUGGESTED ACTION: $NEGOTIATE
INSTANTIATING SCRIPT ROLES
INSTANTIATING
(&ACTOR1 . *US*)
INSTANTIATING
(&ACTOR1 . *RUSSIA*)
INSTANTIATING
(&DISPUTE
  (#CONFLICT ACTOR1 *US*
        ACTOR2 *RUSSIA*
        OBJECT $ARMSRACE
        TOK CONFL0)
INSTANTIATING (&GOAL1
((ACTOR CONFL0 TOWARD (*TF*))
 TOK CON20)

> The negotiation is suggested. &ACTOR1 initiates the negotiation.

> The U.S. goal in the negotiation is to end the conflict.

> *TF* means "transition final", i.e., no more conflict.

INFERENCE: (&GOAL2 . CON20)

THE ANSWER IS:
((< =>
 ($NEGOTIATE
    &ACTOR1 (*US*)
    &ACTOR2 (*RUSSIA*)
    &GOAL1 CON20
    &GOAL2 CON20
    &DISPUTE CONFL0)))

> The result of counterplanning strategy CS-GOAL-9 becomes the liberal response to the arms race scenario.

THE UNITED STATES SHOULD
NEGOTIATE WITH RUSSIA TO
STOP THE ARMS RACE.

7.4 Conclusion

We presented and discussed several examples of reasoning processes exhibited by the POLITICS system. We next turn our attention to what POLITICS cannot do. One limitation is the amount of factual and script-based knowledge actually encoded in the POLITICS system. For instance, we implemented only 12 of a possible hundred or more relevant scripts. POLITICS can handle situations where more than one script interact (e.g., $PARLIAMENTARY-PROC, $FUND and $ARMSRACE in our example), but there are many situations for which we have not written the necessary scripts. Since we are describing an experimental research effort, this limitation is of little consequence. There are other limitations of a more serious nature, such as certain types of human reasoning processes that are not modeled by POLITICS, but of potential relevance to POLITIC's domain. Another limitation is the scope of the domain itself. The next chapter discusses limits to the POLITICS paradigm and analyzes a means of conquering some of these limits.

8

The TRIAD System: Understanding General Conflict Situations

8.1 Introduction: Why We Need TRIAD

In the process of developing and modifying the POLITICS system, we developed new ideas, many of which were rejected as unworkable; gradually our process model of subjective understanding emerged. The feedback we received from our program has proven invaluable, both in situations where the program worked well, and in situations where it failed in interesting and unforeseen ways. Some interesting limitations in the program led us to develop a system in which many different types of conflict situations could be uniformly represented. In this chapter, we discuss a process model for subjective understanding of conflict situations in general.

There is reason to believe that people use the same general decision processes when resolving political, economic, judicial, domestic, and social conflicts. Similarly, understanding such problems and their solutions should entail an integrated, uniform process that depends upon the subjective viewpoint of the understander and the nature of the conflict. In chapter 3 we discussed our goal-tree model of subjective motivations, which was applied to focusing the attention of the understander on his subjective interests and concerns. In chapters 4 through 7 we discussed the decision process which, guided by the subjective perspectives of the understander, is used in counterplanning to resolve conflicts and to understand counterplans applied to conflict situations. This analysis left unspecified one significant aspect of a rather comprehensive subjective understanding model: our model does not address the nature of conflict situations in general.

We discussed the counterplanning process starting from a representation of the goal conflict or plan interference situation. The counterplanning strategies, triggered by the ideological goal trees in POLITICS, provided us with a subjectively oriented model of understanding solutions to conflict situations. However, we said little about understanding the problem itself: What constitutes a subjective understanding of the conflict situation? How is this understanding derived from the natural language account of the conflict event? POLITICS finessed these questions in their full generality by providing specific means to understand specific types of conflicts. Scripts, applied in the event-analysis phase of the understanding, determined conflicting goals or plans that interfered with each other. For instance, the $ARMSRACE script suggested the mutual-exclusion goal conflict between two primary participants, both of whom wanted to be the stronger military power. Most scripts suggest default goals for the various actors. When a script is invoked, the default goals can be checked with the goal trees of the scriptal actors in order to detect possible goal conflicts. Such is the method used by POLITICS to detect goal conflicts. Plan conflicts are detected in a similar manner. Either the main action of the script interferes with an action that another actor is performing, or the normal script used to acheive an actor's goal is blocked by another actor's actions. The interests of the understander determine, to a large extent, which goals are checked for possible conflicts, and whether the conflict is sufficiently serious to merit counterplanning. (A conflict is judged to be serious if it blocks one of the more important goals in the goal tree of an actor. Hence, whether or not to apply counterplanning to a given situation is a subjective decision.)

How do we understand conflict situations when there are no scripts to suggest possible goal conflicts or expected plan interferences? How do we represent such a conflict situation in order that our subjective understanding model make the correct inferences without making superfluous or subjectively irrelevant inferences? TRIAD is a process model of understanding general conflict situations. It uses a new system of representation applicable to social conflicts, including political and military conflicts. We discuss this new representation and the computer system which embodies our process model after we present some examples that show how the POLITICS system makes mistakes based on its lack of a general means of understanding and representing conflict situations.

8.2 Some Interesting POLITICS Errors

All the POLITICS examples we presented to illustrate subjective understanding have been cases in which the event was correctly understood. POLITICS, like any other large AI program, sometimes makes mistakes in understanding new events. Some of these errors provide insights into the intricacies, deficiencies, or contradictions in the model embodied by the program. A computer is a merciless judge of the internal consistency and completeness of a model. If all the details are not clearly spelled out, if an important item is ignored, or if the process is not well specified, the computer program invariably highlights the omission. Consider some examples of POLITICS errors:

*(INTERPRET US-LIBERAL)

INPUT: Russia massed troops on the Czech border.

Q.   What should the U.S. do about it?

A.   THE UNITED STATES SHOULD CONGRATULATE BREZHNEV.

Let us briefly discuss how U.S.-liberal POLITICS arrived at such an answer. In the event interpretation phase, the troop buildup was inferred to be a preparation for an invasion. This information comes from the $INVADE script. If the invasion takes place, the U.S.-liberal goal of preserving world peace will be violated. Therefore, POLITICS sets up an expectation that the U.S. may counterplan to preserve the goal of world peace. When POLITICS is asked for a specific counterplan, it infers that the object of the desired counterplan is to resolve the current conflict. Counterplanning strategy 4.9 (discussed in Chapter 4) suggests that the U.S. and Russia negotiate an end to the Czechoslovakian conflict because the conflict itself can block world peace, a mutual higher-level goal. However, a mediating precondition for negotiation is that both parties be willing to negotiate. POLITICS decided that this was not the case and set out to improve diplomatic relations. How can one country improve diplomatic relations with another country? The only way that POLITICS knows is for one country to support the actions of the second country. Therefore, congratulating Brezhnev was suggested as a subgoal to a U.S. counterplanning action.

There is no individual inference that leads to a logical flaw in the generation of the absurd response. The flaw lies in ignoring global considerations while pursuing local reasoning. POLITICS ignored the U.S. goal of ending the Soviet-Czech conflict while independently pursuing its subgoal of improving U.S.-Soviet relations. The reasoning process was not sufficiently integrated. The purpose of the counterplan should not have been ignored while considering plans to rectify the unfulfilled precondition. The method chosen to fulfill the precondition of improving diplomatic relations precludes the fulfillment of the purpose of negotiating with Russia to end the conflict. One cannot approve of X doing Y in order to be in a better position to ask X not to do Y. POLITICS needs a better understanding of the conflict situation and relations between the participants. This understanding must be used to guide the application of the counterplanning strategies to the requirements of the conflict situation. It was not POLITICS' choice of the negotiation strategy that caused the problem; it was the way in which this strategy was applied to the particular conflict situation that was in error.

Consider another error made by U.S.-liberal POLITICS in answering questions about the previous event. In order to see how U.S.-liberal POLITICS would have answered questions about the Czech problem, we artificially blocked the line of reasoning resulting in the suggestion to congratulate Brezhnev. (This was easily done by temporarily deleting the negotiation rule from the set of counterplanning strategies.)

       *(INTERPRET US-LIBERAL)

INPUT: Russia massed troops on the Czech border.

Q: What should the U.S. do?

A: THE US SHOULD DENOUNCE THE RUSSIAN INVASION IN THE UN.

Q: What if this fails to stop Russia?

A: THE US SHOULD PERSUADE CZECHOSLOVAKIA TO MOVE ITS ARMED FORCES AWAY FROM CZECHOSLOVAKIA.

The first question was properly answered by the application of counterplanning strategy 4.3, threatening a higher level goal to end a lower level goal conflict. The liberal ideology believes that the Russian goal of maintaining a favorable world image is more important to Russia than its goal of directly influencing smaller countries.

The answer to the second question is more interesting. As it reads, this answer appears to be totally wrong. Would a human suggest, or even think about suggesting, such a course of action? We have to be careful in considering exactly what is wrong with this response. Suppose we paraphrase the answer to say "Czechoslovakia should surrender", or "The Czech army should be ordered not to fight." In the 1968 Russian occupation of Czechoslovakia, the Czech army was indeed ordered not to fight in order to avoid bloodshed for what was judged to be a lost cause. It is quite conceivable that this alternative may be judged to be the best option by a liberal or a pacifist.

We could, without substantial effort, modify the English generator used by POLITICS to enable it to generate the phrase "ordered not to fight" from the concept of an army told to avoid contact with the enemy. This, however, would be a cosmetic solution to a more serious internal problem. In general, a country being invaded by foreign armies resists the invasion, no matter how hopeless the resistance might seem. History is full of examples of resistance to invading armies; it is a rare exception for a country to surrender without a fight. Similarly, individual persons and institutions fight for self-preservation regardless of whether or not their chances for success seem promising. POLITICS does not know anything about the Czech situation that may differentiate it from any other case of a threatened self-preservation goal. POLITICS used the plan interference strategy of blocking a mediating precondition (discussed in Chapter 6) to try to stop the Czech-Soviet conflict. In order to fight a battle, both armies have to be in physical proximity to each other. The counterplanning strategy suggested that the U.S. try to block this precondition. Hence, POLITICS arrived at the answer of persuading Czechoslovakia to move its forces away.

Some general rules about conflict situations are necessary for a more intelligent application of the counterplanning strategies. Here, we need rules to the effect that, if attacked, a person or country will defend itself, and that self-preservation is always attempted, regardless of whether or not a workable plan is found. Such rules are easy to state in English, but, in order to integrate them into an understanding system, we need a uniform representation of conflict situations.

Let us see how a better understanding of the conflict situation can help our model of subjective understanding. POLITICS makes, essentially, four kinds of errors typical to any AI system that implements a process model of a theory of understanding. We classify the errors into the following four categories:

1. TECHNICAL ERRORS   Errors in the implementation of the model of understanding.

2. INCONSISTENCY   Parts of the process model embodied in the computer programs are mutually inconsistent.

3. INCOMPLETENESS   Some knowledge (fact, rule, or general process) is not adequately specified in the model.

4. LACK OF INTEGRATION   The component parts of the model are well specified, but the manner in which these components should interact has not been specified.

The first type of error is theoretically uninteresting, although it accounts for the majority of all the programming "bugs". This category includes all the programming "kludges" and instances in which the computer program does not accurately reflect the process model in the mind of the programmer. These errors are invariably the easiest to fix.

The other three classes of errors point out problems in the model, rather than its realization in computer-readable code. In Chapter 3 we discussed the possibility of encoding ideologies as a set of behavioral rules. Later, we decided that this approach was not feasible, and we developed the goal-tree representation for ideologies. The reason for the infeasibility was that we needed mutually incompatible rules to account for different responses to different conflict situations, and any reasonably small set of rules would have been terribly incomplete. Furthermore, we ran into severe difficulties when we had to integrate the specific information encoded in the various rules in order to formulate a coherent model. The goal trees were not subject to these limitations; therefore, they were chosen as the better model for the representation of political ideologies.

On a larger scope, our model of subjective understanding runs into some incompleteness and lack-of-integration problems. The errors caused by POLITICS' lack of understanding of conflict situations suggest that it should have knowledge about conflicts in general, and rules about how this knowledge is to be integrated with the goal trees and the counterplanning strategies as part of the overall subjective understanding process. The first POLITICS error we discussed is the lack-of-integration problem. The preconditions for the counterplanning action were pursued without consideration for their effect upon the conflict situation. Since there is no uniform representation of the conflict situation, the various strategies cannot communicate to each other their effects upon the conflict and upon relations between the parties involved.

The second POLITICS error is primarily one of omission. POLITICS does not have any general knowledge about conflict situations that would suggest the appropriateness of counterplanning strategies as a function of the means invoked to cause the conflict. For instance, it may have been reasonable for Czechoslovakia to appeal for help to any country able to influence Russia to stop the invasion. This is not something we necessarily wish to encode as a counterplanning strategy dependent upon the goals of the actor and the conflict situation. Appealing for help is appropriate to most conflict siutations. What form the appeal takes and who is the recipient of the appeal are factors which depend upon the relations between the disputing parties, the type of conflict situation, the relation between the actor and the recipient of the appeal, and the subjective predisposition of the actor. In the next section we investigate some general principles about conflict situations in order to rectify the omissions in our subjective understanding model.

8.3 The Basic Social Acts

Consider three conflict situations in completely different scenarios.

> EVENT 8.1   Johnny complained to mother that brother Billy took his candy.

> EVENT 8.2   Ralph Nader brought suit against General Motors, but the matter was settled out of court.

> EVENT 8.3:   Ethiopia asked the Soviet Union for help in thwarting the Somali invasion of the Ogaden desert.

What do all of these situations have in common? There is a goal conflict between the two actors in each event. This is what POLITICS recognizes as common to all three situations. However, these three situations share a sizable amount of general information. When we understand event 8.1, the following facts becomes evident: Billy must have invoked some means to take the candy bar from Johnny (e.g., superior strength or a trick-option plan such as stealing the candy). As a result of Billy's action, a dispute over possession of the candy bar exists between Johnny and Billy. Johnny appealed to his mother in order that she do something to make Billy return the candy bar to Johnny. Johnny's mother may tell Billy to return the candy. If Billy refuses to cooperate, she may enforce her order with the threat of punishment. Billy may claim that the candy rightfully belongs to him. The conflict situation between Johnny and Billy is still in effect. Some of these statements must be true about the conflict situation; others are merely plausible inferences which may or may not be made when understanding event 8.1.

Consider the second event. Ralph Nader and General Motors must be involved in some dispute. Ralph Nader appealed to a judicial court to make a ruling on the dispute. We may have expected the court to make its ruling, but Nader and GM invoked negotiation as a means to resolve the conflict. The "but" in event 8.2 tells the understander that one of his expectations may have just been negated. This expectation is the pending court ruling, as the negotiation eliminates the need for further court actions. The negotiation was a successful means in resolving the conflict. The conflict situation no longer exists.

Events 8.1 and 8.2 have some conflict-resolution acts in common. In both cases there was a petition to a higher authority and an expectation that the higher authority might authorize a solution to the conflict; in both cases one party invoked the means to directly resolve the conflict.

Let us see if the third event can be viewed from a similar perspective. Somalia invaded Ethiopia, either creating or perpetuating a dispute between the two countries. Ethiopia petitioned the Soviet Union for help. If the Soviets decide to support Ethiopia, they may pressure Somalia to give up its claim on the Ogaden; they may invoke force either directly or by means of an agent (e.g., Cuba); or, if they have sufficient political authority over Somalia, the Soviet Union may simply order Somalia to stop the invasion. If the Soviets intervene in favor of Ethiopia, Somalia may petition other countries for help, or ask the United Nations to call a halt to the conflict. Once again, the event is represented by a PETITION to an actor in a position of higher power who is expected to AUTH in response. The DISPUTing actors are also INVOKing direct means to resolve the conflict.

Let us list the conflict-resolution acts that appear in the three events:

1. DISPUTE—   A conflict situation is initiated, escalated or terminated between two actors.

2. PETITION—   One actor PETITIONs a higher authority for a resolution to a DISPUTE.

3. AUTHORIZE—   A higher authority decrees a resolution binding over one or more actors. AUTHORIZATIONS are often in response to a previous PETITION, which in turn may have been initiated by a current DISPUTE.

4. ORDER—   A higher authority can ORDER that one of its AUTHORIZA-TIONS be enforced. For instance, a jury's decision that person X should be sentenced to jail is an AUTHORIZATION, but the enforcement of this decision by the appropriate magistrate is an ORDER.

5. INVOKE—   An actor involved in a DISPUTE can INVOKE a direct means to settle the dispute. The means can be any counterplanning strategy, such as negotiation, threats to higher-level goals, and trick options.

6. RESOLVE—   If an INVOKED means results in a solution to the DISPUTE, we have directly RESOLVED the DISPUTE. RESOLVE, like any of other conflict-resolution acts, needs to be interpreted from a subjective perspective. For instance, in event 8.1 Billy may have considered the dispute over the candy bar RESOLVED once he took it, but Johnny certainly did not consider the matter RESOLVED.

7. PRESSURE— If two actors are involved in a DISPUTE, a third actor can
PRESSURE either one towards a particular outcome of
the DISPUTE. Pressure is a netural act, in the sense that it
implies no fixed outcome and no authority relation between
the actor and the recipient.

We call the seven acts listed above the *basic social acts*. The idea of a set
of basic social acts was conceived by Schank, in response to the difficulties encountered in representing social interactions using only the
primitive acts of conceptual dependency (or any other existing representational system). The social acts were later developed and refined jointly
by Schank and Carbonell [1979] as the building blocks of a representation
and inference system for understanding various types of human conflicts.
We define each social act as a knowledge structure with slots that indicate
the actor, object, recipient, and other relevant conceptual cases. Each
basic social act groups a set of inferences that are likely to be true and
relevant to the conflict situation. In this respect, the social acts are akin
to the primitive acts of *conceptual dependency* (Schank [1972, 1975]), but
they form a higher level of description. The basic social acts represent
social interactions that are decomposable into primitive physical acts, but
an understander would almost never have the need to decompose them
in such a manner.

Consider some of the basic acts and the inferences that they group
in some greater detail. The act AUTHORIZE (abbreviated as "AUTH")
requires an actor, a recipient, and an object. The actor is the person or
institution authorizing a change of state that directly affects the recipient.
We present a diagram for AUTH and its respective conceptual case
structure:

Figure 8.1.   The basic social act: AUTHORIZE

```
                                                          A
                    o              r  |--< A'    I        ∧
        A <=> AUTH <--- OBJECT <---|            <---      ||
                                      |--> Z               ∨
                                                         ORDER
```

The diagram in figure 8.1 is read as follows: A is the authority which can
AUTHorize the OBJECT to become true. The OBJECT is a statement
about the state of the world, affecting the recipient Z, that becomes true
by virtue of it being AUTHed. Usually an AUTH signifies a change from
the previous state of the world. The recipient can be a specific person,
two parties involved in a dispute, or an entire nation (e.g., if A is a
government). A' is the "real" authority on whose behalf A AUTHorizes

the object. For instance, a judge often AUTHorizes on behalf of the court; a business executive AUTHorizes on behalf of his company. The theory behind a representative democracy is that the elected officials authorize on behalf of the majority of the population. In all these cases, A acts as agent of the real authority A'. "I" signifies instrumentality. An AUTH may be carried out, or enforced, by means of an ORDER forcing the recipient to comply.

In order to use the basic social acts as a representation of conflict situations, we need to consider the subjective point of view of the understander and the participants in the conflict. Let us see how the act AUTH is affected by subjective considerations. The actor of an AUTH needs to be in an authority relation over the recipient in matters relevant to the object being authorized. A judge can authorize that a doctor pay a malpractice compensation; but, if the judge is seriously ill, the doctor can authorize that the judge remain in the hospital until his condition improves. If the object of the authorization is a judicial matter, the judge has authority over the doctor. In a medical matter, it is the doctor who may exercise authority over the judge. From the point of view of a small child, the parent is the primary authority in all matters. But this is no longer the case as the child grows up and recognizes other authorities. A religious Catholic views the local priest, the church, and the Pope as authorities in many different matters regarding his personal life, but an atheist refuses to accept any church-related authority over his personal life. Therefore, the appropriateness of an AUTHorization and its acceptance by the recipient are subjective matters, depending upon the personal beliefs and social status of the actors involved. Who can AUTH over whom depends upon the nature of the object being authorized, the social relation between the actor and recipient, the acceptance of the actor as an authority by the recipient, and the degree to which the authority can enforce its AUTH by means of an effective ORDER.

The basic social acts fill a representational niche that cannot be finessed by the use of other existing systems for representing knowledge. We can best illustrate the necessity of the act AUTH to represent some functions in our society with an example from Schank (Schank and Carbonell [1979])

EVENT 8.4   The policeman gave the speeder a ticket.

What should the representation of the meaning of event 8.4 look like if we are to model human understanding of the event? At first sight this problem appears to be rather straightforward. Possession of a ticket was transferred from a policeman to a person who was driving a car too fast.

The primitive act ATRANS represents the transfer of possession of an object between two people. Therefore, we could represent event 8.4 as the policeman ATRANSing a ticket to a person who was speeding. However, this representation totally misses the point. The transfer of possession of a slip of paper is irrelevant to the real import of a policeman ticketing a person. It is the legal action brought against the driver (e.g., he may have to pay a fine) which is of interest to the speeder and to a person reading the event. An ATRANS, or any similar representation, neither encodes this information, nor does it provide any means of inferring it. If we represent the ticketing action as an AUTH, we signify the fact than an authority over traffic regulations decreed that the driver must comply with the legal process stemming from his speeding violation. Furthermore, we can infer that if he refuses, the driver may be ORDERed to pay the fine, and that he may PETITION to a higher authority to reverse the present AUTH (e.g., he could ask, or bribe, a judge to dismiss the case). Inference rules enabling us to deduce the possible subsequent ORDER and PETITION are grouped under the act AUTH; therefore, representing 8.4 as an AUTH tells the understander what inferences are likely to be relevant to the situation. Here is the AUTH representation of event 8.4:

Figure 8.2.   Representation of event 8.4 as an AUTH

```
                           driver              driver
                             ∧                   ∧                  |-->driver
  policeman <=> AUTH    o    ||        or        ||         r       
                     <---     ∨                   ∨      <-__-|
                           $TRIAL              ATRANS          |--<govt.
                     (&DEFANDENT  driver)        ↑o
                     (&CHARGE     speeding)     money
                                                  ↑
                                        d |------------| r
                                          |           |
                                          ∧           ∨
                                        driver      govt.
```

Figure 8.2 represents the meaning of event 8.4 in terms of its social import. The ticket is a written manifestation of the AUTH. We could say that the ATRANS of the ticket to the driver is an instrument of an MTRANS notifying the driver that the AUTH has taken place, but this is of no direct relevance to the driver, the policeman, or the reader of event 8.4. The object of the AUTH is that the driver must either do the $TRIAL script in the role of a &DEFENDANT, or he must pay a fine. This is an integral part of the representation, although no trial or fine is mentioned in the event. An understander focuses his attention on the social implications of the AUTH rather than what happens to the piece of paper on which the ticket is written.

8.4 Inference Rules Suggested by the Social Acts

Each social act groups a set of inference rules relevant to situations represented by the social act. Consider the inference rules indexed by AUTH. We classify the inference rules into *antecedent* and *consequent* rules (no connection with the PLANNER use of the words "antecedent" and "consequent"). Antecedent rules infer relevant aspects of the conflict situation that should have been true before the social act took place. Consequent rules infer the consequences of the social act most relevant to the conflict. All the social acts and their respective inference rules are discussed at length in Schank and Carbonell [1979]; here we discuss the inference rules for the social act AUTH. Each inference rule consists of an inferred state plus an additional "IF <test> THEN <action>" statement. Usually, the IF clause looks for confirmation that the inferred state is true. Recall figure 8.1, the diagram of the conceptual cases of AUTH:

```
                                                          A
                    o              r  |--< A'  I          ∧
     A <=> AUTH <--- OBJECT <---|             <---        ‖
                                   |--> Z                 ∨
                                                        ORDER
```

Antecedent inference rules:

1. STATE   Z may have PETITIONed A' to AUTHorize over a particular claim
   before the AUTH.

   IF   this is the case,

   THEN   the OBJECT of the AUTH is a recognition or denial of Z's claim.

2.   IF   the OBJECT is a goal in Z's goal tree,

   THEN   the object of Z's previous PETITION is the same as the OBJECT of
   the AUTH.

3. STATE   Z and others may have been involved in a DISPUTE before Z
   PETITIONED A.

   IF   this is the case,

   THEN   the OBJECT of the AUTH may be a resolution of the DISPUTE.

4.   IF   the OBJECT of the AUTH is a resolution to a DISPUTE, and Z or
   the other disputing party previously INVOKEd a means to
   RESOLVE their DISPUTE,

   THEN   the means was unsuccessful.

Consequent inference rules:

5.   IF   Z does not accept the OBJECT of the AUTH,

   THEN   A may ORDER that Z carry out the necessary actions to bring the OBJECT about.

6.   IF   the OBJECT is a goal in Z's goal tree, and it resolves the DISPUTE,

   THEN   the other party in the DISPUTE may PETITION to a higher authority to reverse the OBJECT.

REFINEMENT   IF   the other party does not accept A' as an authority,

      THEN   the other party may INVOKE some means to RESOLVE the DISPUTE directly with Z, and may possibly initiate a DISPUTE with A.

7.   IF   the OBJECT is an important goal of the other party involved in the DISPUTE,

   THEN   the converse of rule 6 applies.

8.   IF   the OBJECT is a compromise between GOAL(Z) and GOAL(other party),

   THEN   both parties may terminate their DISPUTE.

The usefulness of the basic social acts for understanding conflict situations is largely determined by the inferences they group. The meaning of AUTH, for instance, includes the set of inferences listed above. The social acts form a very convenient unit of representation for conflict situations because they group inferences relevant to the interactions between the conflicting parties and ignore other, less important aspects of the situation. For instance, AUTH ignores information pertaining to the manner in which the OBJECT of the AUTH was communicated to the recipient, and the possible effects of the AUTH on other parties not involved in the dispute. The former is considered to be irrelevant detail, and the latter information, while of potential importance, transcends the understanding of a particular conflict situation.

We present two other basic social acts, PETITION and INVOKE, and the inference rules they group that are relevant to formulating an understanding of events 8.1 and 8.2.

Figure 8.3. The basic social act: PETITION

```
                 o             r  |--> A
       X <=> PETITION <--- OBJECT <---|
                                      |--< X'
```

The conceptual cases of PETITION are read as follows: X is the actor who PETITIONs the authority A for the OBJECT. X can PETITION on behalf of himself (X = X'), or X can PETITION on behalf of someone else (X is an agent of X'; for instance, X may be a lawyer initiating a lawsuit on behalf of his client X'). The OBJECT of the PETITION is a desired change in the state of the world that X wants A to AUTHorize. Often the OBJECT is a solution to a conflict situation involving X' and others. We list the most relevant inference rules grouped under PETITION.

Antecedent inference rules:

9. STATE   There was probably a DISPUTE between X' and some other party before the PETITION.

   IF   this is the case,

   THEN   The OBJECT is fulfilling X's goal in the dispute.

10.   IF   either X or the other party in the DISPUTE INVOKEd a means to RESOLVE the DISPUTE,

   THEN   the means failed to achieve an acceptable solution from X's point of view.

11.   IF   X earlier PETITIONed B, a lower authority than A,

   THEN   B must have AUTHorized against X's OBJECT. X is now PETITIONing to a higher authority to reverse the result of the previous AUTH.

Consequent inference rules:

12. STATE   A will probably AUTH a solution to the DISPUTE between X' and Y, the other party involved in the DISPUTE.

13. STATE   Y may also PETITION A, or a higher authority than A, with his own goal, in the DISPUTE as the OBJECT of his PETITION.

14.   IF   Y believes that the AUTH will be contrary to his own goals,

   THEN   Y may INVOKE some overpower, trick option, or negotiation strategy before A can AUTH.

The application of these inference rules depends upon the social acts that have taken place and upon a subjective interpretation of the goals of the actors involved. For instance, rule 10 tells us something about the goals that one of the disputing parties is actively pursuing. Knowing what an actor considers a satisfactory solution to a conflict determines which counterplanning strategies are applicable, as well as suggesting future PETITIONs to other authorities. Therefore, the inference rules associated with the social acts are useful in subjectively focusing the counterplanning process. On some occasions, knowledge about the goals and beliefs of the actors is necessary in order to apply the social act inference rules. Rule 14 requires that the understander know about an actor's goals and beliefs in order to determine whether he will await an AUTH to resolve the DISPUTE or whether he will take direct action on his own part. We represent the social act of taking direct action to resolve a dispute as follows:

Figure 8.4.   The basic social act: INVOKE

```
               o           s          r  |--< X'
   X <=> INVOKE <--- MEANS <--- SOLX <---|
                                         |--> Y
```

The social act INVOKE reads as follows: An actor X INVOKEs a means to RESOLVE an existing DISPUTE. The MEANS is a counterplanning strategy whose purpose is to achieve SOLX, X's desired solution of the DISPUTE. Y is the other party involved in the dispute, that is, the target of the counterplanning strategy INVOKEd. X' is the party on whose behalf the MEANS was INVOKEd. Often X = X'; otherwise X is an agent of X', as illustrated by the following event:

EVENT 8.5   The Israeli negotiators proposed a new peace treaty with Egypt.

The negotiators are the actors of the INVOKE, but they are negotiating on behalf of the state of Israel. Egypt is the other party involved in the DISPUTE. SOLX contains the terms of the Israeli proposal. The MEANS INVOKEd is a goal-compromise strategy, discussed in Chapter 4.

Here is a list of the most relevant inference rules grouped under the act INVOKE:

Antecedent inference rules:

15.   STATE   X' and Y were probably involved in a DISPUTE that caused the INVOKE.

16.   STATE   SOLX is either a goal of X' or a goal compromise that X' will accept.

17.   IF   X PETITIONed an authority after the DISPUTE,

   THEN   the authority either refused to AUTH or AUTHed against X's goal.

18.   STATE   Y may have either PETITIONed for an OBJECT that violates the goals of X', or Y may have INVOKEd a MEANS that also violates one of X''s goals.

Consequent inference rules:

19.   IF   SOLX does not accord with Y's goals,

   THEN   Y may either INVOKE his own MEANS, or PETITION an authority.

20.   IF   Y accepts SOLX,

   THEN   X' and Y will probably RESOLVE their DISPUTE.

21.   IF   the MEANS requires the use of force,

   THEN   the stronger of X' and Y will probably RESOLVE the DISPUTE by fulfilling its own goal. The weaker party may reject the resolution and PETITION to an authority.

22.   IF   the means is compromise, and the INVOKE results in a RESOLVE,

   THEN   the DISPUTE will no longer exist from the perspective of either party.

Each of the other basic social acts groups a set of inferences similar in nature to the ones listed for AUTH, PETITION and INVOKE. Let us see how we can represent events 8.1 and 8.2 in terms of the social acts, and how these representations are enriched by the above sets of inferences. We reiterate event 8.1:

EVENT 8.1   Johnny complained to his mother that brother Billy took his candy.

Johnny's complaint is a PETITION to his mother with the intent that she AUTHorize in his favor. Event 8.1 does not explicitly state that Johnny is asking his mother to intervene on his behalf by using her greater social authority over the two siblings. We all know that Johnny probably wants his candy back, however, and PETITIONing mother is the most reasonable way to interpret the intentions motivating Johnny's complaint. We represent this PETITION as follows:

```
                            Candy
                        o    ∧     r  |--> Mother
      Johnny <=> PETITION <--- | | | <---|
                             V          |--< Johnny
                        POSS (Johnny)
```

In a different context, we could have interpreted the verb "complained" to mean something other than a PETITION. Consider the following examples:

EVENT 8.6   John complained to his wife that his boss treats him very badly.

EVENT 8.7   The general complained to his aide that his boots were not polished.

In event 8.6 John is airing a complaint without any specific social act suggested. In event 8.7, the general is ORDERing his aide to polish his boots. We may infer that the order is to enforce a previous AUTH stating that boots should always be polished. Therefore, in order to establish the meaning of "complained" in terms of the basic social acts, we must infer the motives of the actors involved in the event. These motives are inferred from the understander's perception of the social relationship between the actors and his beliefs about the goals they are likely to pursue in certain social circumstances.

A parent-child relationship is characterized by the latter's PETITIONing the former to fulfill his needs, and by the parent's AUTHing, often in response to the child's PETITIONs. The somewhat more rigid relationship between a general and his staff aides can be characterized in the same way; the general AUTHs and the staff aides PETITION. A husband-wife relationship is a more balanced relationship (probably a more complex one as well) in terms of who can AUTH and who can PETITION. Therefore, in event 8.6, we do not infer that John is AUTHing or PETITIONing. There is a strong subjective component in the understander's beliefs about the relationships. Consider, for instance, event 8.6 with a slight modification:

EVENT 8.8   Mary complained to her husband that her boss treats her very badly.

In a very informal experiment, events 8.6 and 8.8 were presented to two small sets of people. Everyone concurred in their interpretation of event 8.6, but this was not the case for event 8.8. The interpretations of 8.8 included: "Mary wants her husband to do something about her boss's behavior" (a PETITION); "Mary's boss may be making passes at her"; "Mary may be trying to gain her husband's approval to quit her job" (another PETITION); and "Mary is letting off steam." What can we make of these different (if somewhat fanciful) interpretations? The understander's perceptions of the husband-wife relationship appears to differ in each interpretation. The people who view the husband as the more dominant figure in the relationship (i.e., he who AUTHs), interpret 8.6 as a PETITION by the wife. Other people do not interpret the complaint as a PETITION. Therefore, the understander's perception of the husband-wife relationship affects his understanding of events such as 8.8.

Let us return to the representation of event 8.1. What else do we know about this event? Inference rule 9 tells us that there was probably a DISPUTE that led to the PETITION. Analyzing event 8.1, we see that the DISPUTE was between Johnny and Billy over who should have the candy. Rule 11 states that there may have been an earlier INVOKE of some MEANS to resolve the conflict on Billy's part. Indeed, the focus of Johnny's complaint "Billy took the candy" refers to Billy's INVOKing either force or a trick option. Thus, we conclude that Johnny and Billy disputed over possession of the candy, and Billy INVOKEd force or a trick option before Johnny PETITIONed his mother. These two antecdent rules help us analyze the conflict situation by telling us what has probably transpired in situations in which one actor PETITIONs another.

We can also apply the consequent rules grouped under PETITION. Rule 12 states that the mother will probably decide who should have the candy (or compromise by splitting it). This is a reasonable expectation, especially if event 8.1 is the first sentence in a longer story where we expect the mother to react to the PETITION. Rules 13 and 14 tell us respectively to expect possible PETITIONs to higher authorities or further INVOKEs. We can rule out the former possibility because a parent is usually the highest source of appeal for a small child. These inferences accord with our initial discussion of event 8.1, and what we considered a reasonable understanding of the conflict situation. Rather than diagramming all the social acts, inferred and expected, we use a shorthand notation called *authority triangles*. We diagram the PETITION in event 8.1 and all the relevant inferences as follows: (Dotted lines signify expected social acts; solid lines denote acts that have already taken place, stated or inferred. Crossed-out lines indicate violated expectations.)

Figure 8.5.   Triangle representation of event 8.1: "Johnny
complained to his mother that brother Billy took his
candy."

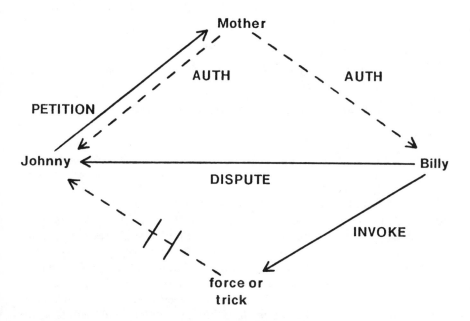

Graphically, the base of a triangle denotes a DISPUTE between the two
actors at each end; the longer the base, the more serious the DISPUTE.
The apex of the triangle is the authority. The sides of the triangle are
PETITIONs and AUTHs. Hence, the upper triangle represents the res-
olution of DISPUTEs via PETITIONs and AUTHs (backed by ORDERs
if necessary). The lower triangle represents direct resolution methods by
INVOKing means (the bottom point of the lower triangle) that may directly
RESOLVE the DISPUTE without recourse to an authority.

We measure the subjective point of view of the DISPUTE by the
relative lengths of the DISPUTE base from the perpendicular. If one party
aggravates the DISPUTE, his half of the base lengthens; if he lessens the
DISPUTE his half of the base contracts. For instance, when Japan attacked
Pearl Harbor, the hostilities were unilateral. Japan's half of the base in
its DISPUTE triangle with the U.S. lengthened. This situation, however,
was temporary; the U.S. declared war on Japan shortly thereafter, length-
ening its half of the base in turn. The notion of equalization of base
lengths introduces a general inference rule about triangles, called the
balance principle.

Rule 23   BALANCE PRINCIPLE
Social act triangles have a tendency to become (and remain) isosceles. That is:

(i)   IF   one actor aggravates the DISPUTE (lengthens his half of the base),

THEN   the other actor will probably react in kind.

(ii)   IF   an actor ameliorates the DISPUTE (shortens his half of the base),

THEN   the other actor will probably react in kind.

REFINEMENT IF   the second actor does not reciprocate,

THEN   the first actor will probably retract his conciliatory overture, and the previous DISPUTE situation will be re-established.

Consider a simple instance of rule 23(ii). Egypt initiated peace overtures toward Israel, thus unbalancing its triangle with Israel by making Egypt's base shorter. Israel reacted to Egypt's peace initiative by negotiating and improving relations with Egypt. This reciprocal action on the part of Israel reduced its half of the base accordingly. If Israel had not responded to Egypt's peace initiative, the dispute would have returned to its former state. Egypt would have withdrawn its peace efforts, and it might have taken a more belligerent attitude. In either case, the triangle will tend to balance itself with time.

We return to the social act representations of our original events. The same inference rules we applied to interpret event 8.1 are useful in understanding event 8.2; indeed, they apply to most conflict situations in our society. Let us see how we can use the basic social acts to understand the conflict situation in event 8.2, reiterated below:

EVENT 8.2   Ralph Nader brought suit against General Motors, but the matter was settled out of court.

Bringing a civil suit in a court of law is a PETITION to a judge. Before reading the rest of the event, let us see what we can infer from this PETITION. Rule 9 tells us that there must have been a DISPUTE between Nader and GM. If we know more about Nader's goals, then we can infer the nature of the DISPUTE and the type of solution he is willing to accept. Hence, knowing Nader's goal tree complements the understanding derived from the fact that he initiated the social act PETITION. Rule 12 states that the court of law will probably AUTH in response to the PETITION. Rule 13 suggests that GM may PETITION a higher authority (e.g., appeal to a higher court), if the AUTH violates its goals. Rule 14 suggests that GM may INVOKE some MEANS to prevent the AUTH, if it believes the AUTH will be against its best interests.

Reading the rest of the event, we see the "but," which signifies that an inferred event will not take place. (This is the "but test" used to distinguish between given facts and inferences, described in Schank [1975].) The strongest expectation we had was for an AUTH by the court that Nader PETITIONed. When we read that the "matter was settled out of court", we realize that someone INVOKEd direct negotiation and RESOLVEd the DISPUTE. This fulfills the expectation generated by rule 14, suggesting that GM INVOKED the goal-compromise strategy fearing an unfavorable AUTH. Since the MEANS of the INVOKE is not force or a trick option, rule 22 tells us that both sides will accept the RESOLVE, thus ending the DISPUTE. Rule 18 states that if an INVOKE follows a PETITION initiated by the opposing party, the INVOKE was motivated by the belief that the expected AUTH would violate one's goals. This strengthens the previous inference that GM INVOKED negotiations to prevent the AUTH by the court of law.

Event 8.2 suggests that an understander processes information by making most of the relevant inferences as the new information is read in. The "but", negating our expectation for an AUTH, confirms our contention that a reader must have understood the first part of the sentence as a PETITION and inferred the probable AUTH before the second part of the sentence was processed. The word "matter" is, by itself, multiply ambiguous, but in the context of the social act suggested by the first part of the sentence, its meaning clearly refers to the object of the DISPUTE between Nader and GM. This example is further evidence for the integrated nature of the understanding process. Inferences from the social act PETITION, analyzed from information in the first part of a sentence, helped the interpretation (including the parsing) of the second part of the sentence.

We diagram the social act representation of event 8.2 in triangle notation. As before, dotted lines denote expected acts; crossed out lines denote violated expectations.

There is a striking similarity between the triangle diagrams for events 8.1 and 8.2. The same social acts and the same inference rules apply to interpret both conflict situations. Although disputes between siblings and disputes between corporations and consumer groups differ in most specific details, the general conflict resolution methods and the ways of interacting with higher social powers transcend the specific circumstances of any single context, and apply equally well to both conflict situations. This is the type of generality that we strove to attain: a single represen-

Figure 8.6.   Triangle representation of event 8.2

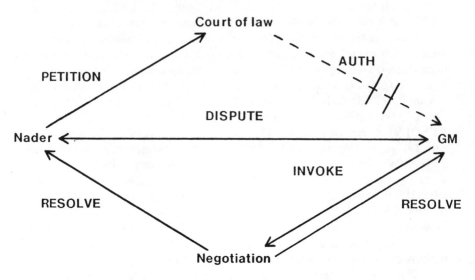

tation system which groups inferences relevant to all human conflict situations.

Conflicts between nations can also be represented by the basic social acts. Recall event 8.3:

> EVENT 8.3   Ethiopia asked the Soviet Union for help in thwarting the Somali invasion of the Ogaden desert.

Ethiopia PETITIONed the Soviet Union as a result of its DISPUTE with Somalia. Somalia INVOKed military force to RESOLVE the DISPUTE, but Ethiopia does not accept this resolution. As a result of the PETITION, Russia may AUTH either to help Ethiopia, stop the conflict, or follow some other course of action, depending upon its goals and the amount of power it is able to wield over Somalia and Ethiopia. Once again, the same social acts and inference rules apply, and their application is modulated by the understander's beliefs about the goals and relative political power of the actors in the event.

8.5 TRIAD: A Computer Program That Understands Social Acts

We are currently in the process of implementing and refining our process model of general conflict situations. TRIAD (TRIangle Applying Device) is a set of computer programs that analyzes newspaper headlines of conflict situations into the social acts representation and applies the inference rules indexed by each basic act. The TRIAD parser integrates linguistic information with the conceptual memory structures that it builds and the social-act inference process. TRIAD has an English generator to output the results of its inference process. Consider the following headline from an article in the *New York Times*:

EVENT 8.9   Catawba Indian land claims supported.

What does this headline mean in terms of the social acts? The land claim is a PETITION by the Catawba Indians. The federal govenment is the authority in charge of Indian affairs; therefore, it is likely that they are the recipients of the PETITION. "Supported", in this context, means that a govenment agency (probably a federal court) AUTHed in favor of the Indian PETITION. The reason for the Indian land claim must have been a prior DISPUTE with some other party over the ownership of the land. The other party, not happy with its goal violated by the AUTH, may PETITION a higher court, or possibly may INVOKE some means directly against the Indians. A later section discusses the language interpretation process in greater detail.

TRIAD makes the inferences discussed above from the PETITION and AUTH directly communicated in event 8.9. We present the TRIAD computer run for this event, and, subsequently, we discuss the analysis processes that interpret English into social act representation.

Start of TRIAD Interpretation and Inference Process

PTYCON LOG FILE   26-May-78 15:46:08

PTYCON> CONNECT (TO SUBJOB) TRIAD
[CONNECTED TO SUBJOB TRIAD (1)]

Yale Computer Science—Research DECsystem20,
TOPS-20 Monitor 3(1371)
TRIFNS-PARFNS-PARDIC-PARREQ-(CATAWBA.REP)-
TRIANGLE analyzer loaded.
TRIANGLE inference loaded.

*(PARSER)

INPUT SENTENCE: Catawba Indian land claims supported.

Run Parser? (Proceed/Halt)
*P

Output token: CON4

[GENERATING THE MEMORY REPRESENTATION OF THE FULL EVENT]

Expanding token: CON4 =
((CON ((ACTOR (*PP* CLASS (#GROUP)
                       CFEATURE (*AMERINDIAN*)
                       TYPE (*ETHNIC*)
                       NAME (CATAWBA) TOK NP1)
          < => (*PETITION*)
          OBJECT (ACTOR (*PP* CLASS (#REGION)
                               TOK NP2 REL Con1)
                        IS (*OWN* VAL NP1))
          TOK CON1)
        FROM NP1
        TO (*PP*CLASS (#INSTITUTION)
               MEM *COURT* TOK NP3))
        TOK CON2)
    IR ((ACTOR NP3
    < => (*AUTH*)
    OBJECT CON1
    RECIP1 NP1
    RECIP2 GAP1
    FROM GAP2) TOK CON3))
        TOK CON4)

** COMMENT **
The memory structure CON4 essentially means that the Indians PETITIONed a federal court for ownership of some land, and that the PETITION initiated an AUTH by the federal court granting them ownership of the land.

Loading generator functions . . .
14703 FREE STG, 6600 FULL WORDS AVAILABLE
Files-Loaded for Generator.

*(GENERATE CON4)

The Catawba Indians asked a Federal Court to rule that they own the land, and it decreed that the land is owned by them.

** COMMENT **
The statement above is the English generation of the social acts analyzed in the input headline, produced by PHLUENT language generator. The sentences below are the result of applying the inference rules grouped under AUTH and PETITION to infer relevant aspects of the conflict situation.

*(INF-APPLY CON4)

[Generating inferences from CON4]

*(TELL-STORY)

The Catawba Indians and the other parties disagreed over the ownership of the land.

The Catawba Indians requested a Federal Court to rule that they own the land.

A Federal Court decided that the land is owned by the Catawba Indians.

The other parties will probably appeal the decision.

The other parties might use force against the Catawba Indians to assert ownership of the land.

The diagram below is the triangle notation for the social acts representing event 8.9, as analyzed by TRIAD.

Figure 8.7.   Triangle representation of a TRIAD analysis

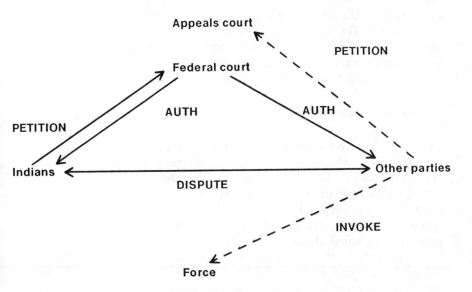

TRIAD normally makes only one level of inferences from the input event. Only if these inferences are confirmed, by further input, does TRIAD continue to expand its inference chain. Thus, the INVOKE inference does not itself produce a RESOLVE inference, unless the INVOKE is confirmed in reading a more detailed account of the event. When we integrate TRIAD with subjective goal trees, the goals will focus the inference process to analyze deeper the consequences that are of high subjective interest.

The importance of making the relevant inferences from the conflict situation is easily illustrated in the above example. Consider the following possible continuation event 8.9:

> EVENT 8.9   (Possible Continuation)
> Catawba chief Okenka proclaimed, "We'll be ready to defend our land if the ranchers try to drive us out!"

Upon reading this continuation we infer that the other party in the land dispute was the group of ranchers. How do we infer this? Why is the chief's statement relevant to the original event? There were two expectations generated in TRIAD's understanding of event 8.9, namely that the other party in the DISPUTE may appeal to a higher court, or that it may INVOKE force to claim the land. If we interpret the chief's statement in light of the latter expectation, we see that an attempt by the ranchers to drive out the Indians matches the use of force by a party DISPUTing ownership of the land. Therefore, we can see that the Catawba chief made the INVOKE inference, and he intends to counterplan to counter a possible INVOKE of force. Matching the chief's statement to the previous inference also tells us that the ranchers and the original party with whom the Indians DISPUTed must be one and the same entity.

8.6 Memory Integrated Parsing

In order to apply the inference rules associated with each basic social act, TRIAD must first analyze the English description of an event into the appropriate social acts. Let us see how this is done. For each social act TRIAD knows the type of concepts that can fill its conceptual cases. Consider the conceptual cases for AUTH: an ACTOR, a RECIPIENT, an OBJECT, an AUTHORITY, and an INSTRUMENT. The table below lists what we know about the concept that can fill these cases.

The constraints on the conceptual cases are characterized by two binary parameters: each constraint is either mandatory or preferential, and its scope is either specific to one conceptual case or dependent upon the concepts filling other conceptual cases. For instance, the first constraint on the ACTOR, the AUTHORITY, and the RECIPIENT is mandatory and specific to the conceptual case. The fact that an ACTOR, AUTHORITY, or RECIPIENT must be a human, or a human institution, is a requirement for the concept filling that slot. (A canary or a bookcase cannot AUTH anything.) This requirement is independent of the concepts filling other cases in the AUTH structure. The second constraint upon the AUTHORITY case is mandatory, but dependent upon the concepts

Table 8.1.   Constraints on the Conceptual Cases of the Basic Social Acts

Conceptual Case	Constraints on the Concept That May Fill the Conceptual Case
ACTOR	1. Must be a HUMAN, or an INSTITUTION run by HUMANS. 2. Must be in a position to exercise authority over the RECIPIENT on matters about the OBJECT. 3. Must either be the same as the AUTHORITY, or must be an agent of the AUTHORITY.
OBJECT	1. Must be a concept signifying a change in the state of the world. 2. Must be consistent with the goals of the AUTHORITY. 3. Preferably consistent with the goals of the ACTOR. 4. Must be in domain where the AUTHORITY has social power to AUTH. 5. Preferably the OBJECT is what the RECIPIENT earlier PETITIONed.
AUTHORITY	1. Must be a HUMAN, or an INSTITUTION run by HUMANS. 2. Its authority over the OBJECT must be accepted by the RECIPIENT. 3. Must be = ACTOR, or the ACTOR must be its AGENT. 4. Preferably has the power to enforce AUTHs over the RECIPIENT with the appropriate ORDER.
RECIPIENT	1. Must be a HUMAN, or an INSTITUTION run by HUMANS. 2. Preferably should accept the power to AUTH of the AUTHORITY on matters relating to the OBJECT. 3. The RECIPIENT should be directly affected by the OBJECT of the AUTH. 4. Preferably the RECIPIENT previously PETITIONed the AUTHORITY to AUTH on matters relating to the OBJECT.
INSTRUMENT	1. Must be a means of communicating the AUTH, or an ORDER whose result is forcing the RECIPIENT to comply with the OBJECT of the AUTH.

filling the RECIPIENT and OBJECT cases. We can infer whether or not the AUTHORITY's AUTHs over the OBJECT will be accepted by the RECIPIENT only if we know the identity of the RECIPIENT and the nature of the OBJECT. For instance, an employee might accept AUTHs from the shift supervisor only on matters pertaining to his job. The company president will not accept any AUTHs from the supervisor, and the employee will not accept any AUTH relating to personal matters from the supervisor (such as AUTHs about whom he should marry or what religion he should practice).

Some constraints are preferential, rather than mandatory. For instance, consider the second and fifth constraints on the OBJECT case. People do not, in general, act against their goals even in situations where they subsume someone else's goals, such as when an actor is acting as another actor's AGENT. Therefore, the OBJECT AUTHed by the ACTOR probably accords with his goals, despite his AGENCY relationship to the AUTHORITY. The fifth constraint states that an OBJECT AUTHed may be an OBJECT previously PETITIONEd. These two preferences help us to analyze events such as 8.10 and 8.11, presented below:

EVENT 8.10   John sued the automobile dealer.
              The judge awarded him $2000.

EVENT 8.11   John assaulted the automobile dealer.
              The judge awarded him $2000.

Who was awarded the $2000? This question has a different answer for each of the two events. In the first case it seems that John was awarded the money, and in the second case the dealer was awarded the $2000. The two events look superficially similar (e.g., they are syntactically identical). How do we account for the different interpretations leading to the establishment of a different referent for the word "him" in the second sentence of each event? We need to analyze the preferential constraints to the conceptual cases of each AUTH. The first sentence in event 8.1 is a PETITION; the second sentence is an AUTH. The OBJECT of the PETITION is to fulfill one of John's goals. Acquisition of money is the usual goal in most lawsuits, and therefore the object of this PETITION. We apply preferential constraint 5 for the OBJECT of an AUTH to conclude that what is AUTHed is often what was earlier PETITIONEd. Therefore, the Judge probably AUTHed (all or part of) John's PETITION object.

In Event 8.11 there is no PETITION. We can only apply preferential constraint 2 for the OBJECT of the AUTH to determine just what the judge AUTHed. Judges have the goal of preserving justice. After reading the first sentence of event 8.11, we may infer that the judge will punish the perpetrator of the assault and/or compensate the victim. Awarding the $2000 to the dealer compensates the dealer and punishes John. Therefore, the dealer is the preferred referent for the word "him" in this example. We may also infer who was awarded the money if we infer the social acts necessary to establish a causal relationship between the two sentences in event 8.11. John INVOKEd force on the dealer causing a DISPUTE. The dealer PETITIONed the court. A judge, acting as an agent for the court, AUTHed in accordance with the PETITION. (This is another example of the second preferential constraint for the OBJECT of AUTH.) Therefore, the OBJECT of the AUTH was probably equal to the OBJECT of the PETITION: The dealer receives compensation from John.

Let us see how TRIAD uses these constraints in parsing headline stories about conflict situations. The TRIAD parser is request-based in the same manner as Riesbeck's parser ELI (Riesbeck [1975] Riesbeck and Schank [1976]) and the POLITICS parser. The TRIAD parser has an advantage in flexibility over other request-based parsers in that it uses facts about the memory structures into which it will parse to dynamically write its own requests. This allows one to expand or change the memory structures, and the parser automatically incorporates these changes into its parsing procedures.

We present an annotated run of TRIAD analyzing event 8.9, the Catawba Indian story.

Annotated Trace of the TRIAD Parser

PTYCON LOG FILE   29-Mar-78 22:36:10

PTYCON> ACCEPT (OUTPUT FROM SUBJOBS) PARSER
PTYCON> CONNECT (TO SUBJOB) PARSER
[CONNECTED TO SUBJOB PARSE(1)]

  welcome to YALE'S DECsystem-20, TOPS-20 Monitor 2(450)
@CONN <TRIAD> (PASSWORD)
@TRIAD
★★★

Triad Run	Annotation

★(PARSE)
  '(CATAWBA INDIAN LAND
    CLAIMS SUPPORTED))	

READING: CATAWBA Considering request: FILTER Considering request: BUILDNP Request fired: BUILDNP	The parser starts a new event by expecting a noun phrase.

*(PSTAT)

!WD = CATAWBA
!NPHOLD = ((NAME (CATAWBA)))
!NPSTK = NIL
!CONSTK = NIL
!REQ = (NIL (FILTER BUILDNP)
         NIL)

The word "Catawba" is unknown.
TRIAD assumes that unknown words
in the context of a noun phrase may
be proper names.

READING: INDIAN
*P
Incorporating requests:
 (REQ0)

TRIAD knows what "Indian" means.
REQ1 is a request stored in the dictionary entry for "Indian" that builds
a noun phrase.

Considering request: FILTER
Considering request: BUILDNP
Considering request: REQ0
Request fired: REQ0

*^NNP1

VALUE
(NP1 #GROUP
     CFEATURE
     (*AMERINDIAN*)
     TYPE
     (*ETHNIC*)
     NAME
     (CATAWBA)
     TOK
     NP1)

This is the noun phrase meaning
"Catawba Indian".

Expunging request: REQ0

READING: LAND

Incorporating requests:
(REQ2 REQ1)

Request fired: REQ2

*^NNP2

VALUE
(NP2 #TERRITORY TOK NP2)

Incorporating requests:
(2. REQ-OWN)

TRIAD reads LAND. This could
mean "territory" or the verb "to
land", as in: "Catawba Indians land
in JFK airport." REQ2 tries to establish the first meaning and REQ1
tries for the second meaning. REQ2
wins by peeking ahead at the meaning
of the next word, "claim".

Land builds a second noun phrase,
NP2, meaning some unspecified
territory. Can the previous noun
phrase be imbedded in the current
one? REQ-OWN tries to answer this
question.

READING: CLAIM
Incorporating requests:
(REQ3 REQ4)
Considering request: REQ3
Considering request: FILTER
Considering request: BUILDNP
Considering request: REQ-OWN

Request fired: REQ-OWN

★ˆNCON1

VALUE
(CON1 (ACTOR NP2 IS
         (★OWN★ VAL NP1)))

REQ-OWN decides that the way to connect "Catawba Indian" to "land" is that the former may own the latter. This uses knowledge about what land is, and who can own what, as well as the linguistic rule that ownership relations may be expressed without a possessive for generic nouns like "Indian".

Considering request: REQ4
Request fired: REQ4

★ˆNCON2

VALUE
(CON2 (ACTOR GP0
        < => (★PETITION★)
      OBJECT GP1
      FROM GP2
      TO GP3) TOK CON2)

"Claim" suggests a PETITION. This calls in the PETITION case frame, where each conceptual case has its own set of constraints.

CREATING REQEST PREDICATES.

(ACTOR => REQ5)
(OBJECT => REQ6)
(AUTHORITY => REQ7)
(AGENTOF => REQ8)

★P

Incorporating requests:
(2. (REQ5 REQ6 REQ7 REQ8)
 3. TESTNPSTK TESTCONSTK)

TRIAD creates a request to fill each conceptual case in the PETITION frame. Each request is formed from a set of predicates constructed so as to find a concept that fulfills the constraints specified for each conceptual case. If these predicates are true for a given concept, that concept is assigned to the case whose constraints generated the predicates.

Considering request: REQ3
Considering request: FILTER
Considering request: REQ5
Considering request: REQ6
Request fired: REQ6

REQ6 found a concept asserting a state that can be the goal of an ACTOR of a PETITION. This state (ownership of land by the Catawba) fills the OBJECT case of the PETITON. This means that someone PETITIONed that the Catawba own the land.

APPLYREQ:
*^NNP2

!WD = CLAIM
!NPHOLD = NIL
!NPSTK = (NP2 NP1)
!CONSTK = (CON2 CON1)
!REQ = ((REQ3)
      (FILTER REQ5
           REQ7 REQ8)
      NIL)
(STATEP !PUT)

This is the current state of parser:
!NPSTK AND !CONSKT store the
concepts already built, and !REQ
stores requests that have not yet been
fulfilled or deleted.

Considering request: REQ7
Considering request: REQ8
Request fired: TESTCONSTK
Considering request: REQ3
Considering request: FILTER
Considering request: REQ5
Request fired: REQ5

REQ5 fills the ACTOR case of the
PETITION. Who is likely to
PETITION that the Indians own the
land? Owning land fulfills an Indian
goal, therefore they are likely to
be the actors of the PETITION.

Considering request: REQ7
Considering request: REQ8
Request fired: REQ8

The Indians PETITION on their own
behalf; i.e., they fill the AGENT
case.

READING: SUPPORTED
Incorporating requests:
(REQ9 REQ10)

PUTREQ:
*P

Considering request: REQ3
Request fired: REQ3

APPLYREQ:
*^NREQ3
TEST:
(AND !NPSTK [OR [NULL NXWD]
     [EQ NXWD @!STOP!]]])
DELREQ:
(= = !THISREQ)
REMTST:
(EQ !WD @!STOP!)
ACTION:
(DV !PASSIVE T)

"Supported" is read in. REQ3, which
was looking for a passive construction
is satisfied because "supported" is
the last word in the sentence; therefore it cannot be a simple past tense.
Headlines usually leave out the auxil-
iary "to be" verb that makes a
grammatical passive. Therefore, we
need to identify passives by other
means.

Considering request: FILTER
Considering request: REQ7

One of the meanings of "supported"
is AUTHed. One can also talk about
a column supporting a building, or
a parent supporting a child. In the
present context, the fact that we are
in the context of a PETITION, gives
preference to the AUTH meaning

Considering request: BUILDNP
Considering request: REQ9

Request fired: REQ9

(ACTOR => REQ11)
(OBJECT => REQ12)
(RECIPIENT1 => REQ13)
(RECIPIENT2 => REQ14)
(AUTHORITY => REQ15)

Incorporating requests:
(2. (REQ12 REQ13 REQ14 REQ15
    REQ11)
 3. TESTNPSTK TESTCONSTK)

*^NCON3

VALUE
(CON3 (ACTOR GA0
       <=> (*AUTH*)
      OBJECT GA1
      RECIP1 GA2
      RECIP2 GA3
      AUTHORITY GA4)
TOK CON3)

Considering request: REQ7
Considering request: REQ10
Considering request: REQ12
Request fired: REQ12

APPLYREQ:
*P
Considering request: FILTER
Considering request: REQ7
Considering request: REQ10
Considering request: REQ13
Request fired: REQ13

Considering request: REQ15
  DEFAULT MEMORY CHECK . . .
Request fired: REQ15

Considering request: FILTER
Considering request: REQ7
Considering request: REQ8
Considering request: REQ10

of supported, because one of the
PETITION inferences expects an
AUTH to occur.

REQ9 brings in the AUTH frame,
and the constraints on the conceptual
cases build the requests to fill these
cases.

The passive rearranges the order of
the requests—to first try to match the
OBJECT and leave the actor for
later consideration.

These are the conceptual cases for
AUTH that the new requests will try
to fill.

The OBJECT of the AUTH is found
to be that which was earlier
PETITIONed. The preference constraint discussed earlier was used
here.

One of the RECIPIENTs of the
AUTH is found to be NP1, the
Catawba Indians. The other recipient
remains unspecified.

Memory is consulted to find out that
federal courts AUTH on Indian
matters. Thus we can fill the
RECIPIENT case of the PETITION,
and the AUTHORITY and ACTOR
cases of the AUTH.

Request fired: REQ10

DEFAULT MEMORY CHECK . . .

*^NCON4

VALUE
(CON4 (CON CON2 IR CON3))
★★★★COMPLETED PARSING★★★★

STRUCTURE POINTER: CON4

REQ10 established the causal connection between the PETITION and the AUTH; namely the former initiated the latter.

CON4 is the full memory structure: the PETITION of the Catawba Indians initiating an AUTH by a Federal court decreeing that the Indians own the land. The fully expanded representation appears below.

```
    ★(TXPN CON4)
    ((CON ((ACTOR (★PP★ CLASS (#GROUP)
                        CFEATURE (★AMERINDIAN★)
                        TYPE (★ETHNIC★)
                        NAME (CATAWBA) TOK NP1)
               < => (★PETITION★)
               OBJECT ((ACTOR (★PP★ CLASS (#REGION)
                                     TOK NP2 REL CON1)
                        IS (★OWN★ VAL NP))
                    TOK CON1)
               FROM NP1
               TO (★PP★ CLASS (#INSTITUTION)
                        MEM ★COURT★ TOK NP3))
           TOK CON2)
        IR ((ACTOR NP3
                 < => (★AUTH★)
             OBJECT CON1
             RECIP1 NP1
             RECIP2 GAP1
             FROM GAP) TOK CON3))
    TOK CON4)
```

8.7 Conclusion

The basic social acts are a very useful representational system for understanding human conflict situations. The social acts provide the appropriate level of representation to group sets of inferences that are applicable and relevant to most conflict situations. Since there are a small number of basic social acts (we have created seven of them), the total number of inference rules is very small, but applicable to a very large domain of conflict situations. Developing a representational system that requires very few rules to understand very large classes of events tells us that we have chosen a very appropriate and useful representational model. It is always the goal of people developing new theories that these theories be as simple as possible and yet account for as many phenomena as possible.

The nature of the social-act representation allows a conceptual, request-based parser to use the memory structures and inference rules to drive the parsing process. We have developed a method of encoding information about the social acts and their conceptual cases into parsing requests built dynamically by the parser at parsing time. This provides for a large degree of generality in the parser. One need only create sufficiently rich memory structures and the parser will create requests to parse into these structures. This facility, of course, assumes that neither the structure of the memory, nor the form of the inference rules changes as the knowledge base of the system is expanded. The procedural encoding of memory information into parser requests reflects Susman's [1973] concern over the fact that a great deal of information is encoded in declarative form, but must be used in a procedural manner.

Furthermore, the broad bandwidth of communication between the parser and the inference mechanism provides for a high degree of integration between the parser and the memory model. The fact that our parser is memory driven, helps us resolve ambiguities, deal with multiple word meanings, and sometimes guess at the meaning of unknown words. For instance, inferring a probable AUTH from a PETITION allows TRIAD to determine the meaning of "support" in "The Catawba Indian land claims supported."

If the parser were totally disjoint from the memory, we could not directly address these problems. We would need a large number of special purpose processes to finesse each type of ambiguity. This would lead to a more fragile and less efficient system, and probably a less plausible model of human understanding.

The social acts can, and often need to, be integrated with the beliefs of the understander. In order to decide what can be a reasonable object of a PETITION we have to know about the goals of the actor of the PETITION. Or vice versa, if we know what has been PETITIONed, we can often determine who must have initiated the PETITION by applying our beliefs about the goals and social relations of the actors in the conflict event. The same process applies to other social acts such as INVOKE or AUTH. People normally AUTH only what is consistent with their goals, and AUTHs, INVOKEs, and PETITIONs are often applied with the express purpose of fulfilling one's goals in a conflict situation. The goal trees of the actors are consulted both in analyzing English into social acts (e.g., to determine whether the constraints on the conceptual cases apply), and in directing the inference process by pruning all inferences that lead to goal violations and focusing on inference paths that resolve conflict situations in accordance with an actor's goals.

The application of counterplanning rules is largely determined by the social acts that have transpired in the course of the conflict situation. If both actors in a conflict have INVOKEd force and other such means against each other, all higher order counterplanning strategies are applicable. After one actor has PETITIONed, the other actor in the DISPUTE may await the AUTH, if he believes it likely to favor his goals. If he believes otherwise, he may pursue counterplanning strategies with possibly more determination than before, in order to RESOLVE the DISPUTE before the unfavorable AUTH occurs. Consider for instance the DISPUTE between Ralph Nader and General Motors. GM may not have expedited its goal-compromise strategies with Nader if Nader had not been awaiting an AUTH in response to his PETITION and if GM had not feared the consequences of the AUTH.

Since social acts integrate naturally with both goal trees and counterplanning strategies, POLITICS should be integrated with TRIAD to produce a system which will model subjective understanding of general conflict situations. This would be an integrated process model that would not be subject to those flaws of POLITICS that were discussed in the first section of this chapter. Our model of subjective understanding will be expanded. Such an approach to modeling human understanding helps us gain insights into the types of processes that focus inferences, and it leads us to formulate more integrated and more general process models. Subjective understanding is both a powerful tool to model human interpretations of different events, and a computational mechanism for more efficient encoding and usage of episodic knowledge and inference rules.

9

Analyzing Human Personality Traits

9.1 What is a Personality Trait?

Goal trees and counterplanning strategies applied to conflict situations are useful tools for modeling most areas of human conflicts and interactions. These tools, applicable to subjective understanding of conflict situations, are also useful in modeling many other areas of subjective human behavior. In this chapter we discuss the necessity of understanding personality traits in order to model subjective understanding of a large class of events and stories. Whenever a story includes character development of one of the actors, this development turns out to be useful and often crucial in formulating an understanding of the story. Here we deal with the most simple form of character development: the attribution of personality traits to actors in simple stories. We analyze personality traits in terms of personal goal trees and predisposition toward applying certain classes of planning and counterplanning strategies. Let us start our discussion with some examples of human personality traits.

Consider the following story:

9.1 John is very ambitious.
He abandoned his invalid mother, worked very hard at his job, and bad-mouthed his co-workers. John was elated when the boss promoted him.

What does it mean for somebody to be ambitious? John's actions in example 9.1 are characteristic of an over-ambitious person. John's emotional reaction to his promotion also characterizes the type of behavior that one may expect from an ambitious person. What happens if we use different personality traits to define John's character? Consider the following story:

9.2 John is very compassionate.
He abandoned his invalid mother, worked very hard at his job, and badmouthed his co-workers. John was elated when the boss promoted him.

Story 9.2 is not consistent. Why not? Compassionate people do not abandon invalid mothers. Badmouthing co-workers does not seem to be consistent with John's being compassionate. The only way we could interpret story 9.2 is to say that John must have been acting "out of character" for some unknown reason. This suggests that the meaning of words describing personality traits are related to certain characteristic types of behavior. In fact, personality traits often express the deviation between socially defined normative behavior and the particular characteristic behavior of an individual.

Before we analzye the meaning and the subjective nature of personality traits, let us see why this is an important issue that requires our investigation. There are psychological reasons which suggest that the way people talk about personality traits may be an interesting subject of study. Here we focus on the relevance of linguistic descriptions of personality traits to subjective understanding of events. Consider the following story:

> 9.3   Bill was very brave, but his brother John was very cowardly. One night the two brothers were walking by the road when a masked bandit surprised them. The younger brother panicked and ran headlong into the forest where he was lost, never to be seen again. The elder brother fought off the bandit, and, in the process, recovered the long lost royal sapphire, stolen years earlier. The king rewarded him handsomely.
>
> QUESTION: Whom did the king reward?

A person reading the above story has little trouble in answering the question: Clearly, the king rewarded Bill. However, it is not particularly easy to see *how* one goes about formulating the answer. In order to answer this question without substantial effort, the reference of "him" in the last sentence of 9.3 must have been determined while the story was understood. Determining this referent is a very difficult task. Many people have worked on the reference problem (e.g., Charniak [1972], Ross [1967], Wilensky [1978], Cullingford [1977]), but resolving this particular referent requires a complete understanding of the story. No simple rule will serve. For instance, the last mentioned character in the story before the "him" is the bandit, but this is obviously not the correct referent.

The first step in determining the referent is to understand the causal relations among the actions in the story. In order to establish a causal relation between the facts that the king rewarded somebody and the sapphire was recovered, one must infer that the sapphire was returned to the king by the elder brother. A story-understanding system such as PAM (Wilensky [1978]) makes this kind of inference and also the inference that the king felt indebted to the elder brother. The state of indebtedness may have caused the king to reward the elder brother. If the story is thus understood, one is able to establish that "him" refers to the elder brother. This is only half of the task. How do we know that Bill is the elder brother who deserves the reward?

In order to determine which brother is which we must use the information contained in their respective character traits. One brother is brave; the other is cowardly. Running away in the face of danger is a characteristic behavior associated with cowardly people. Fighting bandits, or otherwise risking one's life for some worthy cause, is the type of behavior characteristic of bravery. Therefore, we determine that Bill, the brave one, must have been the elder brother who fought the bandit and recovered the sapphire. This determination requires knowledge about certain types of actions characteristic of bravery and other actions characteristic of cowardice. Thus, we need to know, or be able to infer, typical behaviors associated with certain character traits. We need to answer the general question: If actor X has character trait P, is he likely to do action A in situation S? It seems, therefore, that an investigation of personality traits and their associated typical behavior ought to be a worthwhile pursuit.

Let us consider a couple of events in which knowledge about personality traits is necessary to understand the actions of the characters. We present two events that differ only in the characterization of the primary actor. The difference in the actor's personality trait accounts for a difference in the probable meaning of the unknown word "tolliked".

> 9.4 John was a very generous person. When the charity drive asked him for a contribution he put his hand on his wallet and tolliked their request.

> 9.5 John was a suspicious miser. When the charity drive asked him for a contribution he put his hand on his wallet and tolliked their request.

QUESTION: What does "tolliked" mean?

We cannot be sure of the meaning of "tolliked" in either example, but story 9.4 suggests a very different meaning for "tolliked" than 9.5. Generous people are usually willing to share some of their possessions or their time with people in need. Therefore, the reader of 9.4 might expect John to respond in a positive manner to the charity request. The fact that he put his hand on his wallet can be interpreted as a precondition to giving money to the charity, thus fulfilling their request. In light of these expectations, we can determine that "tolliked" probably means "complied with" or "fulfilled". Thus, under the circumstances of story 9.4 the meaning of "tolliked" is postulated to a large extent by the type of behavior one might expect from a generous person.

What about the meaning of "tolliked" in story 9.5? Misers do not share their possession with anybody. Suspicious people distrust the apparent motives of others. Thus, the reader of 9.5 will expect that John does not want to give money to the charity and that he may mistrust the motives of the person asking for a charity contribution. These expectations may lead the reader to interpret John's reaching toward his wallet as a precaution for any trick-option plans that he may suspect on the part of the charity-drive person. The fact that John is a miser and the interpretation of his reaching for his wallet as a precaution suggest the same course of action: John will not comply with the charity request. In this case, "tolliked" takes on the meaning of "denied" or "dismissed". This meaning of "tolliked" is quite different from the meaning suggested by story 9.4. The only difference in the two stories is that different personality traits were attributed to John. Hence, we see that understanding personality traits is important for generating expectations about probable behaviors and, in some cases, postulating the meaning of unknown or ambiguous words.

9.2 How Personality Traits May Be Represented

We might consider defining personality traits, such as "ambitious" and "compassionate", by listing the set of behaviors characteristic of that trait. Recall John's behavior in story 9.1. All his actions are, in a sense, characteristic of an ambitious person, but what do we do with actions that are not characteristic of a particular trait? For instance, neither abandoning one's invalid mother nor working very hard at one's job are characteristic actions of a compassionate person. However, the former action is definitely uncharacteristic of compassion, while the latter action is neutral with respect to being compassionate. Thus, if we are to define character traits by listing characteristic actions, we should also list actions that are typically uncharacteristic of the particular character trait.

We must take into account the monumental nature of the task if we are to list all characteristic and non-characteristic actions for each character trait. There are, in essence, infinite numbers of actions that can be classified as characteristic or uncharacteristic for each personality trait. We will try to narrow the problem by only classifying general types of actions. For instance, consider a very incomplete list of jobs characteristically aspired to by an ambitious person: the president of a company, a trial lawyer, a real-estate king, a shipping magnate, the Governor of California, advisor to the President of the United State, and a movie star. All of these occupations entail power, wealth, and social respect, to different degrees. Therefore, a useful way of classifying these jobs is by the degree to which they imply high social status, power, and wealth. This classification enables us to have only one entry on the list of typical actions of an ambitious person: he wants a job that maximizes these three qualities. Similarly we can generalize some other actions that characterize ambition. Our list of typical actions and wants remains somewhat cumbersome in length. Here is an incomplete list of characteristic and uncharacteristic actions and wants of an ambitious person.

Table 9.1. Characteristic Actions of an Ambitious Person

Characteristic Actions	Uncharacteristic Actions
1. Neglecting relatives in time of need.	1. Anonymous donations to charity.
2. Wanting a job with as much power, respect and wealth as possible.	2. Stepping down to let a more qualified person assume a position of responsibility.
3. Wanting to constantly improve one's present job.	3. Avoiding hard work that leads to self betterment.
4. Using friends to further one's own ends, then discarding them.	4. Helping others at cost to self.
5. Badmouthing competitors.	5. Not being concerned with personal appearance in the presence of one's boss or social peers.
6. Wanting social respect and recognition.	6. Being contented with one's past achievements in life.
7. Want an impressive house.	7. Relinquishing social status, wealth or power.
8. Want a luxury or sports car.	8. Placing honesty above self betterment.
9. Want a socially successful spouse.	9. Tolerant of other people's fault.
10. Dishonest business deals.	10. Happy at another's success.
11. Seeking to be in the presence of successful people.	

The set of characteristic actions and wants of an ambitious person is based on underlying personal motivation. Wanting an impressive house, a luxury or sports car, and a job that yields substantial wealth are instances of acquisition goals (A-goals). Being respected and powerful are instances of A-scont goals. (A-social control means desiring an increase in one's social stature.) Thus, one way of analyzing personality traits is by associating with each trait the goals people described by that trait are likely to have. Once these goals are established, certain behaviors can be inferred in particular situations, such as stories 9.3, 9.4 and 9.5, by a story understander who applies planning and counterplanning strategies. Since we have developed mechanisms for understanding goal-based events (e.g., PAM [Wilensky, 1978] and POLITICS), it seems quite fruitful to reduce personality traits to the pursuit of certain types of goals.

9.3 Goal Trees Representing Personality Traits

Consider the process of understanding a story starting with the following initial segment:

> 9.6   John is a very inquisitive and uncompromising person. He is also rather thrifty in his personal affairs. . . .

There have been no actions thus far in the story, nor any physical or temporal setting that helps the understander establish the situational context. Yet, John's personality traits provide a goal-expectation setting. That is, the understander knows the following information from the above fragment of 9.6: John's goal of increasing his knowledge about most matters is a goal of very high importance. We denote the acquisition-of-knowledge goal as A-know(John,X,+). (The "+" means John wants knowledge about X. A "-" would signify that John's goal is to actively avoid knowing about X, and a "0" signifies that John ignores new knowledge about X. Thus, if we know that Mary is apathetic, we mean A-know(Mary,X,0).) The fact that John is thrifty tells us that he also has the goal of preserving his money. In fact, the word "thrifty" states a relationship between the P-money goal and the set of A-goals that can be accomplished by spending money. John holds the goal of P-money to be more important than most such A-goals.

The fact that John is uncompromising is somewhat more difficult to represent in terms of John's goals. No specific goal is defined by a person's being uncompromising. This personality trait applies to all of John's goals. An uncompromising person is one who does not abandon any goal in the face of opposition from another party; that is, a person who will not yield to someone else's goals. Being uncompromising also carries the implication that one holds the goals of others to be less important than is normally the case. Thus, this personality trait modifies the entire set of goals that a person has, rather than establishing a single specific goal.

Since most personality traits describe deviations from a culturally-defined normative person, we know that John's A-know goals are much more important to him than other people's A-know goals are to them. Similarly, we know that his P-money goal is a little more important to him than is generally the case. We may also infer that John's A-goal of things that cost money may be a little less important to him than other people's corresponding A-goals are to them. The trait "uncompromising" exemplifies an across-the-board deviation from the norm. John will give higher than normal importance to most of his goals.

These importance relations enable us to construct a relative-importance (RI) goal tree for John in the same manner that we constructed goal trees for political ideologies in Chapter 3. Here is the fragment of John's goal tree, constructed from the information contained in the personality traits in story 9.6.

Figure 9.1.   Fragment of John's RI goal tree

$$A\text{-KNOW}(John, X, +)$$
$$\uparrow \text{RI-link}$$
$$P\text{-MONEY}(John, +)$$
$$\uparrow \text{RI-link}$$
$$A\text{-POSSESSIONS}(John, +)$$

Figure 9.1 tells us that John considers acquiring new knowledge to be the most important goal, followed by preserving his money, followed by acquiring new material possessions. Since we know that John is a person and a member of western society, we know that he has certain normative goals common to most people in the society. These goals include:

Goal	Explanation
1. P-health (Self, +)	Self-preservation
2. P-health (Family, +)	Preservation of family members
3. A-possessions (Self, +)	Acquire wealth and belongings
4. P-possessions (Self, +)	Preserve one's belongings
5. A-social respect (others, +)	Be respected by other people
6. A-know (Self, X, +)	Learn new things
7. E-unpleasant activity (Self, −)	Avoid going through unpleasant experiences (e.g., stay out of jail)
8. E-pleasant activity (Self, +)	Have fun doing enjoyable things
9. P-health (others, +)	Help others survive
10. P-anything (enemies, −)	Wish doom upon one's enemies

Enjoyment goals (E-goals) are a third type of goal in Schank and Abelson's [1977] goal taxonomy. These goals are usually of a more fleeting nature, therefore less important then the A-goals and P-goals we discussed earlier.

The set of goals can be ranked in terms of their normative relative importance to a prototypical member of our society. For instance, preservation of oneself and one's family are usually the two most important goals for anybody. However, if we learn that a person is foolhardy, we interpret this as a deviation from the normative goal tree where P-self is a low importance goal to that person. If the person is described as suicidal, the P-health goal is not present in his goal tree; indeed, P-health(self, −) may substitute the normative P-health(self, +) goal. Similarly, wishing doom on one's enemies is, in the normative case, a lower importance goal than most of the other goals listed above. If a person is described as vindictive, we know that his goal of P-anything(enemies, −) is much more important to him than it is in the normative case.

The figure below is the relative-importance goal network for a prototypical, normative person. Since the network is acyclical, it is conceptually equivalent to a tree. This tree is subject to the same inference rules that we presented for ideological goal trees in Chapter 3. Figure

Figure 9.2.   Goal hierarchy for a normative person

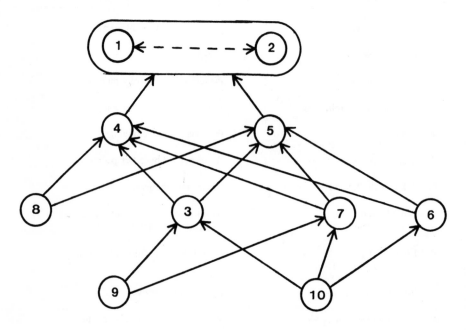

9.2 is an empirical attempt at partially ordering the more common goals that people pursue. The tree includes the goals listed above; it is not meant to be a comprehensive goal tree of all significant goals that may be pursued by people in our society.

In the case of story 9.6, the personality tratis applied to John promote his A-knowledge goal to a higher importance than the other three goals at that level, but keep the higher preservation goals (e.g., P-self and P-family) as most important. The fact that he is thrifty, creates a more specific P-money goal (an instance of the more general P-possessions goal) and places this goal as having higher importance than his A-possessions goal in the goal tree. Furthermore, his A-possession goal is demoted below the other goals found at the level in the normative goal tree. The fact that John is uncompromising makes all his goals in the tree more important to him than in the normative case. Thus, we have represented the meaning of John's character traits in 9.6 as a modification of the normative person's goal tree. How can we use this goal tree representation? Let us continue with the story.

> 9.6 John is a very inquisitive and uncompromising person. He is also rather thrifty in his personal affairs. One day he got an unusually large repair bill for his car . . .

What is John likely to do about the repair bill? The fact that John's P-money goal has high importance suggests that he may not be willing to part with the large amount of money required to pay the bill. His high importance A-know goal suggests that he may want to discover why the bill is unusually large; he may want to know whether he is being cheated by the repair shop. John will pursue these two goals with more than usual determination; this is, in essence, the meaning of John's being uncompromising. We do not think that a reader of 9.6 will predict any specific actions on John's part, but understanding his goals will help one to understand the nature of later actions in the story. We believe that it is crucial for the reader to be aware of the fact that two of the goals which John holds in high importance have been violated by the unusually high repair bill. Without his knowledge one is unable to comprehend the entire story. Furthermore, the general expectation should be made by the reader that John's actions in the immediate future will probably be attempts to fulfill either or both P-money and A-know. We illustrate this claim by giving the conclusion of the story.

> 9.6 John is a very inquisitive and uncompromising person. He is also rather thrifty in his personal affairs. One day he got an unusually large repair bill for his car. John called his brother, a wealthy lawyer, to take care of the problem.

Our interpretation of the last sentence is that John's brother will dispute the repair shop on John's behalf in order to lower the bill. This conclusion is arrived at in light of the goals that John is expected to be actively pursuing, P-money and A-know. How does calling a wealthy lawyer help John achieve these goals? The job of a lawyer is to act as an agent who furthers the goals of his client. A lawyer may be more successful at getting the repair bill lowered. The retaining fee associated with hiring a lawyer (violating P-money) may not apply because of the family relationship. The fact that John is uncompromising supports our interpretation of the conclusion; John is pursuing his violated goals as best he can.

Why did we need to generate the expectations that John would pursue P-money and A-know? The answer is: we need to know John's goals in order to interpret the conclusion correctly. John's goals come directly from the personality traits of the first two sentences. In order to illustrate the necessity of determining John's goals before interpreting the conclusion, we consider the following similar story:

> 9.7   John is an apathetic, happy-go-lucky person. He is also somewhat of a
> spendthrift. One day he got an unusually large repair bill for his car. John
> called his brother, a wealthy lawyer, to take care of the problem.

Our interpretation of this story is that John may have wanted some money to pay for this repair bill. His brother, being a wealthy lawyer, was a possible source for the needed money. (In an informal confirmation of our interpretations we gave story 9.6 to five people and 9.7 to five other people. Everyone was asked to explain the story they read, and their interpretations concurred with ours.) John, being apathetic, attaches little importance to his A-know goal. The fact that he is a spendthrift means that he does not attach much importance to his P-money goal, but he may give more importance to A-possessions or E-things that cost money. Furthermore, someone with a low P-money is not likely to have much money in hand. Therefore, it is reasonable to expect that John may be unable to pay the repair bill. Finally, a happy-go-lucky person does not bother to pursue his goals with much determination. He is more interested in the quickest solution to the present dilemma. With these goals (or the lack thereof) in consideration when we interpret the last sentence of 9.7, we conclude that John only cares about dismissing the problem of the repair bill as quickly as possible. A loan or gift from his rich brother fulfills our expectations of John's probable behavior.

If 9.7 were continued with the statement "John's brother said he had already loaned John too much money," our expectation that John was asking for financial assistance would be confirmed. On the other hand, this continuation makes little sense after event 9.6, because we did not expect John to ask for money in 9.6. The continuation is a response to a non-existent expectation; therefore, it is not surprising that such a continuation following story 9.6 is rather puzzling. Thus, different expectations and interpretations are produced by the different personality traits used in the two stories.

The only difference between stories 9.6 and 9.7 is the characterization of John's personality by a few personality traits. Therefore, once again, we had to rely on goal-based information implied by these character traits in order to interpret the story. This suggests that understanding stories in which the characters are described by personality traits is a similar process to the subjective understanding of events introduced in Chapter 1. In both cases the understander considers only certain inferences and certain interpretations of specific behaviors on the basis of the inferred goals and motivations of the primary characters. For instance, in interpreting story 9.6, one could infer that John would ask his brother for money, for a new car, for moral support, or for the name of a less expensive repair shop. None of these inferences are made in interpreting 9.6 because the understander already expects John's actions to be in service of particular goals. Thus, the same general method of pruning spurious inferences that was discussed earlier is also applicable to stories in which relevant personality traits are attributed to the characters. The primary difference between the events we discussed earlier and these stories is that previously the understander already knew the goal tree of the actor with whom he identified. In the present case, the goal trees must be constructed from the goal tree of a normative person, which has been modified by the goals implicit in the character traits describing the main actor(s).

We list some personality traits and the goals which they imply for the actor whom they describe in Table 9.2. The table lists the deviations from the social norm for each goal implicit in the personality trait. For instance, an ambitious person attributes higher importance to the goals of increasing his social status (i.e., power and prestige) and his wealth and worldly possessions. Ambition also implies less concern for the goals of others, especially if any of their preservation goals conflict with the ambitious person's A-goals. (see Chapter 3 for an analysis of this type of goal conflict.) Thus the goal tree of an ambitious person is the normative person's goal tree (figure 9.2) with the above goals raised or lowered in importance according to the entries in table 9.2

In Chapter 3 we discussed a set of rules to decide which goal in the goal tree a political actor would focus his attention on. These rules are applicable to the current domain, confirming the usefulness of goal trees

Table 9.2   Goal-oriented Personality Traits

Personality Trait	Goals and Their Importance (deviations from the socially accepted norm)	
1. Ambitious	A–possessions (self, +)	higher
	A–scont (self, others, +)	higher
	P–anything (others, +)	lower
	A–know (self, +)	slightly higher
2. Curious	A–know (self, +)	higher
3. Prudent	P–anything (self, +)	higher
	P–anything (others, +)	slightly higher
4. Spendthrift	P–money (self, +)	lower
	P–possessions (self, +)	slightly lower
	E–things/that/cost/money (self, +)	slightly higher
5. Vindictive	P–anything (others who have caused goal failure, –)	higher
6. Powerhungry	A–scont (self, others, +)	higher
7. Compassionate	P.-health (others, +)	higher
	P–anything (others, +)	slightly higher
	E–unpleasant experience (others, –)	higher
8. Playboy	E–sex (self, +)	higher
	E–anything (self, +)	slightly higher
	A–luxurious poss (self, +)	higher
	P–money (self, +)	slightly lower
9. Self-centered	<any-goal>(self, +)	slightly higher
	<any-goal>(others, +)	lower
10. Belligerent	A–scont (self, others, +)	slightly higher
	Cause goal-conflicts	

in different subjective understanding situations. Recall some of the rules in Chapter 3:

RULE 3.10   If progress toward a goal can be achieved by a particular course of action, that course of action should be pursued.

RULE 3.11   If a possible course of action violates a goal, it should be actively avoided.

RULE 3.13   If a course of action affects two goals, and no other rules determine which goal to focus on, the effect on the higher-importance goal determines whether the course of action should be pursued.

RULE 3.14   Relative-importance links in a goal tree are transitive.

Let us apply these rules to the interpretation of the following two stories:

9.8   John, an ambitious lawyer, had to decide whether to accept a lucrative GM contract or devote his time to the free legal-aid society. It did not take long to make up his mind.

9.9   John, a very compassionate lawyer, had to decide whether to accept a lucrative GM contract or devote his time to the free legal-aid society. It did not take long to make up his mind.

The decision confronting John in both stories is whether to pursue the goals of A-money(John, +) and A-scont(John,others, +), or to help others fulfill their P-goals. In the normative person's goal tree, the two A-goals are somewhat more important than the P-anything(others, +) goal. The fact that John is ambitious raises the importance of his self-centered A-goals and further lowers the importance of helping others fulfill their P-goals. Applying rule 3.13 (and 3.14 if necessary) we conclude that John will pursue his A-money and A-scont goals. Therefore, according to rule 3.10, John probably made up his mind to accept the GM contract.

On the other hand, if we modify the normative person's goal tree by entry for "compassionate" in table 9.2, we find that P-goals of others increase in importance. This means that P-anything(others, +) is roughly equal in importance as John's A-money and A-scont goals in story 9.9. Which way did John make up his mind? We cannot tell unless we have some way to measure the relative increase in importance of the P-goals with respect to the base difference in importance between P-anything(others, +) and the two A-goals in the original normative-person goal tree. An alternative solution to this problem involves taking pragmatic considerations of story telling into account when formulating John's goal tree. Why were we told that John is very compassionate? This fact must have some relevance to the rest of the story. The only relevance it could have is to affect John's decision. If we used a normative goal tree for John, we would expect him to decide on accepting the GM contract. In order to affect John's decision (i.e., reverse it) we must change the relative ranking of his goals with respect to importance. Therefore, the reader of 9.9 will probably guess that John's goal of P-anything(others, +) takes on greater importance than his A-money and A-scont goals.

9.4 How Personality Traits Constrain the Application of Planning and Counterplanning Strategies

Some personality traits encode information about the types of planning and counterplanning strategies that a person is likely to use. For instance, consider the following story:

> 9.10 Bill was a capable and trustworthy businessman. After a few years he became vice-president of the company, fulfilling his objective.

> 9.11 Bill was a dishonest and belligerent businessman. After a few years he became vice-president of the company, fulfilling his objective.

> QUESTION   How might Bill have become vice president?

If we enumerate the most likely ways for Bill to become vice-president of his company in each of the two examples above, we have two disjoint sets. Why is this the case? Capable and trustworthy people do different things than dishonest and belligerent people, even when pursuing the same goal. Let us list some plausible answers to the question of how Bill may have become vice-president. First we list some plausible scenarios for example 9.10:

> 1. The company president decided he could trust Bill's integrity and judgment, hence he promoted Bill to company vice-president when the post became vacant.

> 2. Bill was a much harder worker and a more efficient administrator than the previous vice-president. It was decided to fire the inept vice-president and promote Bill to his post.

Neither of the above scenarios is appropriate for example 9.11. Belligerent and dishonest people are not promoted to a position of responsibility because they can be trusted or because they have outstanding abilities. The following scenarios are more plausible in the context of 9.11:

> 1. Bill forged some papers indicating that the previous vice-president embezzeled company funds. After the latter was fired, Bill was promoted into the empty post.

> 2. Bill blackmailed the company president with some prior indiscretions. The president, wanting to maintain his image, promoted John to the vice-presidency.

Some scenarios are plausible, given certain personality traits attributed to Bill, and other, totally different scenarios are plausible given a different set of character traits. These differences are not accountable by differences in the goals that Bill is pursuing. In both 9.10 and 9.11, he wants to become vice-president of the company. How do we account for the differences in plausible scenarios? The two personality traits in 9.10 and the two in 9.11 are examples of traits that specify the types of planning and counterplanning strategies a person is willing (or able) to use. In fact, some personality traits specify types of strategies that a person will specifically not employ. For instance, a trustworthy or honest person will not use trick options; a timid person is unlikely to use threats.

It is often useful for an understander to predict the type of planning or counterplanning strategies that a person is likely to use. Why? Consider the following fragment of a conversation overheard on a bus:

Example 9.12   Fragment of a conversation

Person 1.   Do you remember old Ed?

Person 2.   You mean the incompetent salesman who tries to cheat in our card games?

Person 1.   Yeah, he asked me for a raise today. I pulled out his employee record and you can imagine what I told him!

We certainly can imagine that "old Ed" did not get his raise. How do we know this? How does person 1 know that person 2 will understand him? The answer to both of these questions is determined by what we as readers (and person 2 during the conversation) know about "old Ed"; namely, that he is dishonest and incompetent. This means that he is willing to use trick-option strategies against his boss, and he is unable to choose or carry out the appropriate strategies in his job as salesman. Thus, Ed's boss has two reasons for denying the raise, corresponding to the following two rules:

STRATEGY 9.1   MAKING ENEMIES

IF   an actor X repeatedly counterplans against actor Y,

THEN   Y will not help X achieve any goals in the future.

REFINEMENT IF   X is successful in his counterplanning,

THEN   Y may pursue the goal of terminating any subsumption state that enables X to counterplan against Y.

RULE 3.11   If a possible course of action violates a goal, it should be actively avoided.

The first reason why old Ed's boss should deny the raise is that Ed had repeatedly counterplanned against his boss by trying to cheat at cards, apparently with little success. Thus, according to strategy 9.1, Ed's boss should not be expected to help Ed by giving him the requested raise. It is interesting to note that if Ed had succeeded in repeatedly counterplanning against his boss, then the refinement of rule 9.1 is directly applicable. The boss could fire Ed, thus terminating the subsumption state that makes Ed's boss vulnerable to Ed's trick-option strategies. The second reason why the boss should deny the raise is that giving Ed more money violates the A-money goal that all businesses have. Thus, rule 3.11 vetos any raise to Ed. If Ed was not incompetent he would make more money for the business: thus, no A-money goal would be violated and rule 3.11 would not apply. (Businesses have goals too. In fact, they have goal trees, just like nations, individuals and most other institutions in our society.)

Table 9.3.   Means-oriented Personality Traits

Personality Trait	Types of Suggested Planning and Counterplanning Strategies (deviations from social norm)
1. Ambitious	Higher-order plan boxes (e.g., THREATEN, OVERPOWER) and counterplanning strategies (e.g., BLOCK-HIGHER-GOAL). Trick options if necessary. No compromises if possible.
2. Trustworthy	No trick options used. Preference for lower-order strategies and compromises.
3. Dishonest	Trick options used.
4. Unscrupulous	Higher-order strategies, trick options used disregarding all negative effects on others.
5. Compassionate	Strategies chosen not to harm others and, if possible, to help others fulfill their goals.
6. Capable	Make correct decisions in selecting the proper strategies for each situation. Carrying out strategies without errors.
7. Incompetent	Random or error-prone choice of strategies. Possibly not aware of some strategies.
8. Belligerent	Choice of strategies to maximize plan-conflicts with others. Higher-order strategies used when not necessary.

Here we present some personality traits and the types of strategies likely to be employed by the person with the respective trait.

We emphasize that it is important to understand the strategies implied by certain character traits. Without analyzing the strategies in the previous example we would not have been able to invoke rule 9.1 because we would not have discovered the relevance of the repeated counterplanning on Ed's part. The simple-minded alternative to analyzing the goals and strategies underlying personality traits is to associate all possible outcomes with each trait. For instance, under "incompetent" one would have to store (and consider each time this trait is mentioned) that one may be denied raises, fired from the job, abandoned by one's friends, scorned by neighbors, do badly in studies, lose at most games, have an unhappy life, have a rather low intelligence, etc., ad infinitum. This method of directly associating behaviors with personality traits has many drawbacks, such as the sheer size and inefficiency of the memory required to store all behaviors associated with all character traits.

Let us consider a different reason why such a method is insufficient. How do we deal with the following type of characterization? "Millard Fillmore was an incompetent president." Clearly, we do not mean that Fillmore was scorned by his neighbors and did badly on his studies. On the other hand, most of the above characterizations were true of Galileo. (He was fired, scorned, laughed at, and he led an unhappy life.) We would not say that Galileo was incompetent. Quite the contrary, he applied the proper strategies to physics problems, while his contemporaries may have been the real incompetents.

The strategy-based personality traits are defined in terms of deviations from the social norm, in the same manner in which we defined goal-based personality traits. Thus, asserting that Millard Fillmore was an incompetent president means tht he is less competent than other presidents with respect to his planning and counterplanning abilities in his official role as president. Thus, we have a much narrower social norm for judging the competency of a president. The comparison set of people is narrower, and the domain of application of the strategies upon which he is judged is much better defined. The same principle applies when we refer to a capable janitor or a belligerent priest. We would not expect a capable janitor to make correct strategy decisions in international politics, nor would we expect a belligerent priest to seek out fist fights.

9.5 Combining Personality Traits

Personality traits combine with each other and with other personal attributes such as role themes. (A role theme is a characterization of a person's position in society, largely determined by the person's profession. See Schank and Abelson [1977].) The examples we just discussed are inter-actions of personality traits with role themes. The role theme defines the normative set of people with respect to which the personality trait defines a deviation. As we discussed, the role theme can also define the dimension of applicability of the personality trait. An incompetent president is incompetent with respect to his duties as president. An unscrupulous lawyer is likely to use the higher-order strategies (and not worry about the consequences of his actions upon the goals of others) only within the confines of his role as a lawyer. The unscrupulous lawyer might be con-siderate with friends or family outside the courtroom, regardless of how he carries out his professional activities.

Personality traits combine with each other to give a more complete picture of a person's goal tree and the strategies he is willing to use in furthering his goals. Our previous examples included several instances in which more than one personality trait was used to describe a person. All of these examples had one important property in common: each person-ality trait dealt with different personal goals or different sets of strategies. For instance a description of John as inquisitive, trustworthy, thrifty, and capable is simple to formulate. John has high A-know, high P-money, does not use trick options, and selects and applies strategies correctly. What happens when two personality traits describe the same goal or deal with the application of the same set of strategies? Consider the following examples:

> 9.12   John was trustworthy, but belligerent. When his new car turned out to be a lemon, the dealer ignored his complaints. Later, he sued to recover the purchase price plus punitive damages.

> 9.13   Mary told John, a self-centered playboy, that she was pregnant with his child. John said that he would never change his present lifestyle.

Story 9.12 is in character with John's personality traits. He did not use trick options (trustworthy), but he intensified an existing goal conflict by suing the dealer (belligerent). Hence in this aspect, the personality traits are additive. John's behavior corresponds to the union of the strategies suggested by both character traits. Belligerence, however, suggests that one is likely to use higher-order strategies when not necessary, where as trustworthiness suggests a preference for the opposite inclination. How do these aspects of John's personality traits combine? John did indeed use a higher than necessary strategy (there was no need to sue for punitive damages), but only after first trying the lower-order strategy of voicing his complaint. It seems that if two different personality traits suggest conflicting strategies, the lower-order strategies are likely to describe the person's initial behavior. The higher-order strategies describe his behavior upon failure of any initial attempt.

There are some personality traits that negate the use of particular strategies. For instance, honesty negates the use of trick options, and compassion negates the use of strategies that violate the goals of others. These traits cannot be combined with others that suggest the use of those very same strategies. Thus, it makes no sense to talk about a dishonest trustworthy person, nor does it make sense to describe an individual as compassionate and unscrupulous.

Goal-based personality traits combine in much the same way as strategy-based traits. If two traits refer to disjoint sets of goals, the information that modifies a person's goal tree is treated as purely additive. Story 9.13 is an example of two traits that indicate a disjoint set of goal relationships (see table 9.2) coming together to form a character description of John. People have little trouble understanding such a combination of personality traits, as evidenced by the rest of the story, where John's action appears to be very much in character.

9.6 Reactions upon Failure of Strategies

Many personality traits contain information about people that cannot be encoded in terms of goal trees or preferences for certain types of strategies. However, personality traits in general describe some aspect of the individual that deviates from the socially-defined, normative person. The aspects of personality traits that are outside the scope of our investigation include emotional and attitudinal attributes (but see Schank, et al. [1978]). For instance, there is more to a sensous person than a person whose goal of E-pleasure is high. Similarly, goals or strategies alone cannot fully describe "meek", "moody" or "outgoing" people.

There is, however, one other aspect to personality traits that can be usefully investigated within our paradigm. People have different reactions toward the success or failure of their planning and counterplanning efforts. Some personality traits imply certain types of behavior. A contented or aesthetic person will have a much more restrained reaction to success than an ambitious person, who is likely to be spurred on to further achievements by his past success. Since most stories deal with attempts to fulfill goals that repeatedly fail before (and if) success is ever reached, we focus on reactions to failure situations. The following table classifies the reaction of several personality traits to failure:

In order to see how the information in table 9.4 may be used for subjective understanding, consider the following stories:

Table 9.4.   Reaction-to-failure classification of personality traits

Personality Trait	Reactions to Failure of Planning and Counterplanning Strategies (deviations from social norm)
1. Persistent	Try plan many times before abandoning. Then, if possible, try new plan to fulfill the same goal.
2. Ambitious	Frustration. Try new plan if possible. Otherwise immediately pursue another goal.
3. Resourceful	Analyze failure to correct the plan or to choose a more appropriate strategy.
4. Happy-go-lucky	Abandon plan and possibly goal if not too important. No frustration reaction.
5. Depressed	Frustration. Probably abandon plan and goal.
6. Vindictive	Try to blame others for failure. Direct counterplanning effort to block the goals of whoever caused the failure. (This often takes greater importance than the original goal.)
7. Patient	No overt frustration. Try same or different plan, possibly after some time has elapsed.

9.14   John is a vindictive person. When his vegetable garden was dug up by Bill's dog, he picked up the heavy shovel and went to Bill's house.

9.15   John is a resourceful person. When his vegetable garden was dug up by Bill's dog, he picked up the heavy shovel and went to Bill's house.

QUESTION   Why did John go to Bill's house with the shovel?

Each story suggests a different class of answers to the question. In 9.14 the answer is that John wants to get back at Bill. We do not know whether he will use the shovel to overpower Bill, dig up Bill's garden in revenge, or some other counterplanning act. In 9.15 the most logical explanation seems to be that John wants Bill to fix up his garden, informing Bill that it is his responsibility. In any case, whatever action John intends in 9.15 is focused on the goal of repairing his damaged garden. In 9.14 the stronger expectation is that John wants revenge for the damage. The general expectations that are suggested by table 9.4 help the understander to make a further interpretation of either story. Consider the following as a possible continuation to 9.14 and 9.15.

CONTINUATION   John started digging top soil from Bill's yard.

In story 9.14 this continuation is interpreted as revenge for what Bill's dog did to his garden, but in 9.15 the same continuation makes more sense as part of a plan to repair John's garden. Top soil is necessary for a garden. The reason for the two diverging interpretations is the understander's different expectations about John's currently active goal. In 9.14 the continuation is first interpreted in light of the expected revenge, and a plausible interpretation is found. Hence, an inference mechanism modeling human understanding need not (should not) look further. In 9.15 the continuation is interpreted in light of the expectation that John is trying to repair his garden. As before, a plausible interpretation is found for John's action (stemming from the use of topsoil) and one needs to make no other inferences.

Personality traits define a goal-based context in which further events in a story can be interpreted. Without this context no explanation can be found for many events. If the above continuation occurred as an isolated sentence, we could make many inferences as to John's possible intent. He could be digging for worms to go fishing, laying the foundation to Bill's house, planting trees, or be building a dam with the soil. Neither these nor other spurious inferences need to be made in interpreting the continuation as part of story 9.14 or 9.15.

Some personality traits, such as ambition, encode information about all three aspects: the relative importance of goals, tendencies towards employing certain strategies, and reactions to success or failure. Other personality traits focus on one specific aspect with a higher degree of certainty. For instance, dishonesty refers only to a willingness to use trick-option strategies, but the reader is certain of this aspect of a person's personality. Ambition, on the other hand, suggests many more types of goals and strategies, but with a smaller degree of certainty. An ambitious person will probably use the higher-order strategies, but we can easily conceive of an ambitious scientist who does not spend his time threatening, overpowering, or deceiving people.

9.7 A Note on Integrated Understanding

We have shown the usefulness of analyzing personality traits to infer a person's goal tree, his tendencies toward applying certain classes of strategies, and his expected reactions upon the failure or success of his plan. The fact that goal trees and counterplanning strategies provide a useful way of encoding personality traits gives us good reason to believe that such mechanisms underlie much of human subjective understanding. Furthermore, the existence of a single, computationally effective, mechanism to represent personality traits, political ideologies, and conflict situations, suggests that we have a useful, generally applicable process model. From this model we should be able to create an integrated subjective understanding system using knowledge about people, interactions, conflicts, and human planning and counterplanning strategies.

In order to illustrate the necessity for an integrated mode of subjective understanding, we shall consider an instance in which the integration of personality traits and political ideologies proves very useful. Lee Ross (personal communication, 1978) suggested creating a model of the decision-making process President Truman used in formulating U.S. - Soviet relations in the 1950's. Ross proposed this task as an interesting but difficult endeavor because it involved modeling the personalities of Truman and Stalin as well as United States and Soviet goals and relations. Truman perceived the intentions of the Soviet Union as a mixture of what he thought were traditional Soviet goals and, more importantly, his perception of Joseph Stalin's character and aspirations. Truman relied more heavily on his understanding of Stalin than a fixed ideological perception of the goals of the Soviet Union. Let us see how Truman perceived Stalin, and how this subjective belief came about.

Truman spent a large part of his political career rising through the ranks of the St. Louis Democratic party machinery, at that time dominated by Pendergast. In the political machine one became successful by cultivating political friends, always keeping one's word regardless of changing circumstances, being ruthless with one's opposition outside the machine, and repaying all political favors. From Truman's point of view, Pendergast's character fit perfectly with these parameters. Pendergast had some other personality traits, such as being brusque and not too compassionate. Recall that when Truman became president the cold war had not yet started. In his initial interactions with Stalin, Truman attributed to him all the personality traits he found in Pendergast. (Why he did so is open to speculation. The following factors may have played an important role: Stalin was also brusque, incompassionate, and politically successful.) When Truman dealt with Stalin, he relied on the personality traits he attributed to Stalin, and disregarded the fact that Stalin may well have been acting more in Russia's best interests than in his own best interests.

When Stalin and Truman signed a set of agreements, Truman

expected Stalin, being trustworthy by Truman's perception, to keep his part of the bargain in letter and spirit. Later, Stalin violated the agreements in principle, but was careful to live up to the letter of the agreements. Truman, at first, found this behavior totally incomprehensible. Stalin was supposed to be trustworthy to his friends. What Truman viewed as Stalin's "betrayal" caused him to totally re-evaluate his perception of Stalin. Thereafter, Truman looked for a "hidden motive" behind all of Stalin's actions. In essence, Truman was expecting Stalin to use trick options almost all of the time. This was one of the most important reasons that the cold war started. Truman, worried about the interests of the United States in light of Soviet treachery, decided to take massive counteractions. (Truman considered it a virtue to be ruthless with outside opposition.) It was probably in neither country's best interests at the time to pursue an armaments race, but Truman's perception of Stalin as a totally dishonest and unscrupulous person led him to take counteractions against whatever plans he thought Stalin may have been preparing. Much later in his term of office, it appears that Truman started taking into account the goals of the two nations as his primary consideration in defining U.S.-Soviet policy.

This example illustrates the necessity of understanding personality traits, understanding one person's attribution of certain traits to other people, and the interaction of personality traits with political decision-making strategies. We do not yet have a system that can model such interactions, but building such a system appears to be a worthy goal for future research. We would also like to model the process whereby one person's perception of another person's character traits is radically changed by the former's interpretations of the latter's actions. We believe that modeling integrated understanding processes is the best way to understand human subjective interpretations of most events in the real world. In order to build systems capable of integrated subjective understanding, we need to use and further develop general representational and process-oriented mechanisms such as our goal trees and counterplanning strategies.

10

Subjective Models of
Human Conversations

10.1 Formulating Rules about Human Conversations

Subjective understanding is manifested in many different types of human interaction and communication. We have discussed subjective understanding in conflict situations, human personality traits, and ideological behavior. Modeling human participation in a conversation is another aspect of human cognitive behavior that requires subjective understanding. If we are to model a participant in a human conversation, we need to model his understanding of the topic under discussion and his interpretations of the other participant's knowledge, conversational goals, and interests.

This chapter discusses an empirical approach to understanding the processes that underlie human conversations. Since the task of codifying all the knowledge required for modeling human discourse is monumental, we confine our approach to formulating rules about the conversational intent of utterances in the course of a dialog. We demonstrate why these rules require knowledge structures, such as our goal trees, that encode subjective knowledge of the interests and motives of each conversational participant. This approach leads us to investigate the effects of shared assumptions and knowledge between the speakers, and the social and interpersonal relations between the speakers in the course of a conversation. Our approach toward the problem of analyzing conversations is different from other research efforts, such as those which adopt Searle's speech-acts paradigm (e.g., Levin's and Moore's [1977] dialog games) or a task-oriented approach (Grosz [1977]). Our interests focus on modeling, and hence gaining some understanding, of the mental processes that underlie human conversations. We are less interested in finding linguistic regularities that shed little light on the understanding process itself.

Consider the following conversation fragment between Bill and John, two college students sharing an apartment:

> 10.1   John.   Hi, what's new, Bill?
>   Bill.   I'm going to visit my folks tonight.

We can analyze Bill's utterance in conversation fragment 10.1 in terms of its immediate meaning; that is, a representation of Bill's utterance in conceptual dependency or some other meaning representation. This, however, is a very incomplete analysis of what Bill said. Why did Bill say that he was visiting his folks? Bill could just as easily have said, "I'm going to brush my teeth tonight." This utterance, however, doesn't answer John's question; brushing one's teeth is not "something new". Therefore, we could propose a rather simple conversational rule:

> RULE 10.1   If a question is asked in the course of a conversation, the other participant should answer this question.

Rule 10.1, however, is too naive. Suppose Bill's answer was: "There are a few more microns of dust on the window sill than the last time you asked me that question." This is indeed "something new," but we would think of Bill as a wise guy for answering the question literally rather than addressing what John "must have meant." What did John really mean? John must have been looking for something out of the ordinary and of some intrinsic importance. Let us propose a new rule to incorporate this principle:

> RULE 10.2   In the formulation of an answer, the speaker should address the true significance of the question, not just its literal meaning.

What is the true significance of a question? In conversation fragment 10.1, Bill might have answered: "The J-particle angular momentum of +3/2 was confirmed today." John, a literature major who does not understand physics, may not be inclined to continue the conversation. Therefore, Bill's answer is not what was called for, unless Bill intentionally wanted to end the conversation. This example suggests that Bill missed something in establishing the true significance of John's question. John did, indeed, explicitly ask to hear something new; implicitly he meant something important and out of the ordinary. The J-particle answer conforms to these requirements, but it is still an inappropriate response. Therefore, the true significance of John's answer must include John's conversational goal. Why did John ask "What's new"? The answer is, obviously, to start a conversation with Bill. Bill, being aware of this conversational goal, needs to choose an answer that attempts to initiate conversation. That is, Bill should choose a topic of conversation that John can talk about and that John may be interested in. Conversational rule 10.3 summarizes this discussion:

> RULE 10.3   In introducing a new topic of conversation, the topic should be chosen so that both speakers have some knowledge and interest in its discussion.

The process of understanding the conversational import of an utterance may be conceptually divided into two primary subprocesses: 1) determine the conversational goal of the utterance, and 2) establish the real, often implicit, meaning of the utterance. Both of these processes require subjective analysis of the question. The conversational goal of an utterance depends on one speaker's beliefs of the motives of the other speaker. Establishing the real meaning of an utterance depends on the knowledge that the speaker believes he shares with the other conversational participant. Lehnert [1978] analyzes the process of establishing the real meaning of questions as a function of the way in which the question is asked and knowledge about what a person generally considers important. Our analysis focuses on the conversational goals of the participants and the establishment of a shared knowledge base between the participants. It is this shared cultural, personal, and factual knowledge that the conversational participants leave implicit in each communication. To illustrate this fact, consider conversational fragment 10.2:

> 10.2 *John.*   Do you want to go out and try the bar at Monument Square?
>
> *Bill.*   I'm going to visit my folks tonight.

Real significance of Bill's utterance:

   i.   No, I cannot go to the Monument Square bar.

   ii.   The reason why I cannot go is that I made a previous commitment, and I cannot be in two places at once tonight.

  iii.   The previous commitment is a visit to my folks.

  iv.   I am telling you about the reason why I cannot go drinking with you rather than just saying "no" because I do not want you to get angry at me.

   v.   I might also wish to shift the topic of conversation to a discussion about my family.

Bill knows that John will interpret his answer so as to conclude its real significance; otherwise Bill would have chosen to explicitly state the real significance. How does Bill know that John will understand him correctly? Clearly Bill and John must share some common sense knowledge such as:

    a.   A person cannot be in two places at once.

    b.   Previous commitments should be honored.

    c.   If X's invitation or suggestion is turned down by Y without apparent reason, then X is likely to get upset at Y.

    d.   If a person introduces a new topic in a conversation, he may want to discuss the current topic further.

Both Bill and John are aware that they share a common cultural knowledge base. This knowledge is very crucial in determining what is said in the conversation. Bill must have considered items (i) through (iv) before deciding that it was sufficient to say only (iii). How did Bill decide to say only (iii)? He must have concluded that John would infer (i), (ii), and (iv) without difficulty. Thus, Bill knew about John's general knowledge because of their common cultural background (i.e. they are both members of the same culture). In addition, the personal relation between Bill and John can establish a larger context of shared knowledge between them. Bill used this knowledge to decide what to say in the conversation.

In the course of a conversation, people make assumptions about each other's knowledge. It is sometimes easier to see what these conversational assumptions are when they turn out to be incorrect, as in the following example:

10.3 *Pete.*   How are you going to vote on Proposition 13?

    Mary.   On what?

    Pete.   You know, the property tax limitation.

    Mary.   Oh yeah. I'm not registered to vote. Which way were you trying to convince me to vote?

    Pete.   I was hoping you would help me make up my mind.

    Mary.   Actually, I don't give a damn about politics.

At the beginning of the conversation Pete assumed that Mary knew what Proposition 13 was, that she was able to vote, that she would vote, and that she had already decided how to vote on Proposition 13. All of these assumptions turned out to be incorrect, and the course of the conversation turned towards clarifying the incorrect assumptions. This example is an instance of a more general rule of conversation:

RULE 10.4   If a participant in a conversation discovers that his assumptions about the shared knowledge between the two speakers is incorrect, then he will steer the conversation to

1.   establish a common knowledge base on a specific topic, or

2.   discover what their shared knowledge is in general, or

3.   shift the conversational topic to some matter where a common knowledge base is more likely to exist, or

4.   end the conversation.

Assumptions are also made about the conversational intent of the participants and about their interest in the conversational topic. Mary inferred Peter's conversational intent incorrectly: he was seeking advice, not trying to lobby for or against Proposition 13. Pete started the entire conversation on the wrong topic by assuming that Mary was interested in politics or taxes. A conversation about a topic that one of the participants finds uninteresting will usually digress to other topics or fizzles out as the uninterested party volunteers no new information, finds an excuse to do something else, or states outright that the conversation is boring (as was the case in our example).

Erroneous assumptions about conversational intent lead to misunderstandings because each speaker will address the perceived intent of the other speaker's utterance. It is, therefore, imperative to infer correctly the other speaker's conversational intentions in order for the conversation to proceed naturally. The type of misunderstanding that often results from incorrectly perceived conversational intentions is, on occasion, exploited in creating certain types of jokes, as in example 10.4:

10.4   *Son.*   Dad, I robbed the liquor store yesterday.
      Dad.   How could you ever do such a thing, son?
      Son.   Well, I got me this gun, and I pointed it at the cashier . . .

The father's conversational intentions were expressing shock and disbelief at his sons' action, and asking what motivated his son to do such a terrible thing. The son, possibly not sharing Dad's (and the reader's) assumption that armed robbery is necessarily a bad thing, misinterpreted Dad's intent to be a query about the plan he used to rob the store.

To illustrate the importance of the implicit conversational goals and shared knowledge between the participants in a conversation, we present a few more dialog fragments between Bill and John, the two college students who share an apartment. In each example, as in conversations 10.1 and 10.2, Bill utters the same response, but its meaning is significantly different, depending on the context of the conversation.

> 10.5 *John.*   Are you broke again? You are going to have to come up with your
> share of the rent this month.
>
> *Bill.*   I'm going to visit my folks tonight.

Meaning of Bill's utterance:

    i. Yes, I'm broke again.

    ii. Yes, I'll try to contribute my share of the rent.

    iii. My parents might give me some money if I ask them.

    iv. If I visit them and ask them in person I have a better chance of getting some money.

    v. I'll visit them tonight and then I'll ask them for money.

When we read conversation fragment 10.5, we infer that Bill may be going to ask his parents for money. How do we do this? We do not share knowledge with Bill to the effect that his parents have money or that Bill is willing to ask them for money. The answer is based on a conversational rule:

> RULE 10.5   The utterances in a conversation should be connected by continuity
> of topic, common conversational goals, and attention to the intent of
> the utterances of the other participant.

Since the reader assumes that rule 10.5 is true for conversation fragment 10.5, he concludes that there must be a connection between Bill's need for money and the visit to his parents. The reader then infers the most likely connection: Bill will ask his parents for money. John must also make this inference, based on rule 10.5, unless he already knows that Bill regularly visits his parents to ask for money. The significant point illustrated in example 10.5 is that the conversation focused the inference mechanism to find a connection between the respective utterances. Therefore, conversational principles can play an important role in focusing human reasoning processes. The principle of focusing inference processes on significant or interesting aspects of conversational utterances is the underlying assumption of our theory of human subjective understanding. We reiterate our principle below:

Conversation rules constrain the inference process in generating and understanding conversational utterances. The subjective interpretation of the utterances and the conversational goals of both participants further narrow the focus of the inference process.

Let us continue with fragments of Bill and John's conversation:

10.6 *John.* How come you never see your family?

    Bill. I'm going to visit my folks tonight.

Meaning of Bill's utterance:

  i. I do visit my family.

  ii. Supporting evidence: I'm going to visit them tonight.

  iii. Therefore, what you just said is not true.

10.7 *John.* Can I borrow your car? I got this heavy date tonight.

    Bill. I'm going to visit my folks tonight.

Meaning of Bill's utterance:

Alternative I:

  i. No, you cannot borrow my car tonight.

  ii. I am going to visit my folks tonight.

  iii. I need to drive there.

  iv. The car cannot be in two places at once.

Alternative II:

  i. Yes, you can borrow my car tonight.

  ii. I am going to be at my folks' place where I don't need to use it.

In order to interpret the above conversational fragment, we need to use conversational rule 10.2 in conjunction with rule 10.6, stated below:

RULE 10.6   If the form of the expected response to one's last utterance is totally violated by the other speaker's actual response, he is probably:

1. Supplying more detailed information from which the original expected response can be inferred, or

2. Temporarily digressing to a subtopic, or

3. The current topic violates his conversational goals, and therefore he shifts topic.

Thus, to understand Bill's response in 10.7 we first apply rule 10.2, which tells us to expect a yes/no answer. Bill said, "I'm going to visit my folks tonight." This violates the expected response, making rule 10.6 applicable. In order to determine whether the yes/no answer can be inferred from Bill's response, the inferencer is called to see how Bill's PTRANS can relate to the use of a car. Once the inferencer is focused in such a manner, it should be easy *for John* to determine whether Bill does or does not need the car for his PTRANS. We, as third party observers, cannot make this determination, although the first alternative may be preferred because "no" answers require explanations more often than "yes" answers. However, John's subjective interpretation of Bill's response should clearly establish in his mind whether Bill meant yes or no. John, being Bill's roommate, probably shares with Bill the knowledge of whether or not Bill drives his car to his folk's house.

It is often the case that a speaker will expect his listener to make a subjective interpretation of his remarks that a third party overhearing the conversation may not be able to make. For instance, consider the meaning of the following utterance:

McGovern is running for president, and we all know what will happen in this country if he wins!

If the above utterance is part of a conversation between two ultra-conservatives, it has a very different subjective meaning than if the utterance takes place in a conversation between two liberals. In the first case the utterance means that McGovern will ruin the country, and in the latter case it means that he will greatly improve the U.S. government. Therefore, conversations are subject to the same differences in interpretation as narrative events. Each speaker has to take into account, to some degree, the beliefs of the other speaker if he wishes to be correctly understood.

Let us consider one more conversation fragment which will illustrate the importance of conversational context in interpreting utterances. Understanding the following exchange requires one to use rule 10.2 and rule 10.6 in the same manner in which they were used to understand conversation fragment 10.7.

> 10.8 *John.*   Can I have the apartment to myself?
> I got this heavy date tonight.
>
> *Bill.*   I'm going to visit my folks tonight.

Meaning of Bill's utterance:

   i.   Yes, you can have the apartment.

   ii.   What you want is for me to be elsewhere.

   iii.   I was planning on that anyway, since I am visiting my folks tonight.

In each of our conversational fragments the same utterance on Bill's part is understood differently, depending on the context established by John's previous utterance. Utterances in a conversation do not usually have a meaning independent of the rest of the conversation; their meaning is part of the context of the entire conversation. Thus, it is easy to see why quoting only a short passage from a conversation (or a political speech) can give that passage an entirely different meaning from what was originally intended.

The shared knowledge between two speakers depends on many different factors. Two speakers share a large amount of basic knowledge by merely being members of the human race (e.g. the basic drives that motivate humans such as hunger, self preservation, etc.). More knowledge is shared if the two speakers are members of the same culture. (Much of the cultural and more basic human knowledge necessary to understand natural language is discussed in Schank and Abelson [1977].) If the two participants hold the same type of job, are professional colleagues, or have the same special interests, then they will share some rather specific knowledge. Two people with the same special interests (such as football or radio astronomy) will usually steer the conversation to a discussion of their common interests.

RULE 10.7   The topic of a conversation may drift to a subject on which the conversational participants share a great amount of knowledge.

10.2 Social Relationships in a Conversation

Social relations establish the perceived goals of conversational participants and the type of knowledge shared by the participants. For instance,
the relationship between John and Bill in conversational fragment 10.7
establishes their shared knowledge about whether Bill needs his car. Let
us consider some examples of how different social relations affect the
meaning of a conversational utterance.

> 10.9   Army general.   I want a juicy hamburger.
>   Staff Aide.   Right away, sir!

> 10.10   Seven-year-old.   I want a juicy hamburger.
>   Mother.   Maybe next week. We are having chicken today.

> 10.11   Prison Inmate 1.   I want a juicy hamburger.
>   Prison Inmate 2.   Me too! Everything here tastes like cardboard.

The utterance "I want a juicy hamburger" is interpreted differently
in each dialog fragment. The difference in the interpretations is based on
the different social relations existing between the two conversational participants. In dialog 10.9 the utterance was interpreted to mean a direct
order to the staff aide: "Get me a hamburger and make sure it is juicy!"
In dialog 10.10, the 7-year-old was expressing a request to his mother,
hoping that his mother might comply. A paraphrase of the 7-year-old's
statement is: "I like juicy hamburgers, can you please make me (or buy
me) one?" In dialog 10.11, the same statement was interpreted as nothing
more than wishful thinking: "Wouldn't it be nice if I could eat a really
juicy hamburger." The first inmate made no order or request to the second
inmate. Hence, the first utterance of each dialog fragment reflects a different conversational goal, one which is dependent on the differences in
the social relations of the conversational participants.

The social context and the relationship between the two speakers
generate expectations that guide the course of the conversation. A staff
aide expects to be ordered about by a general. A mother expects her son
to ask her for favors. Prison inmates cannot expect each other to do
things that are made impossible by their incarceration. These expectations
lead to a formulation of different conversational goals for the utterance,
"I want a juicy hamburger," in each conversational fragment. The conversational principle exemplified in our discussion is summarized in the
following conversational principles:

> *The social relationship between the participants in a conversation generates expectations about the intentional meaning of utterances in the conversation. These expectations are used to determine the conversational goals of each participant.*

> *Each speaker's perception of the conversational goals of the other speaker determines his interpretation of the other speaker's utterances.*

Differences in interpretation of conversational goals lead to different responses in a dialog, as illustrated in conversation fragments 10.9, 10.10 and 10.11. We saw how a social relationship between two people can influence their interpretations of each other's conversational goals. Two strangers can also make assumptions about each other's conversational goals based on appearances, social circumstances, and each other's occupation. Let us analyze an example presented in the first chapter. There are several responses to John's question below; each response is appropriate in its social context:

Scenario: John walked up to a person on the corner and asked: "Do you know how to get to Elm Street?"

10.12.1   The stranger replied: "You go two blocks toward that tall building and turn right."

10.12.2   The cab driver on the corner replied: "Sure, Hop in. Where on Elm do you want to go?"

10.12.3   The person, who was holding up a map and a piece of paper with an Elm Street address on it, replied: "No, could you tell me how to get there?"

10.12.4   The child answered: "Yes, I know how to get there!"

We can explain the different responses in terms of each person's goals and his perception of John's conversational goal. The stranger believed that the reason behind John's utterance, i.e., John's conversational goal, was D-KNOW(John, location of Elm Street). (D-KNOW(X,Y) means that X has the goal of finding out Y. D-PROX(X,Z) means that X has the goal of being at location Z. See Schank and Abelson [1977] for a full discussion of D-goals.) Furthermore, most people have the goal of being helpful when doing so costs them nothing. The goal of being helpful translates into the conversational goal of answering questions when divulging information is not detrimental to the goals of the responder. Hence, the combination of the following three items led the stranger to answer with response 10.12.3:

1. John probably has the goal:
   D-KNOW(John, loc. of Elm Street).

2. The stranger inferred John's conversational goal.

3. The stranger has the goal of being generally helpful.

The other three responses can also be explained in terms of the conversational goals of the participants. The taxi driver interpreted John's question as a request to drive him there. That is, the taxi driver inferred that John's goal was D-PROX(John, Elm Street). One can infer in general that if a person wants to know the location of a particular street, it is likely that he also has the goal of going to that street. Why is this inference more appropriate for a taxi driver than a random person on the street? A taxi driver makes his living by fulfilling other people's D-PROX goals. Therefore, it makes sense for him to look for people who have D-PROX goals but lack means of achieving them. Since it is the goal of a taxi driver to find people with unfulfilled D-PROX goals, it is extremely useful for him to make the D-PROX inference discussed above. A stranger on the street corner has no reason to make the D-PROX inference—it does not help him fulfill any goals. Therefore, the goals of a conversational participant guide him to infer a different goal for the other participant.

The third response to John's question illustrates again how the goals of the other participant affect his interpretation of John's conversational goal. The person with the map has the goal of D-KNOW(self, location of Elm Street). Furthermore, he can infer that John knows his D-KNOW goal; the map and Elm Street address are clearly visible. When John asks him whether he knows how to get to Elm Street, the person with the map infers that John has the goal of being helpful, i.e., of providing him with the desired information. This is the reverse of the situation in 10.12.1

Why does this person *not* make the inference that John has the goal D-KNOW(John, location of Elm Street)? After all, John can see the map, a source of information for D-KNOWing the location of streets. It is perfectly conceivable that John wants to tap this source of information for his own ends, counting on the general helpfulness of the person with the map. The person with the map, trying to fulfill his D-KNOW goal, will give preferential interpretation to utterances by others as directly relevant to his goal. Therefore, John's question is interpreted with respect to how it can affect the D-KNOW goal and found to be quite relevant. Once a satisfactory interpretation of an utterance is achieved, people do not continue to search for other possible interpretations. The person with the map never considers the possibility that John was pursing a D-KNOW goal of his own.

This argument is analogous to the argument against parsing a sentence with semantically ambiguous words or ambiguous syntactic structures by generating all possible parses and, subsequently, selecting the most appropriate parse. People use situational context and semantics in generating only one parse for almost all English sentences (Schank [1975]). In the same manner, people do not analyze for later evaluation all possible conversational goals which may underlie an utterance in a dialog. One can always hypothesize an endless list of possible motives for any utterance in a conversation, each new motive more bizarre than the previous one. Once a sufficiently adequate conversational goal is inferred, people do not continue searching for other possibilities. As illustrated in the above examples, the search for a conversational goal starts with a subjectively centered inference process. A conversational participant first tries to see how an utterance may be related to his own conversational goals. This process, to some extent, explains why people often hear what they want to hear in a sufficiently ambiguous conversation or speech, such as an interview or press conference given by a politician or diplomat.

Response 10.12.4 illustrates that the responder may have inferred yet another conversational goal for John. Children are often quizzed by adults; they have the goal in some conversational situations, such as school, of showing how much they know. The child, therefore, infers that John's goal in asking the question was related to his goal of demonstrating his knowledge. Essentially, the child assumed that John's goal was D-KNOW(John, does child know location of Elm Street). None of the other responders inferred this conversational goal on John's part. The different subjective assumptions about someone else's conversational goals leads to different types of conversations (and different topics being discussed) between different people. If it were not for the subjective component in the interpretation of conversational goals, human conversations would be much more predictable and repetitive than they actually are.

If a person in a conversation has more than one active or relevant goal, then the goal focused on by the inference process is the higher-level goal in that person's goal tree. (See Chapter 9 on personality traits.) For instance, the responder in 10.12.3 had both the D-KNOW(self, location of Elm Street) goal and the goal of being generally helpful. In his present situation, the D-KNOW goal was more important; therefore he focused on the possible relevance of John's question to this goal, rather than trying to interpret it as a request for help. Similarly, the taxi driver may also have the general helpfulness goal, but the inference process does not focus on this goal unless the higher importance goal of getting a fare is not relevant in the current situation. The following dialog illustrates this instance:

10.13   *John.*   Do you know how to get to Elm Street?

    Taxi Driver.   Sure, hop in. Where on Elm do you want to go?

    John.   Oh, no, thank you, I wasn't looking for a cab.

    Taxi Driver.   Elm Street is a mile and a half from here, that way.

10.3 MICS: A Process Model of Human Conversation

The phenomenon of human conversation is too complex for any single study to do justice to more than a narrow aspect of the problem. In order fully to understand human conversations we may have to understand all human cognitive reasoning processes. Thus far we have focused our efforts primarily on the subjective interpretation of conversational goals. In building a system of programs to model human conversations and to test our ideas of subjective focus of inference in the course of a conversation, we pursued the following general approach: (1) study many sample conversations; (2) try to establish some relatively general rules of conversation; (3) encode these rules into a process model; (4) see if this model accounts for certain aspects of human conversation; (5) realize that we solved hardly more than a minute part of the problem, and (6) reiterate the research process in a (hopefully convergent) feed-back loop.

The conversational rules and principles discussed in the previous sections primarily illustrate the subjective aspect of human conversation. There are other processes in human discourse that need to be analyzed if we are to create a functional process model of human conversation. We demonstrated the need to understand shared knowledge between speakers, social relationships between speakers, and the conversational goals motivating each utterance in a dialog. All these aspects are subjective phenomena; knowledge about particular topics, conversational goals, interests, and social relations may vary greatly among different speakers. There are other mechanisms, not as dependent on subjective viewpoints, that also need to be modeled in order to create an integrated process model of a conversational participant. For instance, the problem of topic selection in a conversation needs to be addressed. How does a person change the topic in a conversation? How are new topics chosen? How is the continuity of a conversation preserved? These questions are analyzed in Schank [1977]. Here we propose some additional ideas on the impact of shared knowledge and interests on topic selection.

MICS (Mixed-Initiative Conversational System) is a fully implemented computer program which generates one side of a natural-language conversation. MICS embodies the conversational rules discussed in this paper, a topic transition mechanism based on Schank [1977], and the idea of a conversational form. We define conversational form by a set of rules which helps to characterize well-formed conversations. For instance, the following seven rules are among the twenty conversational-form rules in MICS:

RULE 10.8   Do not repeat information in the course of a conversation unless explicitly requested.

RULE 10.9   Do not say things that the other speaker already knows about.

RULE 10.10   If the other speaker says something that violates one's belief, then respond in kind by re-asserting the violated belief.

RULE 10.11   If insulted, insult the other speaker or end the conversation.

RULE 10.12   If the other speaker rejects the current topic, do not return to it in the course of the conversation.

RULE 10.13   If the previous utterance activates no conversational goals, give any information relevant to the topic. (i.e., maintain the conversation.)

RULE 10.14   If the entire conversation activates no goals, then find a way to terminate the dialog.

The conversational-form rules are useful in producing a coherent conversation. A sequence of utterances that does not accord to the rules above would not be labeled a "well-formed" conversation by a person reading the transcript. These rules are used by MICS for two primary purposes: interpreting the conversational import of an utterance from its immediate meaning representation and guiding the English generation of most utterances.

The conversational-form rules were formulated because without some process notion of what is appropriate to say in the course of a conversation, MICS could not produce coherent dialogs. It is also the case that without topic transition rules, or without a model of the subjective import of the conversational goals of the speakers, MICS cannot generate reasonable utterances of any form. MICS illustrates that the conversational rules, topic-transition rules, and conversational-form rules provide a sound, if possibly incomplete, approach to the modeling of human conversation.

MICS is able to generate reasonable conversations on domains about which it has some knowledge, but there are still many shortcomings, as illustrated in the examples that follow.

MICS "knows" about itself as a person (e.g. it believes itself to be a computer programmer) and uses a model of the other conversational participant that contains certain information about him, such as his social status, his occupation, his relationship with other people, his areas of special interest, and his personal goals relevant to conversational situations. The model of the other speaker is a necessary part of the conversational model, since it enables MICS to apply the conversational rules. When MICS talks to a stranger, it builds a model of this person; in fact, one of its conversational goals is to learn about the person with whom it is conversing.

We first re-introduce a MICS dialog, presented in Chapter 2, with some comments on what MICS does in the process of formulating its utterances. Then, we describe the conversational process model embodied by the MICS programs. Finally, we analyze MICS's processing for a short dialog in greater detail. In the conversation that follows (an actual computer run), MICS starts out knowing nothing about Dave.

MICS CONVERSATION LOG   OCT-11-77

HELLO, WHAT IS YOUR NAME?

I am Dave.
WHAT'S NEW TODAY, DAVE?

Nothing, What's your name?
MY NAME IS MICS.

What is your job?
I AM A COMPUTER PROGRAMMER

That's nice.
WHAT DO YOU DO FOR A LIVING?

COMMENT
MICS takes the initiative by asserting its conversational goal of learning about Dave.

I am still a student.
DO YOU LIKE BEING A STUDENT?

For the time being yes.
WHAT WILL YOU DO AFTERWARDS?

★★COMMENT★★

MICS knows that most people who are students have the goal of qualifying for a profession. Achieving one's desired profession is a high importance goal for most people, thus MICS tries to find what this goal is for Dave.

I want to be a professor some day.
WHAT DO YOU DO FOR FUN?

★★COMMENT★★

MICS formed a person frame for Dave. At this point, the conversational goal of trying to establish an area of mutual interest and shared knowledge is activated.

I smoke dope.
YOU MIGHT GET STONED IF YOU SMOKE TOO MUCH.

I know, that's the idea.
YOU MIGHT GET IN TROUBLE IF THE COPS CATCH YOU.

All right, stop moralizing, what do you do for fun?
I LIKE TO PLAY CHESS

That sounds boring.
NO, IT IS A LOT OF FUN!

My brother Eric plays chess.
HE MUST BE SMART.

I have to go. Bye Mics.
NICE TALKING TO YOU, DAVE

As a result of the conversation, MICS knows something about Dave, in particular that one of his life goals is to become a professor. MICS's conversational goals cause it to establish its own conversational topics. When a new topic is introduced by the human speaker, MICS stays on the chosen topic or chooses a closely related topic. Another rule of conversation is invoked in the above dialog:

> RULE 10.15   Each participant in the conversation has the conversational goal of saying things that are important to the other participant.

When the human participant says that he likes to smoke marijuana, MICS finds in its memory that smoking marijuana is illegal and can lead to the smoker getting stoned. According to MICS's beliefs getting stoned is illegal and doing something illegal leads to undesirable consequences. MICS determines that it is important for Dave to know about the bad consequences of his acts. Therefore, applying rule 10.15, MICS warns Dave about the evils of marijuana. It is evident that MICS should have known that Dave knows that smoking marijuana leads to getting stoned, and that getting stoned is, in fact, Dave's primary purpose for smoking. If MICS had known this fact, conversational-form rule 10.9 would have applied and prevented MICS from warning Dave about getting stoned. Therefore, MICS needs a better mechanism for deciding what knowledge it shares with the other speaker. It is very difficult to determine what the other person already knows and what he is able to infer, but this is a problem that cannot be circumvented if we are to model human discourse.

The conversational-form rule of reacting to a belief violation (rule 10.10) causes MICS to object when Dave says that playing chess (MICS's favorite pastime) is not exciting. Since the two participants can not find a common area of interest, the conversation ends without any substantive dialog. This illustrates conversational rule 10.4, discussed in the previous section. If neither participant in a conversation is able to satisfy his subjectively defined conversational goals, the conversation is likely to terminate in short order.

Let us see how the MICS paradigm uses the various conversational rules, knowledge of its goals and interests, and knowledge of other speakers to produce a coherent conversation. Consider the control-flow diagram outlined in figure 10.1.

Figure 10.1 is a diagram of the control flow of MICS. As a process model of conversation, MICS is a useful tool, but it is far from a complete or even an entirely correct model of human conversation. MICS is essentially a three-module production system. Each module knows about a different aspect of conversation. A production corresponds to a rule of conversation, including the rules discussed in this chapter. The productions do not have any formal constraints, like Newell's [1973] PSG model. Some productions, such as rule 10.6, suggest more than one alternative course of action.

Let us trace the processing typically performed in formulating an appropriate response to an utterance in the course of a conversation. First, the meaning of the utterance is analyzed by a set of expectations generated from the active conversational context. These expectations range from specific answers to questions posed by MICS, to general expectations about topic transitions motivated by MICS considerations of what the other conversational participant is interested in discussing. If these expectations fail to determine the meaning of the utterance, MICS analyzes the utterance for its immediate meaning, which it later tries to relate to the topic of the conversation. Next, the conversational-form rules apply to this analysis. These rules determine both the eventual form of the response and constrain the topic selections possible at the second module.

Figure 10.1. MICS control-flow diagram

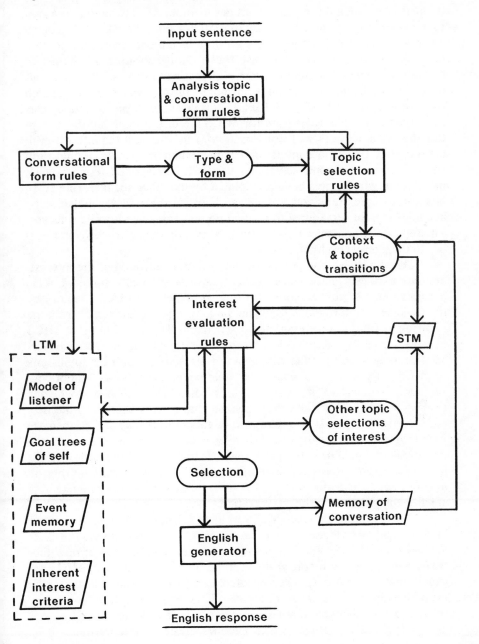

The second module consists of a set of rules that suggests transitions in the conversational topic and searches memory for information relevant to the current topic. Some items in the MICS memory are tagged as being inherently interesting; other items are interesting only in a specific context. The topic selection rules use these static measures of interest to retrieve information items on a most-interesting-first basis. This is analogous to the best-first technique in more conventional heuristic search (Newell and Simon [1972]). Schank [1977] discusses topic selection rules in conversation. The rules used for MICS are of the same nature, except that they interact both with conversation-form rules and the interest-evaluation rules. The former interaction occurs when the conversational-form rules block a set of topic selection rules from being tested. For instance, in a case in which one's belief is violated by the other speaker, rule 10.10 blocks all topic transition strategies. That is, the violated belief itself becomes the conversational topic, and no new topic needs to be selected. The topic-selection rules pass on the information they retrieve from memory to the interest evaluation rules.

The subjective component of the system is encoded in the interest-evaluation rules. These rules evaluate several (typically three or four) possible items of conversation that have been retrieved from memory by the topic-selection rules. A topic can be judged as "interesting" from the viewpoint of either conversational participant. The algorithm that MICS uses to decide on the most interesting topic to introduce in the conversation functions in the following manner: if discussing an item fulfills one of MICS's conversational goals, that item becomes the new topic of conversation. Otherwise, if an item fulfills what MICS believes to be the conversational goal of the other speaker, that item is chosen as the new conversational topic. If two items are of equal interest to MICS, then the item that may interest the other speaker is chosen. If no items fulfill the conversational goal of either participant, MICS chooses the item with the highest inherent interest. The annotated MICS run appearing on the following pages illustrates how MICS uses this algorithm to generate reasonable things to say in the conversation.

Our algorithm requires MICS to have substantial knowledge of the interests and knowledge of the other speaker. This is not always the case; MICS is not well-versed at inducing the conversational goals of the other participant (a very difficult problem in its own right!). Hence, MICS assumes that the other speaker is interested in discussing the topics he introduces in the conversation, topics related to his goal tree, and topics related to any other goal that people in general are likely to have.

MICS has a goal-tree which encodes the relative importance of its conversational goals. When we model the other speaker with a full goal tree of his own, we can often infer which goal was addressed by the other speaker's utterances. Thus, knowing the goals of the other speaker is of great help to MICS in generating meaningful conversations. For instance the conversation between MICS and Pete (presented below) is much more interesting than our earlier conversation between MICS and Dave, a stranger for whom MICS had no goal tree from which to derive its interest-evaluation rules.

Once the topic selections are evaluated for relevancy to the goals of each speaker, the most relevant item of information is chosen as the next utterance to express in the conversation. The other possible topic selections that are of interest (either subjective interest or inherent interest) are stored in a short term memory. These items are used if the other speaker does not change the conversational topic and MICS is called upon to give more information on a particular item. The preferred topic selection is expressed by a template-based English generator that uses any relevant information abstracted by the conversational-form rules. For example, in the MICS-Dave dialog MICS generated the utterance "No, chess is a lot of fun!" from the information item that playing chess gives pleasure to the two players and the conversational form that called for an emphatic denial of the other speaker's last utterance.

We illustrate the internal workings of MICS by analyzing in some detail the processing exhibited by MICS in its conversation with Pete, someone who MICS believes to be its friend. Recall the previous conversation with Dave; MICS uses the information it learned about Dave in the following dialog.

Start of MICS Conversational Dialog

PSEUDO LOG FILE	12-Oct-77 23:57:01

@RUN MICS[37,104]

Program Run	**Annotation**

*(CONVERSE)

HELLO, WHAT IS YOUR NAME?

Pete.

	Rule S12 is the conversational rule
FULFILLED EXPECTATION	which states that if a specific item of
FROM RULE#S12	information is requested then the
	other participant will provide it. In

PETE PERSON FRAME FOUND
PETE GOALTREE LOADED

TOPIC SELECTION INVOKED . . .
    (NO ACTIVE TOPIC)

RULE#T4 FIRED

WHAT'S NEW TODAY, PETE?

Professor Stevenson is
giving us an exam Friday.

TOPIC SELECTION INVOKED . . .
    ((STEVENSON N1 N2 N3)
    ($EXAM N4 N5 N2 N3))

SEARCHING GOALTREE: MICS
INTEREST EVAL INVOKED . . .
    (NO MICS GOALS ACTIVATED)

SEARCHING GOALTREE: PETE
    INTEREST PRIORITY
RULE#G2 FIRED

RULE#G6 FIRED
    ((N2 N3) (N4 N5) (N1))

(PP N2)
    ((< = > ($EXAM
            CLASS: NIL
            PROF: STEVENSON

            STU: NIL
            DIFFICULTY: +10
            OUTCOME: NIL))

STEVENSON GIVES DIFFICULT
EXAMS.

Yeah, do you know that Dave
is probably going to flunk?

TOPIC SELECTION INVOKED . . .

this case the specific item was a
name.

When there are no topic selections to
choose from, the interest-evaluation
rules are not called. Rule T4, a topic-
selection rule, states that if one has
nothing to say, one should invite the
other party to introduce a topic.

MICS finds in memory several items
(given temporary nodes N1, N2,
etc . . .) that are relevant to Stevenson and taking exams. N2 and N3 are
relevant to both topics.

MICS does not find anything relevant
to its own goals among the topic
selections.

MICS knows Pete's goal tree. Pete is
more interested in passing exams than
in the personal lives of others. Therefore, the items relevant to $EXAM
are ranked as more important than
those relevant to Professor Stevenson.
Of course, the items relevant to both
topics are the most important. Rule
G6 checks for an item being relevant
to more than one topic. N2 is chosen
over N3 (N3 is: Bill passed Stevenson's exam last year) because it is of
higher inherent interest. The +10 in
N2's representation (left) indicates
that N2 is an unordinary event. (Our
scales range for 0 to 10; 5 indicates
a normative value.)

Pete stays on the $EXAM topic but
ignores Stevenson. Topic selection
rule 17 detects that this is the second
utterance by Pete on the same topic;
therefore, other topic selection rules
give preference to $EXAM related

RULE#T17 FIRED
   (TOPIC PRIORITY $EXAM)
   ($EXAM PREVIOUS-TOPIC)
   (DAVE N6 N7 N8)

SEARCHING GOALTREE: MICS

RULE#G2 FIRED
   (D-KNOW ACTOR: MICS
      MOBJECT: (*SPEC* REL
         DAVE))

SEARCHING GOALTREE: PETE

RULE#G5 FIRED
   ($EXAM FOCUS: OUTCOME)

CALLING INFERENCER . . .

FOCUS: (MERGE (GOAL7 . MICS)
         (GOAL4 . PETE)

CHECKING PRIMARY EFFECT OF:

   ((< => ($EXAM
         CLASS: NIL
         PROF: STEVENSON
         STU: DAVE
         DIFFICULTY: +10
         OUTCOME: FAIL)))

VIOLATES PRECONDITIONS FOR:

((< => ($GRADUATE
         UNIVERSITY: NIL
         STU: DAVE
         FIELD: NIL
         DEGREE: NIL)))

CHECKING PRECONDITIONS FOR:

(#GOAL
   TYPE: (ROLE-THEME-INIT)
   ACTOR: DAVE
   STATE: (TH-PROFESSOR
      ACTOR: DAVE))

PRECONDITION VIOLATED:

items. Pete also introduces Dave into the conversation. The previous items about $EXAM are once again considered, except N2, which is blocked by conversational syntax rule 10.8 (do not repeat information).

The interest-evaluation rules find that MICS is interested in knowing more about Dave, his new acquaintance. Searching Pete's goal tree, MICS finds that Pete is indeed interested in the outcome of taking exams (as suggested by Pete's last utterance).

MICS tries to find something relevant to both its present conversational goal (talking about Dave), and Pete's interest in the outcome of exams.

Hence, the inferencer focuses on the most significant consequence of Dave's flunking and on how this can affect Dave's goals. From the previous conversation with Dave, MICS knows that Dave has the goal of becoming a professor. Establishing a career is an important goal for most people; therefore success or failure on this matter is interesting.

If Dave flunks, he cannot graduate.

If Dave wants to become a professor, he needs to graduate first.

Therefore Dave's flunking prevents the achievement of his goal. Violated high-importance goals are considered inherently interesting.

ACHIEVE G1 REQUIRES
  $GRADUATE

THAT'S GOING TO MAKE IT
HARD FOR DAVE TO BECOME
A PROFESSOR.

Too bad, Dave is not too
smart anyway.

RULE#S7 FIRED

CALLING INFERENCER . . .

FOCUS: (REASON CON6)
(PP CON6)
((ACTOR DAVE
        IS (*MENT-ABILITY*
                VAL (2))))

SEARCHING DAVE FRAME . . .
FAILURE

FOCUS: (INSTANCE CON6)
SEARCHING DAVE FRAME . . .

FOUND:
(PSPEC (DAVE HOBBY))
 ((CON
   ((DAVE < = > *INGEST*
        OBJECT
   (SMOKE SOURCE MARIJUANA)))

VIOLATES GOAL (PERSON . G5)

YES, DAVE LIKES TO SMOKE
DOPE.

I've got to go and study.

TOPIC SELECTION INVOKED . . .
((STUDY N9 N10))

SEARCHING GOALTREE: PETE
INTEREST PRIORITY

The inference process itself is rather
simple. The significant point in
MICS's processing is that the inferencer was focused on the conversational
interests of MICS and Pete. Therefore, the resulting inferences were
likely to be interesting to both conversational participants.

Conversational-form rule S7 decides
that Pete's utterance expresses a
belief. Rule S7 triggers either rule S8
or rule S9 depending on whether
MICS agrees with the opinion. Rule
S9 was responsible for MICS's disagreement with Dave about chess.
Here rule S8 is applicable. (If MICS
neither agrees nor disagrees with a
belief, the topic selection proceeds
normally.)

MICS tries to find a reason for a
belief, but finds no reason why Dave
should or should not be smart.

MICS's working definition of intelligence is how well one can act in
pursuit of one's goals. All people have
the goal of staying out of danger.
Dave, insists on smoking dope, in
spite of MICS's warning that this can
lead to danger (i.e., being arrested).
Therefore, Dave is not pursuing
his goals well, and is, by MICS's
definition, not too smart.

The normal topic selection rules were
not triggered in this case because
the conversational-form rules decided
to focus on the topic of Pete's belief.

MICS treats this comment like any
other utterance. There are two items
about studying in memory. N9 says
that studying leads to passing exams
and N10 says that MICS himself used
to study hard.

RULE#G3 FIRED
   (PREVIOUS GOAL TOPIC)
      ((N9) (N10))

(PP N9)
   ((< = > ($EXAM
         CLASS: NIL
         PROF: STEVENSON
         STU: PETE
         DIFFICULTY: +10
         OUTCOME: PASS)))

YOU WILL DO WELL IN THE
EXAM.

The interest-evaluation rules decide that since N9 refers to the previous topic relating to Pete's goal, it is a more interesting item.

The problem here is that MICS's analysis of this utterance is totally off base. Pete probably meant to end the conversation with his remark about going to study. We discuss this problem below.

The above conversation illustrates the usefulness of understanding the knowledge shared by the two participants and each participant's awareness of the other's subjective interests. Pete and MICS both know about taking exams, and they both know Dave. MICS is able to use what it learned about Dave in its previous conversation. MICS's response to the possiblity that Dave might flunk the exam illustrates conversational rules 10.3, 10.5 and 10.7. The continuity of the conversation is preserved. Rule 10.7 applies because in the social relationship between Pete and MICS (they are friends) it is acceptable to talk about mutual acquaintances. (It is not necessarily acceptable for a judge and a defendant to chat about mutual acquaintances in the course of a jury trial.)

Focusing the inference process by importance criteria (as in the example about Dave's not being too smart) was found to be necessary in order to keep conversations from digressing into uninteresting topics. The conversational rule (S7) guiding the response to opinions is presented below:

> RULE S7   If a speaker in a conversation states an opinion, the other speaker should consider whether or not he agrees with the opinion, and express his agreement or disagreement. The first speaker usually has the conversational goal of wanting feedback (usually agreement) on his opinion.

The last exchange in the above dialog illustrates a deficiency in MICS's determination of the conversational goals. When Pete says, "I've got to go and study," he means, "I want to end the conversation," but to infer this conversational goal one must understand what it means to study. One cannot infer from the phrase, "I've got to go . . .", that the conversation should terminate. For instance, if Pete says, "I've got to go to Europe," he probably wants to introduce his upcoming trip as a new topic of conversation. The knowledge that studying and talking cannot proceed simultaneously is necessary in order to conclude that Pete wanted to end the conversation.

The primary usefulness of the MICS system is that it sheds light on problems about the rules of conversation that might otherwise remain unnoticed. The feedback from testing the implementation of our conversational model forces us to be more precise and complete in the formulation of our ideas about human conversation. The following is a conversation fragment from a later version of MICS which has a more sophisticated inference capability for determining the knowledge that it shares with the other speaker. For instance, MICS infers that if a person voluntarily chooses to pursue a certain activity, then that person is aware of the intended consequences of his activity.

> Ashtrays.
> WHAT ABOUT ASHTRAYS?
>
> Ashtrays are useful.
> DO YOU SMOKE?
>
> Yes.
> YOU MIGHT GET CANCER IF YOU SMOKE TOO MUCH.
>
> Who cares, anyway I smoke dope, not tobacco.
> I SEE, YOU LIKE TO GET HIGH.
>
> ★★COMMENT★★
> *Once again MICS will react to an opinion, finding a fact that contradicts the other speaker's statement. Stating and responding to opinion occurs very often in non-technical conversations.*
>
> It is better than getting drunk.
> NOT NECESSARILY. YOU MIGHT GET CAUGHT BY THE COPS.

The purpose of the first part of the conversation fragment above is to illustrate the topic-selection rules in the absence of a conversational goal. MICS does not know what to make of "ashtrays", but, when the other speaker says they are useful, MICS realizes that the other speaker may be interested in the function of an ashtray. Thus, it changes the topic to "smoking". When the other speaker confirms the topic to "smoking". When the other speaker confirms that he smokes, MICS's conversational goal of warning people of pending danger is activated. The new rule, stating that people are probably aware of the consequences of their actions, is not applied because a high-importance P-goal is threatened. Threats to high-level goals take precedence over normal conversational rules. (Cancer is simply defined as something that disenables the goal state of being alive.)

When MICS discovers that the person smokes dope, the rule that people know the consequences of their actions, coupled with the rule of not saying something the other person knows, prevents MICS from giving its warning about the evils of dope. The final remark is in response to the belief stated by the other speaker. MICS knows that drinking may lead to sickness, and smoking dope may lead to arrest. Both courses of action lead to goal violations of equal subjective importance (to MICS). Therefore, MICS expresses doubt, rather than agreement or direct disagreement, with the other speaker's stated belief.

10.4 Beyond MICS, Some Unsolved Problems

When MICS considers two possible topic transitions, one of high inherent interest and the other of high subjective interest, the latter is given preference. There is, however, a serious unresolved issue in this matter: How do we combine two different measures of importance? Subjective importance is the focus of most of this dissertation, but there are many happenings in the world that are of high intrinsic importance (see Schank [1978]). For instance, I was involved in more than one conversation in which the KLM-Iberia airplane accident in the Canary Islands was introduced as a topic of conversation and discussed at some length. Why is this topic interesting? Clearly, the airplane accident did not directly affect the lives of the people who mentioned it in their conversations; therefore, it could not have been of direct subjective interest. The fact that people brought up the topic in a conversation argues for the necessity of evaluating the intrinsic importance of most events. MICS only knows about the intrinsic importance of events if such importance is explicitly coded into memory. Thus, two significant factors that will improve the MICS conversational paradigm are a means of evaluating the intrinsic importance of new events and a method of somehow combining both subjective and intrinsic importance measures in guiding the course of a conversation.

The high degree of modularity between the three sets of rules has not proven to be a blessing, but rather a hindrance in disguise. It seems more logical that a person decides what he is interested in discussing simultaneously with his considerations of what is relevant and appropriate to say in the conversation. Rather than having several topic selections made and then discarding most as not interesting, the interest-evaluation process should provide the memory search with some notion of what it is interested in with respect to the context of the conversation. With this extra guidance, the memory search should become more focused. As some items that activate a conversational goal are retrieved, the search should narrow on the relations of these items to the conversational goal itself. Thus, if the other speaker introduces "whales" into the conversation, and the MICS conversational goal is to impress the other speaker, the topic-selection rules should specifically search for facts about whales that other people are not likely to know. (e.g., The finback faces imminent extinction, with a present population of under 500 individuals.) The present control structure of MICS first finds all facts about whales that are inherently interesting (e.g., whales surely do not look like mammals), and only then tries to see if any of the retrieved facts can help the conversational goal. Unfortunately, this paradigm may bypass facts such as the expected extinction of the finback whale if other items are considered intrinsically more interesting. Thus, the topic-selection process itself should be goal directed, merging the topic-selection and interest-evaluation rule modules into one integrated system.

The knowledge and rules built into MICS have all been designed with the sole purpose of producing a psychologically plausible model of human conversation. Other programs such as POLITICS and TRIAD have totally different sets of knowledge. The next logical step in modeling conversations is to integrate ideological, social, and counterplanning types of knowledge with the conversational rules. In theory, this process should produce a system that can carry on political arguments and discuss social disputes. Many of the conversational goals of an integrated reasoning system would be derived from its ideology and from its understanding of complex situations. In MICS all the conversational goals must be previously coded into memory.

We believe that the best way to analyze a problem as difficult as modeling human discourse is to forge ahead by creating rules that capture important aspects of the conversation process. The usefulness of these rules should be tested in a reactive environment, such as an interactive computer program. Since conversation is not a problem that can be isolated from other aspects of human cognitive behavior, we are researching it in conjunction with other aspects of Artificial Intelligence. A process-based theory of human conversation highlights the necessity of goal-directed subjective understanding in mundane human situations.

11

Conclusion

11.1 A Brief Comparison with Other Models of Belief Systems

We have seen how the process of subjective understanding applies to many areas of human interaction. Subjective understanding is crucial in formulating interpretations of political events; understanding conflicts among people, institutions, and countries; modeling human discourse processes; and understanding personality traits. Modeling the subjective understanding processes in these areas is necessary for understanding natural language descriptions of events which depict many types of human interaction.

Other researchers have analyzed and modeled belief systems, but their efforts differ from ours, primarily in terms of different objectives and different scopes of the models. Let us briefly consider three other models of subjective belief: Colby's PARRY [1973], Schmidt's and Sridharan's BELIEVER [1978] (also Bruce [1975]), and Abelson's "Goldwater Machine" [1965, 1973]. PARRY simulates a neurotic person who believes that the Mafia wants to kill him. Colby's objective is similar to ours only in that he strives to see how a belief system affects the responses formulated by his system. However, PARRY's understanding is limited to associating and outputting a pre-formulated response to each statement produced by a human in the course of a dialog. PARRY's model of a belief system consists of a few emotional-state monitors and associations between input patterns and output responses. The "belief system", as such, is implicit in the type of responses built into the system. PARRY has no analog to the POLITICS goal trees that focus the understanding process and the application of counterplanning strategies. Finally, since PARRY has no internal conceptual representation, its belief system cannot, in principle, be disassociated from the computer implementation to apply to other domains of subjective belief.

BELIEVER was designed with a different objective than POLITICS. Schmidt and Sridharan are primarily interested in inferring plans and associated beliefs from sequences of actions. Rather than using beliefs to guide and focus understanding processes, their concern appears to be in guessing the plans and beliefs that an actor must have had in order for him to have selected the particular sequence of actions he chose to perform. In this respect, the objective of BELIEVER more closely resembles the motivations for developing the PAM system (Wilensky, [1978]) than the POLITICS system. There are other differences between the BELIEVER and the POLITICS paradigms. BELIEVER embodies the "hypothesize and revise" method for guessing plans, revising its hypotheses, and refining its belief structure as new information is introduced. POLITICS has a fixed set of beliefs—its goal trees—but exhibits the capability of interpreting input actions in different ways to suit preconceived beliefs. Hence, understanding in POLITICS is more model-driven, whereas in BELIEVER it is more data-driven. Both POLITICS and BELIEVER deliberately avoid any method requiring substantial backtracking or re-interpreting the input, since both systems are targeted at creating a psychologically plausible models of human subjective understanding. Psychologists, most notably Bransford and Johnson [1973], have shown that people exhibit great difficulty in backtracking when forced to re-interpret previous input in light of new data. BELIEVER, unlike POLITICS, does not address serious issues in natural language understanding, such as the reference problem, since its input is in pre-analyzed symbolic notation.

Abelson developed a model of Senator Barry Goldwater's ideologically right-wing belief system. His model made ideological inferences from various propositions representing events pertaining to the cold war. The model was implemented as a computer program called the "ideology machine", also referred to as the "Goldwater machine". Abelson's goal was to model "hot cognition", that is, to reproduce the rhetoric typically voiced by a "cold warrior". The ideological responses were directed against perceived communist threats at the height of the cold war. In this respect, the program was moderately successful and demonstrated that certain types of ideological behavior could be reproduced by a computer program.

Abelson's original motivation for formulating his ideology machine was his impression that Goldwater's reasoning about ideological matters was relatively uncomplicated, and that a relatively small set of rules in the computer could duplicate much of this reasoning. Abelson produced a "master script", which encoded the basic decisions motivating the rhetoric used by a right-wing ideologue when responding to actions that could be interpreted as communist threats.

There is one very serious problem with Abelson's model, however: it fails to understand mundane reality. This problem is best illustrated by an example from the ideology machine. From the fact that leftist students in South America threw eggs at Richard Nixon, the program would conclude that Castro would throw eggs at West Berlin. Why? The ideology machine knew that communists do bad things to the free world. Throweggs-at must be a bad thing because leftists did it to an American. Therefore, Castro, who is communist, would throw eggs at West Berlin, part of the free world. This reasoning process obviously lacks an understanding of what it means to throw eggs. In fact, the ideology machine did not attempt to analyze the meaning of any actions; it merely classified them according to ideological criteria.

The master script, as a concise model of Goldwater's ideology, was an important concept. A relatively small memory structure guided the behavior of the program in all its responses. In essence, the master script encoded Goldwater's beliefs, and the way these beliefs were to be applied, as one concise and integrated unit. This represented a quantum from other systems that had no unified model of a belief system.

POLITICS was originally motivated by Abelson's ideology machine. The advent of conceptual dependency (Schank [1972, 1975]), frames for representing real-world knowledge (Minsky [1975]), situational scripts, planning units and other memory structures (Schank and Abelson [1977], Abelson [1975]), in addition to more sophisticated computing facilities, led us to believe that we could re-create a much better version of the ideology machine. The new version would analyze the actions in the input events and deal with mundane reality in modeling ideological behavior. In the process of working on the new system, we first relied on situational scripts and goal-directed inference rules. Later, as we expanded our scope to model more than one ideology and events other than East-West confrontations, we developed goal trees and counterplanning strategies. These structures formed the basis of our subjective understanding model. Abelson's master script modeled only one important aspect of one ideology, although the concept could have been somewhat generalized. The paradigm we developed can model any reasonable ideology, and has been extended to model other types of subjective beliefs.

Our model of subjective understanding transcends ideological behavior to encompass focus of attention and idiosyncratic interests in understanding events in general. Furthermore, we apply goal trees and counterplanning strategies in order to understand personality traits, certain aspects of human discourse, and human conflict situations. Hence, what started as an interesting application of current developments in memory representation and natural language understanding to the reformulation of a previous system, resulted in the creation of a general process-model of subjective understanding. The scope of application and the computer implementation of the various aspects of our subjective understanding model far exceeded the original expectations of creating a more sophisticated version of Abelson's ideology machine.

11.2 The Role of Integrated Understanding

One of the more significant side effects of the POLITICS project is demonstrating the usefulness of an integrated approach to modeling complex understanding processes. We cannot build a natural language understanding system, except in well-defined micro-worlds (such as Winograd's SHRDLU [1972]), without taking into full account its interactions with memory and inference processes. In essence, "context free" understanding is impossible, as was amply demonstrated by the repeated failures of the machine translation projects of the 1950's (Bar-Hillel [1960]). (Machine translation, however, is feasible as an integral part of an understanding system—see Carbonell, Cullingford, and Gershman [1978].)

In response to the realization that various sources of knowledge were necessary for understanding natural language text, many researchers built sequential modular systems. Each module encoded a different class of knowledge to be used at a different phase of the understanding process. The stipulation of these modular systems was that the various classes of knowledge were quite separable; there should be little, if any, need for communication across the different modules. This general paradigm led to the following configuration in several natural language understanding systems:

Figure 11.1. Modular Natural Language understanding paradigm

Natural				Memory
Language →	SYNTAX →	SEMANTICS →	PRAGMATICS →	Representation
Input				

The natural language text was first subjected to a syntactic analysis. The resultant phrase markers were then subjected to semantic interpretation. Finally the "pragmatics" were supposed to take care of all the unsolved problems such as context, non-linguistic reference, memory integration, and inference rules. (Wood's [1972] LUNAR system is an example of such a multi-phase understanding system.) In practice, many researchers devoted much of their effort to the SYNTAX module, less effort to the SEMANTICS module, and ignored the PRAGMATICS component completely. Many of the unsolved problems were relegated to this un-implemented module by stating "Oh, that's just a matter of pragmatics." In fact, this pitfall is exemplified in the LUNAR system. LUNAR can retrieve facts from memory only if they are explicitly referenced in the input. LUNAR failed to understand any semantic paraphrase of the input, as it lacked the ability to reason about the objects and actions in its memory.

With the realization that the different modules need to exchange information, the configuration of many understanding systems has changed to permit more complicated interactions. (This was the case for Wood's speech understanding system, when the linear application of the separate modules proved insufficient.) With further study of the "pragmatics" black box, many researchers came to the conclusion that the bulk of the interesting problems in understanding systems lies in this previously ignored realm.

In the SAM system (Cullingford [1977]), the syntax module, the semantics module, and part of the pragmatics module were mapped into a single module, ELI (The English Language Interpreter, Riesbeck and Schank [1976]). The rest of the pragmatics box was divided into the script applier and the memory-tokenizer module. This shift in emphasis suggests a realization of where the difficult problems in understanding are. One cannot arbitrarily subdivide a problem into several modules, produce a working model of some of these modules, ignore the others, and claim to have solved a significant part of the problem. The hardest part of the problem may lie in the other modules (as has been the case with the "pragmatics" module in many natural language understanding projects), or it may lie in the interaction between the various modules.

The SAM system proved somewhat fragile, largely as a result of its modularity. ELI had no access to the memory, and the expectations of the script applier were not used by ELI to facilitate language interpretation, with the exception of some help in verb-sense disambiguation. In response to these problems FRUMP (DeJong [1979]), and POLITICS were created as unified, integrated understanding systems. Modularity has always been hailed as a virtue in all computer systems. This is largely a result of our scientific training which teaches us to attack problems by simplifying them, dividing them into component parts, and independently conquering the subparts. There is nothing wrong with this approach, except that it does not apply very well to modeling human thought processes. There is no evidence to suggest that the mind is neatly compartmentalized into the "syntax" module, the "semantics" module, or the "script application" module. In fact, since people interpret events as they read them, without waiting for the completion of syntactic or semantic units, it appears that human understanding is indeed quite integrated. Any process model that requires a complete syntactic analysis of a sentence before considering its semantic interpretation, which in turn must be completed before any conceptual processes such as inference rules are applied, is of necessity an incorrect model of human understanding.

POLITICS contains no separable modules; it is a fully integrated system. As we saw in chapter 8, information derived from scripts and goal trees is used in the natural language analysis phase. Moreover, in the process of analyzing natural language text, conceptual structures built from the input text are assimilated into memory, often triggering situational inferences. Throughout this process, the goal trees of the actors are consulted in order to focus the attention of the understander on those aspects of the event being analyzed that the understander is most interested in pursuing. The fact that POLITICS is an integrated understander does not mean that it lacks diverse sources of knowledge and inference rules—quite the contrary. POLITICS uses all of the following sources of knowledge in its subjective understanding of political events:

1. Goal trees of the actors in the event.

2. Rules that determine the application of the goal trees.

3. Counterplanning strategies.

4. Script application process.

5. Situational inference rules triggered from scripts.

6. Factual token memory about the actors and objects in the world.

7. Episodic memory about past events.

8. Parsing expectations generated by memory structures.

9. Parsing expectations stored in the dictionary.

10. Rules of English syntax.

11. Working memory containing currently active context.

12. Question analysis and answering strategies.

POLITICS's ability to draw upon the multiple sources of knowledge as needed gives it a measure of flexibility and generality not found in many previous systems. The overall success of integration in POLITICS leads us to believe that modularity may often be more of a hindrance than a virtue. The more knowledge a system can draw upon, the better its performance will be, as long as the interaction between the sources of knowledge does not produce contradictory suggestions. We found that redundancy occurs much more often than contradiction. Redundancy may also be a hidden benefit in integrated systems. It appears that people rely on redundant information to make sense of garbled speech, incomplete sentences, and partially readable text. Integrated understanding also allows the understander to ignore large amounts of information that he may not be interested in, without requiring him to first understand it all and then discard it. (Schank [1978] discusses ways of controlling inferences and unnecessary conceptual analysis of uninteresting material.)

There are some engineering drawbacks to fully integrated systems such as POLITICS. It is much more difficult to modify and debug those programs in which a change in one source of knowledge can have repercussions throughout the system. This, indeed, is the primary reason why computer scientists, especially system designers, prefer modular systems. Our position is that the benefits of integrated understanding far outweigh the extra complexity in programming and modifying such systems.

11.3 A Final Note on Subjective Understanding

Most models of human understanding should exemplify some subjective behavior, since the humans whom they strive to model demonstrate such behavior in understanding events and in interacting with other people. Researchers have often circumvented the problem of subjective understanding by either trying to model a normative, totally stereotypical person, or by building systems that do not claim to model human behavior. There are really few areas of human endeavor for which an accepted normative model exists; such areas are mostly restricted to technical fields which require expert knowledge, (for example), chemical analysis as exemplified by DENDRAL (Feigenbaum, Buchanan and Lederberg [1971]), and medical diagnosis systems such as MYCIN (Shortliffe [1976])). In such objective endeavors, there is no attempt to model mundane human understanding, but rather the goal is to model, or improve upon, technical expertise. For instance, DENDRAL uses the generate and test paradigm, reinterpreting previous computations as new results are obtained. This method does not parallel mundane human reasoning, but instead tries to maximize the accuracy of its chemical analysis.

As the complexity of AI systems that model human behavior increases, the need for formulating the subjective component of the system increases. A system that tries to understand relatively complex events about human conflicts and interactions requires a subjective point of view in order to focus the attention of the inferencer. As the volume of knowledge, including inference rules, encoded in an AI system increases, so does the need for mechanisms that constrain and focus the application of the inference rules. We demonstrated in earlier chapters that the number of possible inferences applicable at any given step in the interpretations of an event can be quite staggering. If we follow each inference path for several steps we create an exponentially increasing proliferation of inferences, the vast majority of which will be totally irrelevant to the concerns of the understander. (Rieger's [1975] model of unfocused inference ran headlong into the problem of a combinatorial explosion.) This problem suggests the need for creating a process-model of the subjective interests of the understander. Such a model guides the inference processes by pursuing only the inference path(s) that are relevant to the interests of the understander. Furthermore, a method that uses subjective concerns to guide the inference according to the goals and motivations of the understander is a more reasonable model of human reasoning than any unfocused inference system.

Our process-model, which incorporates goal trees and counterplanning strategies, provides a solution to the inference proliferation problem. This solution is consistent with our criterion of maximizing the psychological plausibility of our model. Different people often pursue different lines of reasoning in understanding events. Our model of subjective understanding accounts for this phenomenon by having the subjective component be a major part of the mechanism that chooses which inference paths to pursue. We found our subjective-importance goal tree model to be useful in modeling ideological behavior, understanding conflict situations, simulating human discourse, and representing personality traits.

Bibliography

Abelson, R. P. and J. D. Carroll. (1965). Computer Simulaton of Individual Belief Systems. *American Behavioral Scientist*. 8, 24-30.

Abelson, R. P. (1973). The Structure of Belief Systems. In R. C. Schank and K. M. Colby (eds.) *Computer Models of Thought and Language*. Freeman & Co. San Francisco.

_____. (1975). Concepts for Representing Mundane Reality in Plans. In D. Bobrow and A. Collins (eds.), *Representation and Understanding: Studies in Cognitive Science*. Academic Press. New York.

Anderson R. C. and Pichert, J. W. (1978). Recall of Previously Unrecallable Information, following a Shift in Perspective. *Journal of Verbal Learning and Verbal Behavior*. 17, 1-12.

Axelrod, R. (1976). *Structure of Decision: The Cognitive Maps of Political Elites*. Princeton University Press, Princeton, N.J.

Bar-Hillel, Y. (1960). The Present Status of Automatic Translation of Languages. *Advances in Computers*, vol. 1, 91-163.

Barstow, D. R. (1977). *Automatic Construction of Algorithms and Data Structures Using a Knowledge Base of Programming Rules*. Ph.D. Thesis. Stanford University, Memo AIM-308.

Bobrow, D. G. and Colins, A., editors. (1975). *Representation and Understanding: Studies in Cognitive Science*. Academic Press. New York.

Bourne, L. E., Dominowski, R. L. and Loftus E. F. (1979). *Cognitive Processes*. Prentice-Hall, Englewood Cliffs, N.J.

Bransford, J.D. and Johnson, M. K. (1973). Consideration of Some Problems of Comprehension. In W. Chase (ed.), *Visual Information Processing*. Academic Press, New York.

Bruce, B. C. (1975). Belief Systems and Language Understanding. Computer Science Dept., Rutgers. NIH Report CBM-TR-41.

Carbonell, J. G. (1978). POLITICS: Automated Ideological Reasoning. *Cognitive Science*, vol. 2, no. 1. 27-51.

_____. (1981). "Problem Solving and Learning by Analogy" in R. Michalsky, J. Carbonell, and T. Mitchell (Eds.) *Machine Learning*. Palo Alto, CA: Tioga Press.

_____, Cullingford, R. E., and Gershman A. V. (1978). Towards Knowledge-Based Machine Translation. *Proceedings of the Seventh International Conference on Computational Linguistics*. Bergen, Norway. Research Report #146, Yale University.

Charniak, E. (1972). *Towards a Model of Children's Story Comprehension*. Ph.D. Thesis, M.I.T. AI TR-266.

_____. (1977). A Framed PAINTING: The Representation of a common sense knowledge fragment. *Cognitive Science*. vol. 1, no. 4. 355-394.

Colby, K. M. (1973). Simulations of Belief Systems. In R. C. Schank and K. M. Colby (eds.) *Computer Models of Thought and Language*. Freeman & Co. San Francisco.

Collins, B. E. and Raven, B. H. (1968). Group Structure: Attraction, Coalitions, Communication, and Power. In G. Lindzey and E. Aronson (eds.) *Handbook of Social Psychology.*, vol. II. Addison-Wesley, Reading, Mass.

Cullingford, R. (1977). *Script Application: Computer Understanding of Newspaper Stories.* Ph.D. Thesis. Research Report #116, Yale University.

DeJong, J. (1979) *Partial Understanding of Connected Natural Language Text.* Ph.D. Thesis, Yale University. (forthcoming).

Feigenbaum, E. A., Buchanan, B. G., and Lederberg, J. (1971). On Generality and Problem Solving: A Case Study Using the DENDRAL Program. *Machine Intelligence 6.* Edinburgh University Press.

Grosz, B. J. (1977). The Representation and Use of Focus in a System for Understanding Dialogs, *Proc. of the Fifth IJCAI.*, MIT, Cambridge, Mass.

Lehnert, W. (1978). *The Process of Question Answering.* Lawrence Erlbaum. Hillside, NJ.

Levin, J. A. and Moore, J. A. (1977). Dialogue-Games: Metacommunication Structures for Natural Language Interaction. *Cognitive Science.* vol. 1, no. 4, 395-420.

Meehan, J. R. (1976). The Metanovel: Writing Stories by Computer. Ph.D. Thesis. Research Report #74, Yale University.

Minsky, M. (1975). A Framework for Representing Knowledge. In P. Winston (ed.) *The Psychology of Computer Vision.* McGraw-Hill, Inc. New York.

Newell A., and Simon, H. A. (1972). *Human Problem Solving.* Prentice-Hall, Inc., New Jersey.

_____. (1973) Production Systems: Models of Control Structures. In W. G. Chase (ed.), *Visual Information Processing.* Academic Press. New York.

Norman, D. A. and Rumelhart, D. E. (1975). *Explorations in Cognition.* W. H. Freeman and Co., San Francisco.

Rieger, C. (1975). Conceptual memory. In R. C. Schank, (ed.), *Conceptual Information Processing.* North-Holland Pub. Co. Amsterdam.

Riesbeck, C. (1975). Conceptual Analysis. In R. C. Schank *Conceptual Information Processing.* North-Holland Pub. Co. Amsterdam.

_____, and Schank, R. C. (1976) Comprehension by Computer: Expectation-Based Analysis of Sentences in Context. Research Report #78, Yale University.

Ross, J. R. (1967) On The Cyclic Nature of English Pronominalization. *To Honor Roman Jakobson.* Mouton & Co. The Hague.

Sacerdoti, E. D. (1977). *A Structure for Plans and Behavior.* Elsevier North-Holland Pub. Co. Amsterdam.

Schank, R. C. (1972). Conceptual Dependency: A Theory of Natural Language Understanding. *Cognitive Psychology*, 3, 552-631.

_____, and Colby, K. M. (1973). *Computer Models of Thought and Language.* Freeman & Co. San Francisco.

_____. (1975), *Conceptual Information Processing.* North Holland Pub. Co. Amsterdam.

_____, and Abelson, R. P. (1977). *Scripts, Goals, Plans and Understanding*, Lawrence Erlbaum. Hillside, NJ.

_____. (1977). Rules and topics in conversation, *Cognitive Science.* vol. I, no. 4, 421-441.

_____, Wilensky R., Carbonell, J. G., Kolodner, J. L. and Hendler, J. A. (1978). Representing Attitudes: Some Primitive States. Research Report #128, Yale University.

_____, (1978). Interestingness: Controlling Inferences. Research Report #145, Yale University.

_____. and Carbonell J. G. (1979) RE: The Gettysburg Address, Representing Social and Political Acts. In Findler (ed.) *Associative Networks.* Academic Press. New York.

Schmidt, C., Sridharan N. and Goodson, J. (1978), The Plan Recognition Problem. *Artificial Intelligence.* vol 11, no. 1,2, 45-83.

Sears, D. O., Hensler, C. P. and Speer, L. E. (1977). Whites' Opposition to Busing: Self-interest or Symbolic Racism? Paper presented at the 85th annual meeting of the American Psychological Association. San Francisco.

Shortliffe, E. (1976). *Computer Based Medical Consultations: MYCIN*. Elsevier. New York.

Slovic, P. (1974). Consistency of Choice Between Equally Voiced Alternatives. *Oregon Research Institute Bulletin*, vol. 14, no. 11.

Sussman, G. J. (1973). *A Computational Model of Skill Acquisition*. Ph.D. Thesis. M.I.T. AI TR-297.

Taylor, S. E., Etcoff, N. L., Fiske, S. T. and Laufer, J. K. (1978). Imaging, Empathy, and Causal Attribution. Unpublished manuscript. Harvard University Press.

Wilensky, R. (1978). *Understanding Goal-Based Stories*. Ph.D. Thesis, Research report #140, Yale University.

Wilks, Y. (1975). A Preferential Pattern-Seeking, Semantics for Natural Language Inference. *Artificial Intelligence*. vol. 6, 53-74.

Winograd, T. (1972). *Understanding Natural Language*. Academic Press. New York.

Woods W., Kaplan R. and Nash-Webber B. (1972). *The Lunar Sciences Natural Language Information System: Final Report*. Bolt Beranek and Newman Report No. 2378. Cambridge, Mass.

Index